Praise for
The New Influencers

"There are a lot of people who don't want you to read *The New Influencers*. Your competition, for starters. And the media rep who sells you TV time for another. Ignore them. This is essential reading for anyone who missed the blogging train when it left the station."
—Seth Godin, author of *Small Is the New Big, Unleashing the Ideavirus*

"How can we understand this new force? How should we engage with it constructively? How can we protect ourselves from its darker side? These are the questions this book seeks to address, and I commend you to it. It is timely indeed, for we are seeing not just marketing campaigns, but political and social ones as well, playing out in this new venue."
—Geoffrey Moore, author of *Crossing the Chasm, Inside the Tornado, The Gorilla Game*

"Instead of another how-to book on blogging, Gillin expertly unwraps the dynamics behind this fast-evolving phenomenon—and its profound implications for marketers. Using a large number of case studies, he shows how "influencers" are changing the marketing equation."
—Ellis Booker, editor-in-chief, *BtoB* magazine

"Everything you ever wanted to know about social media rests safely inside the mind of Paul Gillin—lucky for us he's willing to share."
—*Ragan's Web Content Report*

"*The New Influencers*...is one of those landmark books that has everyone talking and for good reason. This book is an important contribution to discussions of the change in marketing and public relations techniques. I highly recommend *The New Influencers*...for anyone who wants to explore the leading edge of the new social media revolution."
—Wayne Hurlbert, *Blog Business World*

"*The New Influencers* definitely has the right parts...it positively excels in highlighting the opportunities that open up when the responsible marketer is exposed to social media."
—Phil Gomes, *iMediaconnection*

"By showing what methods work and which ones tank, Gillin tells us how to gain media exposure. Experimenting with novel techniques is a great way to climb toward triumph."
—MarketingSherpa

"Paul Gillin goes beyond trends such as blogging, podcasting, or social networks to look at the underlying dynamics of influence and conversation marketing. Marketers need to understand, embrace and participate in this brave new world."
—Eric Kintz, vice president, Global Marketing Strategy
   & Excellence, Hewlett-Packard Company

"As 'word of mouth' loses opinion-forming power to 'word of blog,' companies are faced with a revolution in how their brands and corporate image will be shaped in the future. Paul Gillin provides a very insightful and well-written guide on how to effectively benefit from these dramatic changes. A must-read!"
—Patrick J. McGovern, founder and chairman,
   International Data Group (IDG)

"I'd suggest this book for any manager or senior executive who doesn't 'get' social media."
—Sam Decker, Decker Marketing

"Between consumers transforming into producers, branding occurring not in the boardroom but from the bottom up, and customers, not CMOs, calling the shots, today's companies are presented with a choice: embrace these tools to improve and innovate or face irrelevance in this evolving landscape."
—Christina Kerley, ckEpiphany Marketing

The New INFLUENCERS

A Marketer's Guide to the
New Social Media

Paul Gillin

To Tim,

Enjoy the conversation!

Paul Gillin

9/17/99

Quill
Driver
Books

Fresno, California

Printed in the United States of America.

Published by Quill Driver Books
an imprint of Linden Publishing, Inc.
2006 South Mary, Fresno, California 93721
559-233-6633 / 800-345-4447
QuillDriverBooks.com
Info@QuillDriverBooks.com

Quill Driver Books' titles may be purchased in quantity at special discounts
for educational, fund-raising, training, business, or promotional use.
Please contact Special Markets, Quill Driver Books at the above address, toll-
free at 1-800-345-4447, or by e-mail: Info@QuillDriverBooks.com

Quill Driver Books project cadre:
Doris Hall, Linda Kay Hardie,
Stephen Blake Mettee, Carlos Olivas, Andrea Wright

Quill Driver Books and colophon are trademarks of
Linden Publishing, Inc.

135798642

ISBN 1-884956-94-7 • 978-1-884956-94-2

To order another copy of this book, please call
1-800-345-4447

Library of Congress Cataloging-in-Publication Data
Gillin, Paul.
    The new influencers : a marketer's guide to the new social media / by Paul Gillin.
    p. cm.
    Originally published in 2007.
    Includes bibliographical references and index.
    ISBN 978-1-884956-94-2 (pbk. : alk. paper)
1. Marketing—Blogs. 2. Social media—Economic aspects. 3. Customer relations.
4. Interactive marketing. I. Title.
    HF5415.G5424 2009
    658.8'72--dc22
                                                                    2009008087

Contents

Foreword vii

Acknowledgments ix

Introduction xi

How to Use this Book xvii

1. The Origins of Social Media 1

2. From Chaos, Structure 15

3. Enthusiasts 33

Influencer Profile—The Gadget King 57

4. Measures of Influence 63

5. Corporate Conversations 79

Influencer Profile—The Corporate Renegade 103

6. Small Is Beautiful 113

7. Putting "Public" Back Into Public Relations 123

Influencer Profile—The Marketer 135

8. The Talkers 139

Influencer Profile—The Sound Man 157

9. Tools of the Trade 163

Influencer Profile—The Toolmaker 173

10. Going Viral 179

Influencer Profile—The Guerilla 191

11. Next Steps 195

Appendix A—The Numbers 207

Appendix B—Leveraging Technology 209

Glossary 219

Index 225

About the Author 238

Please visit
NewInfluencers.com
for additional, continually updated material.

To Dana, who said, "Go for it!"

Foreword to
The New Influencers

When I first became involved with the technology sector, there was no such thing as high-tech marketing. Regis McKenna changed all that with a book called *The Regis Touch.* It explained how, in markets where buying decisions were high-risk and issues were technologically complex, traditional forms of advertising and promotion were ineffective. Instead one had to "influence the influencers," and thus high-tech PR was born.

The high-tech PR model reigned throughout the 1980s and 1990s. Organized around the product launch, it consisted primary of a press tour focused on the technical press (including *Computerworld,* where Paul Gillin worked). Such a tour was done in conjunction with an analyst tour, with visits to the Gartner Group, Yankee, Forrester, and the like, to brief the industry experts to whom reporters would turn for validation of the company's claims. Customer references were carefully teed up for these experts to interview, and partners dutifully chimed in. Finally, as the art form continued to mature, business press and financial analysts were added to the mix. But the key principle always remained the same: *Orchestrate the influencers in order to communicate marketing messages to the audiences you seek to reach.*

Such were the days when media were tightly held, influencers were a recognizable clique, and reporters held sway. Alas, those institutions, if not completely gone, are sliding from the scene at an alarming pace. In their place appears this new phenomenon of *social media.*

How lasting the impact of social media will have is yet to be determined, but one thing for sure, it has turned the chain of influence upside down. Today the *reader*, the lowly reader, that presumably passive consumer of all the great insight handed down by the reporter, confirmed by the analyst, attested to by the reference customer—this reader, I say, has now become the *writer!*

Except it is not *a* reader/writer. It is *reader/writers at large,* many readers, the wisdom (or madness) of crowds. We have embarked upon the world's largest and longest cocktail party, and every issue imaginable is up for grabs. The orchestrators of old are valiantly trying to practice their craft in these turbulent waters, but the results are still largely unpredictable. For now there are few rules—only risks and opportunities and emerging principles, all swirling in electronic space.

How can we understand this new force? How should we engage with it constructively? How can we protect ourselves from its darker side? These are the questions this book seeks to address, and I commend you to it. It is timely indeed, for we are seeing not just marketing campaigns, but political and social ones as well, playing out in this new venue. And these campaigns are having an impact, and they will become a growing force in our lives. Whether as vendors or consumers, candidates or citizens, we cannot afford to be ignorant of the dynamics of this new world.

Geoffrey Moore
Managing Director, The Chasm Group
Author of *Crossing the Chasm, Inside the Tornado, The Gorilla Game, Living on the Fault Line, Dealing with Darwin: How Great Companies Innovate at Every Phase of Their Evolution*

San Mateo, California
November, 2006

Acknowledgments

The New Influencers evolved out of a passion for social media that developed in late 2005 as a result of a career shift. Software legend Dan Bricklin gave me my first exposure to the power of the blogosphere and later conceded to an extended interview and profile. Ellis Booker, editor-in-chief of *B2B Magazine*, indulged me with early assignments that helped develop my knowledge in this area and gave me a standing column that I continue to use as an opportunity to stay engaged.

I am indebted to Quill Driver Books and publisher Steve Mettee, in particular, for taking a chance with a new author and a proposal that other publishers had dismissed as being "another book about blogging." Steve got the message that the book was really about influence, which is more interesting, in my view. He also encouraged me, without hesitation, to post draft chapters of the book on my blog for feedback. Whether this eventually helped sales is an open question, but there's no doubt that the experiment helped greatly with prerelease buzz, and the strong early interest indicates that there was no adverse impact on sales.

Quill Driver Books' publicist, Andrea Wright, constantly prompted me for new ideas and followed up promotional opportunities. Catherine Marenghi, who's a dear friend and an ace publicist, secured more media recognition than I probably deserved.

Neil Salkind, my agent, kept plugging away even after more than 100 publishers had rejected the title. He was a constant source of encouragement and wisdom, and I am particularly indebted to him for helping me through numerous revisions of the proposal.

Peggy Rouse of Whatis.com read the entire draft and provided me with valuable feedback, particularly some early advice that led me to completely restructure the order of the chapters. Her team also wrote the book's glossary. Whatis.com was Wikipedia a decade before there was a Wikipedia. It is still an incredibly valuable source of technology knowledge.

Christina Kerley of CK'sBlog was an early fan and continually told me that what I was doing was valuable. She now contributes to the popular Daily Fix blog at MarketingProfs.com, which you should read every day.

I contacted Philipp Lenssen because he was an influencer, but he became a valuable source of intelligence on the culture of the blogosphere and his early comments on the draft chapters were enormously helpful.

Incidentally, both Christina and Philipp contributed sidebars to the book. Like Tom Sawyer, I have no hesitation about putting my friends to work!

Many of the influencers gave generously of their time for interviews and follow-up questions. My thanks to everyone quoted in the book, particularly those who agreed to multi-hour interviews for profiles. I want to extend special recognition to Andy Abramson, Renee Blodgett, Stowe Boyd, Ted Demopoulos, Jody DeVere, Vincent Ferrari, Natalie Glance, Paige Heninger, Mike Kaltschnee, Doug Kaye, Geoffrey Moore, Katie Paine, Peter Rojas, Steve Rubel, Eric Schwartzman, Robert Scoble, David Meerman Scott, Gretchen and Paul Vogelzang, Larry Weber, David Weinberger and Kevin Whalen.

Network World's editor-in-chief John Gallant encouraged me to write for years and I finally did, although I think he had a novel in mind. Former *Computerworld* editor-in-chief Bill Laberis has been my friend and mentor for more than two decades. He gave me a chance to observe a fascinating industry from one of the best perches in the business and I'll always be grateful to him for that.

Special thanks to my many friends and colleagues at TechTarget, who taught me by baptism of fire the intricacies of Web publishing and the beauty of small markets. Particular thanks to Greg Strakosch and Don Hawk, who understood both my skills and limitations and who made it possible for me to devote significant time to this book.

My children, Ryan and Alice, thought it was pretty cool that dad was writing a book and showed remarkable restraint in finding something else to do while I was hammering away at the keyboard on weekends. They are not only my pride and joy, but also two of my best friends. They also contributed valuable insight into what motivates people their age, which is wisdom I could have found nowhere else.

This project began during a particularly difficult period of my life. If it hadn't been for the unceasing support, encouragement and love of Dana McCurley, it would never have been completed. She has helped me accomplish things I never thought were possible and given me confidence that I never thought was in me. This September, I will be proud to make her my wife.

Introduction
To Set the Stage

"Blogging's wave has already crested, now that millions of online diarists are realizing that not that many people actually read this stuff."

I wrote those words in December 2003 in an annual year-end forecast of trends in the computer industry. In more than a decade of writing that annual column, I have never been more wrong about anything.

In January 2004, there were about 1 million blogs on the Internet. A year later, there were 8 million and the year after that, more than 30 million. As of mid-2006, the population of the "blogosphere" was well past 50 million and climbing. Podcasts, those radio programs delivered digitally over the Internet to PCs and portable media players, exploded in popularity during the same time period. MySpace.com, a social networking site targeting teens, grew from nothing to almost 100 million users between 2004 and 2006. YouTube.com and more than fifty other video-sharing services began to change the television landscape by giving ordinary people the power to publish their own programs. All of this happened in a little more than twenty-four months. The revolution whose demise I forecast in December 2003 had, in fact, not even begun.

I was the last person who should have missed the signs. At the time I publicly dismissed blogging, I had been working for a successful Internet startup for four years. Prior to that, I had covered the computer industry as a journalist for fifteen years. Newspaper, TV and radio reporters frequently called to ask my opinion on tech trends. I thought I understood the media world. And yet I completely missed the most important development in media of the last fifty years. It's not surprising a lot of others made the same mistake.

In October 2004, *Wired* magazine editor Chris Anderson crystallized the power of this emerging media in an article entitled "The Long Tail." Anderson demonstrated how the power of the Internet was in its ability to serve small groups of people organized around very specific interests:

The average Barnes & Noble carries 130,000 titles. Yet more than half of Amazon's book sales come from outside its top 130,000 titles. Consider the implication: If the Amazon statistics are any guide, the market for books that are not even sold in the average bookstore is larger than the market for those that are. In other words, the potential book market may be twice as big as it appears to be, if only we can get over the economics of scarcity.

Marketer's dilemma

The shift to small markets served and influenced by an entirely new breed of opinion-leaders is a sea change for marketers. Most marketers still have no idea what to do about it. That's understandable. In the half century leading up to 2005, the whole focus of marketing had been on optimizing mass markets. The skills that led to success in marketing were analytical and mathematical. Marketers learned to analyze response rates down to a thousandth of a percentage point and to tailor campaigns that would appeal to maybe 3 percent of an audience of millions. "Twenty-plus years ago…the profession was still mostly about applying mathematical odds in the effort to increase chances of ads being seen," wrote Lisa Seward, media director at Fallon in Minneapolis, in a column in *Media* magazine in June 2006. "Excellence in media was pretty much defined by gross ratings points levels and costs per thousand."

The waste was incredible, but there was no alternative in a market that had no way to efficiently speak to communities of customers. Websites helped, but they were basically an online version of a printed brochure. The tools to enable interactivity already existed, but they were either too expensive or too hard to use to be of much use to the average business.

That changed suddenly in the first few years of the new millennium. Consumers and businesses have gravitated to social media with awesome speed. While we're all still sorting this out, the extent to which communities and influencers have already emerged in this new media world is stunning.

The New Influencers is a book about influence. It's not about blogs or podcasts or viral videos.[1] Those are channels of influence that are important and that will change over time. What's captivated me about social media is the extent to which new centers of influence have emerged in communities that have no rules, no governing structures, no standards and no hierarchy. You can say or do anything you want in a blog, podcast or Web video, and you can publish it to the world. No one can stop you, at least not at this point.

1. There are several fine books that will help you get going in these areas. Among them are *Blogging for Business* by Ted Demopoulos and Shel Holtz (2006, Kaplan Publishing); *The Corporate Blogging Book* by Debbie Weil (2006, Portfolio) and *Naked Conversations* by Robert Scoble and Shel Israel (2006, Wiley).

Common sense says that a medium with so little structure should degenerate into chaos. But remarkably, exactly the opposite is happening. Complex patterns of governance are already emerging, driven by a set of shared values that aren't codified but just understood. The blogosphere rejects structure, yet it's making up a structure as it goes along. Powerful voices are emerging: people and groups who have the capacity to move markets and challenge institutions. As these media mature, new voices are entering. Increasingly, they are people who already command respect and authority in their disciplines. As they add their voices to the global conversation, the quality of the discourse improves. The blogosphere, which was the Wild West in its early years, has rapidly matured to become a valuable information channel, one which now commands the respect and attention of mainstream media. As each new voice is added, the community gets stronger.

Marketers need to understand, accept and participate in this new world. They really have no choice. The tools they've been using to reach their customers for the last fifty years are becoming less and less effective. Newspapers are losing readers and having an increasingly hard time justifying their high advertising rates. Television viewership has been declining for years. Radio has consolidated into a few basic formats that deliver predictable demographics and ignore large swaths of the population that has simply tuned out. Even conventional Internet channels are becoming exhausted. Spam and list exhaustion are undermining e-mail marketing. Web users ignore banner ads, except for the intrusive ones, which they despise. Publishers and ad reps engage in pointless debates over a few hundredths of a percent in the response rate.

Social media offers marketers a chance to break this gridlock and engage with their customers in a whole new way. The new discipline is coming to be known as "conversation marketing." It means creating a dialog with customers in which useful information is exchanged so that both parties benefit from the relationship. As trust builds, customers develop loyalty that makes them long-term partners, leading to a more lasting relationship.

Conversation marketing requires a completely different set of skills than those which have dominated the marketing profession for the last two generations. It means throwing out the spreadsheets and the mailing lists. It means ditching terms like "reach," "frequency," "impressions" and "click-through rates." It means understanding who your customers are, who influences them and how to engage with those influencers. It means exchanging information, not delivering a message.

Demographic shift

Conversation marketing is going to become more and more crucial to reaching young customers and addressing changing customer preferences. That's because traditional mass media is being replaced by networks of individual and small-group influencers. MediaPost noted that in 1977, 67 percent of people polled in a research study said they were moved to take some sort of action by word-of-mouth influence. In 2003, that number was 92 percent.

Customer relationship management expert Paul Greenberg described the buying behavior of so-called Gen X and Gen Y consumers (those born after 1961) in a March 2006 article in *CIO* magazine:

> As customers, Gen X-ers and Gen Y-ers are more volatile and high-maintenance than any other generation in history. They are voracious in their desire for immediate information and have sophisticated behavioral approaches to filtering that information, no matter how many sources it comes from.
>
> In a recent study, for example, Yankelovich [Partners] found that 63 percent of this group will research products before they consider a purchase. What makes this statistic even more compelling is that these new customers are creating extensive communities to exchange information. Even though nary a handshake occurs, the information swap is trusted—and thus is more powerful than any marketing pitch ever could be.

In other words, young people are so convinced of the value of peer networks that they will trust the advice of a total stranger over that of a professional marketer. Until a few years ago, technology limitations prevented those networks from forming. Now that dam has broken and the landscape will look very different from here forward.

And the younger the consumers, the more likely they are to want to engage with each other online. Forrester Research reported in August 2006 that people between the ages of 18 and 28 are 50 percent more likely than people 28 to 40 years old to send instant messages, twice as likely to read blogs, and three times as likely to use social networking sites like MySpace.

Research firm Frank N. Magid Associates looked at the media habits of the 79 million Americans between the ages of 9 and 28 and concluded that they consume twenty hours worth of media a day in seven hours of actual time. They're super-multitaskers who pass messages back and forth via e-mail and frequently have multiple media streams running simultaneously. A Burst Media study of 800 college students found that a third spend at least ten hours a week online, while less than 20 percent spend that much time with TV or radio.

They don't have the patience to listen to marketing messages. There are too many other things to do. As my 14-year-old daughter, Alice, said, "Constant advertising is annoying."

It's not that the younger generation shuns the media. They just shun the media their parents use.

How to Use this Book

The New Influencers is intended to help marketers understand the new patterns of influence that are emerging in social media and to begin to engage with the influencers. I've tried to do this by telling stories. In the chapters that follow, you'll meet a lot of these influencers and hear them describe their aspirations and motivations in their own words.

Chapter One introduces blogs and tells how they came to be so influential. It covers the many different kinds of blogs, although I'll suggest that only three are really meaningful to marketers, and discusses the complex interdependency that is forming between mainstream and social media.

Chapter Two looks at the fascinating ethical and behavioral standards that are developing in social media. Even if you're an experienced blogger, you'll probably be interested in reading how communities, standards and conventions are being shaped without any formal mechanism for doing so. This chapter is the foundation for understanding the rest of the book.

Chapter Three is about the enthusiasts. These are some of the most fascinating people I met in the course of researching this book. They're passionate about their interests and many are building large communities of like-minded readers who are shaping markets. These people are the essential New Influencers.

Chapter Four gets into the nitty gritty of influence. It gathers up a body of research and opinion from people who are out in the field trying to understand influence and suggests some models for making sense of it all.

Chapter Five tells how big business is using social media to communicate with customers and the media and to become influencers themselves. Even if you choose to skip this chapter, check out the remarkable opening anecdote about General Motors.

Chapter Six is about blogging and podcasting in the small/medium business world. More and more businesses are using these low-cost media to raise awareness and grow sales and it really works. There are lots of good case studies here.

Chapter Seven looks at public relations, a profession that I believe will be transformed by new media. It's a pretty scary new world for a lot of PR people right now, but some industry leaders are setting the direction and the PR profession is getting very animated by the potential. Social media is a chance for them to shine.

Chapter Eight is about podcasting, those digital radio shows that are increasingly turning up on people's iPods in the gym and the car. This is grass roots media at its finest, even though some of it is not so fine right now. But it's getting better.

Chapter Nine is a practical guide to the tools you can use the keep your digital ear to the ground. It's a big new world out there. Fortunately, most of these services are free and they're not nearly as hard to use as you may think.

Chapter Ten looks at the fascinating new field of viral marketing, in which social networks are used to create awareness and, ultimately, sales. There are some wonderfully clever ideas being tried in this area. The downside is that a lot of them don't work.

Chapter Eleven is the to-do list. It sums up some issues to consider in deciding whether and how to join the global conversation. And it issues a challenge to marketers to grasp this opportunity to reinvent themselves and enhance their visibility in the business.

There are also six profiles of people who have had a notable impact on markets through their use of blogs, podcasts, Web video and word-of-mouth marketing. Finally, two appendices look at the remarkable and unpredictable transformative power of information technology and statistics about social media practitioners and their motivations.

I wrote *The New Influencers* to help marketers understand the changes in influence patterns that social media is creating in their customer base. Every market is different, of course. Some have already been transformed by these trends while others will change much more slowly or hardly at all. But the forces of change that have been set in motion will be dramatic and irreversible. The worlds of media and marketing will be transformed forever. Get ready for it.

CHAPTER 1
Origins of Social Media

On June 13, 2006, Vincent Ferrari decided to cancel his America Online account. Ferrari, an active blogger, had heard complaints about AOL's customer service. The company's high-pressure tactics were legendary; sales reps were trained to make it uncomfortable for a customer to leave.

Ferrari thought it would be an interesting experiment to record his phone call with the AOL representative. If there was something funny there, he'd share it with a few friends and everyone would have a laugh. "I didn't expect much," he says.

The call was cosmic. After spending fifteen minutes on hold, Ferrari was connected to a rep named John, who spent the next five minutes trying to convince Ferrari that it would be a terrible idea to disconnect the service. Even though Ferrari demanded fifteen times to "cancel the account" during one three-minute stretch, John persisted. The height of absurdity was reached when the rep asked to speak to Ferrari's father. Ferrari was 30 at the time.

Vincent Ferrari's been blogging for four years. His Insignificant Thoughts blog gets good traffic: about 350,000 page views a month, enough to make the top 3,000 on the Technorati blog search engine. But he's hardly an A-list blogger.[1] Ferrari didn't think much about the re-

---

1. There actually is no formal "A list," but the term is commonly accepted to mean the most popular bloggers as defined by Technorati, the leading blog search engine.

cording and sat on it for a week. On June 20, he posted the audio file on his blog. "Anyone else have an interesting 'cancellation' story from AOL or some other company?" he asked. Ferrari also sent an e-mail notification to Consumerist.com, a consumer advocacy site that specializes in telling nightmare stories, and to digg.com, a social media site where readers vote for their favorite articles.

What happened next was indeed a nightmare—for AOL. Consumerist published a link to Ferrari's blog post, calling the recording "The Best Thing We Have Ever Posted." An hour later, Ferrari's Internet server crashed under the crushing load of an estimated 300,000 requests for downloads of the audio file.

Within forty-five minutes, the server had crashed again, as it would a couple of more times before the saga ended. In fact, Ferrari's server logged fifteen times its usual network bandwidth in June, almost all of it in the last ten days of the month.

By June 24, the state of the servers didn't matter any more. The story had a life of its own. Copies of the phone call were turning up all over the Internet. On Saturday, a friend called to tell Ferrari that the story had been covered in the *New York Post*. On Sunday, a squib ran in the *New York Times*. The servers crashed again.

On Monday, CNBC called for a phone interview. Then NBC. On Tuesday, June 30, just six days after he had posted the recording, Vincent Ferrari was interviewed by Matt Lauer on the *Today* show, which played a full three-minute clip of the phone call. "How did you remain calm?" an incredulous Lauer asked. Another twenty-five to thirty media calls followed; Ferrari lost count. On July 14, he was on *Nightline*.

And that was just mainstream media. Thousands of blogs and websites picked up the story, including A-list blogs like BoingBoing.net, Metafilter.com and Fark.com. On July 19, Consumerist posted what it said was an AOL retention manual, an eighty-nine-page document with detailed flowcharts showing how to head off a customer cancellation. The site ran a photo of a smoking cigarette protruding from the barrel of a gun. By August 1, a Google search on "Vincent Ferrari" and "AOL" returned more than 150,000 results.

Through it all, AOL remained grimly stoic. The company issued an apology, said it fired the rep (who was probably guilty only of overzealousness) and declared the incident "inexcusable." But it couldn't ignore the comments that were accumulating on Insignificant Thoughts;

more than a thousand of them, most of them outraged at AOL, some by AOL employees. "I'm so glad someone recorded this," read one. "I work at AOL so I know what a shit company it is." Added another self-described AOL employee, simply, "I finally feel like I have my soul back." Thousands of similar comments were logged on other sites that played the sound clip.

On August 2, AOL announced that it would stop charging certain customers for access to its service. The process of dismantling its customer retention organization had begun. A spokeswoman said the decision was reached after months of analysis and had nothing to do with the Ferrari incident.

And she was probably right. At least to a point. Vincent Ferrari may not have caused AOL to change it business model, but he must have influenced it. He lit a match that set off a conflagration of customer complaint. AOL probably knew that its hard-sell tactics were unpopular, but it probably didn't know the degree to which those tactics inspired rage among its customers.

Try this yourself: Type "aol customer service" into Google and look at the first page of results. This company had a problem. Vincent Ferrari wasn't AOL's enemy. He was merely a catalyst for the enemies to make themselves known.

Blog swarms

What happened to AOL is sometimes called a "blog swarm" and it is one of the most awesome meteorological phenomena of the social media atmosphere. Blog swarms of AOL proportion don't happen very often, but smaller cloudbursts occur every day in different corners of the blogosphere. And outright swarms are becoming more common.

Understanding how these clouds of dissension form turns out to be about as difficult as modeling the real weather. No one really has the answers. But some patterns are beginning to emerge as experts try to model the complex patterns of influence in this vast peer network.[2]

The disruptive[3] power of social media is made starkly real in crises like the AOL swarm and it's something businesses will have to learn to

2. In Chapter 4, we'll look at these patterns in greater detail.
3. Throughout this book I'll use the word "disrupt" to refer to fundamental change. I don't mean the word to have a positive or negative connotation, for disruption can often set the stage for rebirth and new growth.

adjust to. "Just about every company will have a problem with a product or service, resulting in unhappy customers," wrote Marqui, a developer of Web-based marketing automation software, in a 2006 white paper. "What has changed…is that disgruntled customers now have a greater reach, a louder voice, than they ever did in the past. News travels very, very fast in the Web 2.0 world—and bad news can spread through the blogvines like wild fire."

Conventional marketing wisdom has long held that a dissatisfied customer tells ten people. But that's out of date. In the new age of social media, he or she has the tools to tell 10 million. How did this all happen so quickly?

Online economics enabled new businesses to germinate and re-write the rules of media.

It's now possible to address small audiences cost-efficiently, audiences that could never have been served in print. In the first decade of the Web, new-media publishers like CNet, MarketWatch, TechTarget,[4] Motley Fool, Slate and many others grew and prospered by building affinity groups that hadn't existed before and by delivering information at a velocity that was impossible in print. eBay offered the first glimpse of what would come to be called the "long tail."[5]

But the first decade of the Web wasn't about publishing so much as it was about reading. Early browsers had a forms capability that enabled the

> ### What's a Technorati?
>
> Throughout this book, you'll find many references to Technorati or BlogPulse rankings. These are two popular blog search engines that, in addition to indexing the blogosphere, attempt to identify the most popular bloggers. Their formulas for doing this are imperfect and a bit controversial, but the rankings are closely monitored by many bloggers. For more detail, see Chapter 9.

4. TechTarget is a company that understood the looming shift to targeted markets and built a business on it. I was fortunate to be there for the first six years and describe the company's success in more detail in Chapter 4.
5. The Long Tail has become an overused marketing buzzword, but the basic principle is critical to understanding the value of small markets. Chris Anderson published a book on the subject: *The Long Tail: Why the Future of Business Is Selling Less of More* (Hyperion, 2006). The original Wired article is at http://www.wired.com/wired/archive/12.10/tail.html. Recently, the long tail idea has come under fire. The *Wall Street Journal*'s Lee Gomes took issue with Anderson's thesis in a July 2006 column, citing factual errors and quoting the author's own sources to argue that the long tail isn't nearly as great a market opportunity as Anderson claimed. A debate continues on Anderson's blog (thelongtail.com).

user to input information to a website. But the tools to actually publish that information were rudimentary. Yes, you could build a personal website but updating was a chore. Most people who built personal websites pretty much left them alone once they were running. Even if you did update your website, there was no way to tell anyone about it other than by e-mail.

Some students of social media like Stanford law professor Lawrence Lessig have called that first decade the "read-only" Internet. While it was possible to create websites, it wasn't easy. So the people who created them were mostly organizations, who saw the Web as a billboard or a way to take orders from customers. The "read/write" Internet wouldn't emerge until a few years ago.

The interactive Web

Blogs give individuals a way to express their voices in a way that is highly personal and controllable. Blogs are revolutionary because they make it possible for people to publish quickly and easily under their own names. And whether for reasons of ego or control, that characteristic has struck a mighty chord with Internet users.

A survey of 7,012 people by the Pew Internet & American Life Project in mid-2006 found that 39 percent of U.S. Internet users read blogs while 8 percent write them. More than half of bloggers are under the age of thirty and more than half also said they had never published before they started blogging, podcasting or videocasting. Women represent 46 percent of the blogosphere and men 54 percent.

The dynamics of social media today are rooted in the competition between bloggers to achieve greater influence for their personal points of view, attached to their names and their identities. They're an evolution of discussion groups, the early online conversational tools that were a hit with a small group of computer enthusiasts. Blogs are different from discussion groups, though, because they put the author in control. They do have their shortcomings; for example, their reverse-chronological format limits flexibility. But the value of personal expression is compelling for so many frustrated writers that newly empowered Internet diarists have seized blogs—and their companion, podcasts—with a passion previously unseen in the media world.

"Thousands of new Web communities have popped up offering twists on MySpace and YouTube," wrote *Washington Post* technology columnist Leslie Walker in a retrospective article in August 2006. "Partly, these start-ups are the result of something I didn't anticipate—Internet publishing costs falling through the floor, at a time when Web software grew more powerful…Falling costs will turbo-charge personal publishing even more by letting the good ones reach the Web quickly." Walker is actually wrong about the cost. If you have a computer, and an Internet connection, there are at least a dozen websites that will give you a blog for free.[6]

Understanding blogs

The online encyclopedia Wikipedia.org defines "blog" as:

> …a website where regular entries are made (such as in a journal or diary) and presented in reverse chronological order. Blogs often offer commentary or news on a particular subject, such as food, politics, or local news; some function as more personal online diaries. A typical blog combines text, images, and links to other blogs, Web pages, and other media related to its topic. Most blogs are primarily textual although many focus on photographs, videos or audio.

Wikipedia makes some distinctions that are important for marketers to understand. While the popular image of a blog is as a personal diary, the reality is that the most popular—and commercially influential—blogs on the Internet are topical. They offer a personal voice, but usually on an issue that's compelling to a number of people. They're a new style of publishing that emphasizes timeliness and opinion over comprehensiveness.

Types of blogs

Among the fifteen varieties of blogs listed by Wikipedia.org are business blogs, cultural blogs, gossip blogs, link blogs, online diaries, photo blogs, political blogs, video blogs (vlogs) and travel blogs. For practical

6. The underlying technology forces that sparked the social media revolution are a continuation of a trend that has developed over the last twenty-five years and which I call technology leverage. Small changes in technology can have enormous economic and societal impacts years down the road, but we're rarely even aware of their potential at the time. In the case of blogs, the incredible deflation in the price of computer storage and the rise of so-called open-source software were the catalysts for change. In Appendix A, I explain this phenomenon in more detail and explain how a few technology forces came together early in this decade to create the social media craze.

The Search Phenomenon

Blogs have a few distinctive features that standard web sites don't. A *permalink* is a unique blog entry—or article—with its own URL. Every blog entry has a corresponding permalink. A blog is actually a series of permalinks strung together. Most blogs simply list permalinks in reverse chronological order by default. But using "categories" or "tags," permalinks can be combined in many different ways. This gives blogs flexibility that conventional websites typically don't have. A blogger may choose to assign an article post to one or more categories or add tags that are a more flexible equivalent of categories. A reader can then view all blog posting in a particular category or by date, with the corresponding permalinks organized according to that selection.

Permalinks have another very powerful feature. They do very well on search engines. This is because permalink file names usually correspond to the headline on the entry. Google pays a lot of attention to file names in its Page Rank algorithm, the result being that a blogger who posts extensively on a particular topic or company name can swiftly rise up the stack in Google search results. For example, HackingNetflix, a popular blog about the mail-order DVD service, was the number two result in a Google search on "Netflix" just a few months after it was launched.

This can be a problem for marketers because critics can quickly become as prominent in search results as their own brands. In a 2005 incident that came to be known as "Dell Hell," popular blogger Jeff Jarvis posted a rant on his Buzzmachine.com blog about a negative experience he had with Dell Computer's customer support operation. Thousands of readers added their comments and linked to the Jarvis page from their own blogs. The story was picked up by the *New York Times*, the *Washington Post*, *BusinessWeek* and other mainstream media, many of which linked to Jarvis' blog. The result: by the end of 2005, Dell Hell postings were showing up in the first page of Google search results on the keyword "Dell."[1]

Many blogging software packages also support TrackBack, which is a mechanism for bloggers to automatically notify other bloggers when their work has been cited. The original entry can automatically display the URL from a later commenting entry, which can help both rise in search ranks. Even casual bloggers are sometimes amazed to type search queries into Google and find their own entries within the top few results.

purposes, though, most blogs fall into one of four categories: online diaries, topical blogs, advocacy blogs and link blogs.

Online diaries like Yarn Harlot, CourtingDestiny and Wil Wheaton are mainly focused on recounting personal experiences, often in touching or hilarious detail. They tend to get less traffic than linked commentaries, but the readers who visit them are often passionately committed to the blog and the blogger. They read every day.

Topical blogs are the most popular and commercially successful. They include leading titles like Engadget.com, Gawker.com, Lifehacker.com and TechCrunch.com. Often written by multiple authors, they provide highly focused and passionate coverage of subjects like consumer electronics, politics, media and sports. Their audiences may be large or small, but they are often just as passionate about a subject as the authors of the topical blogs. In my view, these are the most important blogs for marketers to watch, since they have the most potential to move markets.

Advocacy blogs (my own terminology) are usually written by individuals and are intended to reflect a point of view on a variety of topics. Examples include Instapundit, Daily Kos, Huffington Post and Michelle Malkin. Usually authored by an individual, advocacy blogs offer the blogger's opinion—often very pointed—on current events. They also inspire a passionate following of readers who share the author's point of view.

Advocacy blogs are a mixed bag for marketers. A lot of them are about politics, which makes them of limited interest to business. However, many focus on workplace rights, consumer affairs, corporate governance, lobbying and other topics that may affect businesses. Wal-Mart, for example, has fought an ongoing battle against bloggers who criticize its employee relations practices. Some advocacy blogs have very large readership. On the other hand, some companies have such passionate followings (Apple and Harley-Davidson, for example) that they spawn a community of enthusiastic fan blogs. As we shall see in Chapter 3, this community can be tapped for feedback and viral marketing, often at nominal cost.

Link blogs are also very popular. They include BoingBoing.net, Metafilter.com, Fark.com, Waxy.org and RobotWisdom.com. These sites are essentially collections of commented links to other information on the Internet, but their distinctive voices can make them hugely influential. BoingBoing, for example, can send hundreds of thousands of visitors to a website with a single link.

Link blogs frequently have distinctive voices and political or social agendas. Fark.org, for example, is known for biting sarcasm while the somewhat more intellectual BoingBoing has been a vocal critic of digital rights management. Although these sites don't do original reporting in the conventional sense, they initiate and guide conversations based on where they choose to link. The lines between topical and link blogs are usually fuzzy, because so much of blogosphere content consists of links between sites.

Style points

Different content requires different formats. Online diaries are generally the least frequently updated blogs, but the posts can be carefully crafted personal essays, often of 1,000 words or more. Diarists' stock-in-trade is their personality and voice. Their topics are drawn from life experience and they are likely to link to other bloggers in a close-knit community of people with similar interests.

Advocacy blogs are also all about personality but the author's objective is to promote a point of view. Advocacy blogs typically link to and comment upon news stories and other blog entries, often with frenetic frequency.

Instapundit is a prototypical advocacy blog. Written by Glenn Reynolds, a law professor at the University of Tennessee, it's the 17th most popular blog in the Technorati rankings. Reynolds posts fast and furiously. On June 16, 2006, he posted twelve blog entries from 7:52 A.M. to 6:18 P.M. ranging from five words ("GEORGE W. BUSH: Gun felon?") to three hundred words.

Reynolds' postings are typically a mix of uncommented links to other articles on the Web that reinforce his conservative political agenda and impassioned opinions seeded with extensive excerpts from speeches and blog postings. This style is part of Reynolds' voice and his readers—some 200,000 daily—respond to it. Reynolds' frenetic posting schedule is also part of his style. There's always something new on Instapundit and that keeps readers coming back.

Actually, June 16 was a light day for Reynolds, who frequently posts more than twenty entries daily. But he could be excused for that. He was on vacation.

Topical blogs

Topical blogs are the closest thing in the blogosphere to mainstream media because many of them report on current events. Frequently they are political, but some of the most popular topical blogs—like Engadget, Gawker, TechCrunch and Make—write extensively about products and companies. They most closely resemble mainstream media in the blogosphere.

Autoblog is an example. Ranked 131st by Technorati, the site serves a dedicated audience of hard-core car lovers. It was launched in 2004 by Weblogs, Inc., the blogging network that also owns Engadget. The idea was to take the Engadget formula and extend it to a new market, according to David Thomas, 30, the founding editor of Autoblog.[7]

The small staff used the Engadget editorial guidelines: find something interesting on the Web, describe it, comment on it, link to it, find a photo and get in on the site. Then start looking for something else. It's a rapid-fire, manic work style with few items running more than a couple of hundred words. But the staff posts new content, on average, every hour or two, seven days a week.

Autoblog and topical blogs like it leverage the unique characteristics of blogs, which are speed and links. The site doesn't pretend to be a major source of breaking news, but it keeps readers apprised of what other people are saying in near real-time. It is more likely to post an unverified rumor than its mainstream media counterparts, but that's part of Autoblog's voice.

In that respect, Autoblog is like a wire service. "You're not so much creating stories yourself as finding stories, pointing to them and explaining their relevance," Thomas says. "It's a really fast, as-it's-happening, one-stop kind of place." And there's an important dimension of blog protocol: always cite the source.

This near-real-time news style is what's made it possible for Autoblog to prosper in a market that's chock full of car sites. That and voice. Voice is very important in the blogosphere. In fact, any successful blogger can tell you in detail what his or her voice is.

Voice is the way you speak to readers. Your voice may be friendly, edgy, snarky, academic, sagacious or enthusiastic. Two blogs can cover much the same material yet be successful with different audiences because they have different voices.

Autoblog's voice "is how you'd sit in a bar talking to your buddies about cars," Thomas says. "It's informal but informed. Some of the car sites are dry as can be. They're lab reports. We know we're speaking to the kind of people who see a new Mustang and just have to have it."

7. Engadget's successful formula is explained in more detail in "The Gadget King," a sidebar to Chapter 3 that profiles founding editor Peter Rojas.

To demonstrate the importance of voice, Thomas talks about a recent project: launching a blog for auto site Cars.com. The Cars.com audience is completely different from Autoblog's, he says. Visitors are consumers looking to make intelligent buying decisions. They aren't enthusiasts. So the Cars.com blog will emphasize facts and recent news, presented with a serious and authoritative voice. "Autoblog is an enthusiast publication. Cars.com is a tool for helping people," he says. The voices may be different, but both can succeed with their audiences.

Mainstream media meets the blogosphere

Some social media advocates like to portray bloggers as being in conflict with mainstream media. The implication is that one side is set against the other, as if there will be a winner and a loser.

In fact, mainstream media and the blogosphere are remarkably complementary. Bloggers need newspapers, magazines, radio stations and their accompanying websites to provide a constant stream of source material. Mainstream media, though it may not want to admit it, can use bloggers to provide feedback on the work it does. A struggle is playing out there, but it's a constructive struggle.

If you think of mainstream media as the news section of the Internet, then the blogosphere is like the op-ed page. Few blogs report breaking news, although some bloggers do cover events like conventions and trade shows through their medium. But the format and organization of a

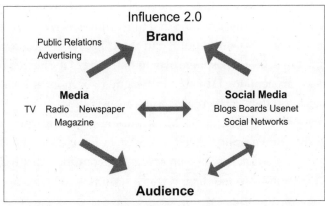

In Influence 2.0, a model proposed by influence measurement firm Cymfony, mainstream and social media are intertwined, forming an idea and feedback loop that is unlike anything marketers have ever encountered. *Source: Cymfony*

blog really doesn't lend itself to news reporting. Blogs have no hierarchy and relatively poor indexing. There's no "front page" on a blog. It's just one continuous narrative that starts at the end and goes back to the beginning.

Newspapers and news sites are designed to deliver a wide range of topics in a random-access format. Front pages and home pages present the reader with a lot of choices. Navigation is by category and chronology has little to do with it. You read a news site completely differently than you read a blog.

Topical blogs and advocacy blogs need mainstream media, which is why the vaunted clash between the two sources is so improbable. Instapundit, Michelle Malkin, Engadget, Autoblog, 43 Folders, Huffington Post and many other blogs would be nowhere without mainstream media sites to mine for news. When pushed, bloggers will admit that mainstream news organizations do the leg work and grunt work that they won't. The two groups have an odd love-hate relationship. Mainstream media feeds the blogosphere but increasingly get story ideas and tips from it. Bloggers criticize mainstream media for its well-publicized lapses but link to newspapers and magazines far more than any other source.[8]

That symbiosis can sometimes get pretty heated. In a notable incident in 2004, bloggers attacked a *60 Minutes* report that claimed to have documented proof that President George W. Bush had evaded the draft. CBS posted the documents online and bloggers immediately cried foul, pointing out that fonts used in the documents were unavailable on typewriters at the time they were allegedly published. After a couple of weeks of denial, CBS eventually admitted that the documents were suspect and issued an apology. The story didn't end there, however. CBS continued to suffer attacks in the blogosphere over its handling of the incident. When *60 Minutes* commentator Dan Rather resigned six months later, many media-watchers cited "Rathergate" as a leading factor.

In the fall of 2005, blogger Mark Russinovich unearthed a backdoor security vulnerability called a rootkit in Sony BMG music CDs. Rootkits can enable hackers to gain access to a computer that had come in contact with the infected disk. It was a serious security compromise,

8. In my survey of 163 bloggers (Appendix A), mainstream media was the bloggers' second most often-cited external source of ideas (57 percent) behind other bloggers (70 percent). However, link analyses by professional researchers shows that bloggers in general cite mainstream media sites as sources far more than other blogs.

particularly in a product that was not sold as computer software. Russinovich posted a detailed account of his discovery on his blog on Halloween Day and the blogosphere immediately exploded. More than 1,500 people commented on Russinovich's discovery and the story was quickly picked up by news sites like Slashdot.org and TheRegister.com. From there, it spread into mainstream media.

Sony first denied, but eventually admitted to its overzealousness in including the hidden software on music CDs.[9] It offered a fix, but Russinovich found that the fix actually worsened the security vulnerability. The blogosphere, again, went nuts. The story generated mainstream media coverage in the *New York Times*, the *Boston Globe*, the BBC, *BusinessWeek* and dozens of other major publications. For two months, it seemed that Sony could do nothing right. Every attempt it made to quell the criticism resulted in more blog rants, sparking more media coverage and more demands for compensation. Dozens of class action suits were filed against Sony in New York and California. The state of Texas also filed suit.

Sony eventually admitted that at least fifty-two CD titles had been released with the hidden rootkit. Researchers estimated that a half million customers in 165 countries had been infected. Sony agreed to pull hundreds of thousands of CDs out of stores, compensate affected customers and tighten its policies on the disclosure of copy protection methods in the future. There's no clear estimate of how much the mistake cost the proud Japanese firm, but the damage was easily in the tens of millions of dollars. And that's not counting the hit that Sony's reputation took as the story spread. Six months after the incident, mainstream media were still covering the scandal. "We made a mistake and Sony paid a terrible price," Sony CEO Howard Stringer told Walt Mossberg of the *Wall Street Journal*.

The Sony story dramatizes two important truths about the blogosphere. One is that the mainstream media and bloggers can work together constructively to develop a story. In this case, not only did bloggers alert journalists of the existence of a problem, but they also provided detailed explanations of the technical factors at hand. Coverage in newspapers like the *New York Times* openly complimented bloggers for defin-

9. Press accounts later revealed that many Sony executives weren't even aware that the software was there; it had been authorized by a few overzealous officials who were worried about intellectual property protection.

ing and explaining the issues. And for the first time since blogs exploded on the scene, mainstream media coverage was genuinely positive about the contributions of the blogging community.

Another truth with the blogosphere is that transparency is key to working in this medium. Sony's biggest mistake arguably was not that it planted the spyware platform on the music CDs but that it failed to respond quickly and openly to complaints. The company's ducks and dodges in the face of a storm of blogger complaints and mounting pressure from the media made the company look evasive and sneaky. In fact, it was probably just confused.

This premium on transparency may be the single greatest cultural shift that businesses will face as they engage with social media. The move from messages to conversations will tax many marketers and swamp some. The emerging culture of transparency and openness in social media is a story taking shape, but it's clear that companies that choose to participate will need to speak to their communities in very different ways.

CHAPTER 2

From Chaos, Structure

Years from now, anthropologists may look back on the early years of the blogosphere as the greatest experiment in social self-organization ever attempted. Millions of writers of all ages, interests, languages and motivations are together forming a set of shared principles, operating standards and behaviors without any kind of central coordination.

MIT's David Clark, who was one of the architects of what would become the modern Internet, once said, "We reject kings, presidents and voting. We believe in rough consensus and running code." In many ways, the blogosphere is the embodiment of that principle.

The blogosphere is perhaps unique in human history in that respect. There are no standards organizations, governing bodies or representatives. There is no written constitution or bill of rights. There are no organizations to enforce acceptable behavior. There is no elected or appointed leadership although, as this book will argue, sophisticated patterns of influence are emerging. In short, there is no one actively trying to organize or govern this global community in any meaningful way. And bloggers like that just fine.

Conventional wisdom holds that a large group of people without leadership or governance will make bad decisions, if they can make any decisions at all. But recent research indicates that isn't necessarily so. In *The Wisdom of Crowds*, author James Surowiecki cites case after case in which large groups of people collectively make wiser choices than any individual expert within the groups would have made alone.

For example, Surowiecki points to the popular game show *Who Wants to Be a Millionaire*, in which contestants, stumped for an answer, could phone an expert or ask the audience for help:

> *Everything we think we know about intelligence suggests that the smart individual would offer the most help. And, in fact, the "experts" did okay, offering the right answer—under pressure—almost 65 percent of the time. But they paled in comparison to the audiences. Those random crowds of people with nothing better to do on a weekday afternoon than sit in a TV studio picked the right answer 91 percent of the time.*

In another example, using the popular carnival game in which contestants try to guess how many jelly beans are in a jar, he cites a similar result.

> *When finance professor Jack Treynor ran the experiment in his class with a jar that held 850 beans, the group estimate was 871. Only one of the fifty-six people in the class made a better guess.*

Of course, groups can make colossal mistakes, too. An example with sometimes fatal consequences is the tendency of a group of panicked people to run toward the same door without considering other means of egress. The same behavior causes people to choose a restaurant with a few patrons rather than an empty one across the street, on the assumption that the people in the restaurant have made a wise choice. In fact, most of them may be there for the same reason: because they saw others inside.

Author and teacher Clay Shirky maintains that communities without rules or supervision inherently become unmanageable. Structure is needed to "defend the group from itself." Shirky cites numerous examples of online communities, such as Yahoo! message boards, in which the lack of governance leads to chaos. Without someone to keep order, the spammers, flamers and nuts take over.

One of his examples is Communitree, an early online bulletin board system that was founded on the principle of open access. The experiment went fine until a group of high schoolers entered and turned the discussion into a free-for-all of juvenile behavior. He told the Etech conference in April 2003:

> *The adults who had set up Communitree were horrified, and overrun by these students. The place that was founded on open access had too*

much open access, too much openness. They couldn't defend themselves against their own users. The place that was founded on free speech had too much freedom. They had no way of saying "No, that's not the kind of free speech we meant."

In another example, the *Los Angeles Times* in June of 2005 launched an experimental wiki, which is a kind of free-form collaborative software. The paper issued an open invitation for users to contribute to its morning editorial. "Who knows where this will lead? It may lead straight into the Dumpster of embarrassing failures," the invitations read, prophetically.

Early revisions were modest but the tone grew more shrill as the day went along. By the next day, obscenities began to appear. Eventually, a vandal replaced the editorial with a two-word expletive and the *Times* sheepishly terminated the experiment.

So the question is which way will the blogosphere go? Will an army of individuals follow the Surowiecki model and achieve a higher level of intelligence as a group? Or will the group inevitably become so big that it collapses into chaos, as Shirky has suggested?

Efforts to organize the blogosphere are proceeding on multiple lines. An informal network of prominent writers, sometimes called the "A-list," attracts so much attention and readership that they are able to articulate standards that are broadly accepted by others. A-list bloggers are all too aware of the risk of chaos and are determined not to let it happen to their neighborhood. Their efforts are proceeding along multiple lines with no formal coordination but a kind of shared goal. The leaders sometimes don't even know they're leaders. They see themselves as part of a feedback loop in which their audience keeps them in line while they, in turn, guide a discussion that engages the audience.

This constant reader-blogger interaction can also make bloggers more inclined to take risks. A-list bloggers, in particular, count on their readers to help them focus and even fact-check a story and they take those comments very seriously. "I'm happy to publish something that I've heard but isn't confirmed because someone who has knowledge will comment on that story," says Steve Hall of Adrants. "People know that Adrants is not the place to come for absolute fact. If I'm not absolutely sure something is right, I'll say that. Readers will set me straight if I'm wrong."

When I mentioned to Robert Scoble, formerly Microsoft's #1 blogger, that he wields great influence in the blogosphere, he demurred:

> *This is a two-way medium. You can't snow your audience for long. My audience is far smarter than I am, far better connected and far more powerful. If I say something is true and it isn't, they're going to let me know in the worst way.*

Scoble told how he once posted a compliment and a link to perceptive comment from a political blogger. However, it turned out that blogger was a political extremist. "My audience responded within fifteen minutes," he said. "I pulled the post down. Part of being a good blogger is listening and learning from your audience."

Standards of behavior

One prominent voice of reason is Dan Gillmor, formerly the technology columnist for the *San Jose Mercury News*. Gillmor is a leading proponent of "citizen journalism," in which individuals play an active role in reporting and disseminating information. These people usually aren't professional journalists, but can act in that capacity for brief periods of time. "The person who documented the London subway bombing was a journalist, if only for a moment," he says.

Gillmor has made it a mission to advocate standards of quality and accuracy in social media that rival those of commercial news outlets. He proposed, for example that major media organizations enlist citizens to blog about the cleanup from hurricane Katrina in New Orleans. The vision is being realized, in rudimentary form, by sites like ibrattleboro.com, backfence.com and Korea's OhMyNews. The standards promoted by Gillmor and practiced by citizen journalism sites are percolating out through the blogosphere.

Viable forms of social media self-governance are taking shape. Wikipedia.org, the online encyclopedia that anyone can edit, has become the largest reference source on the Web, with an archive of information considerably larger than that of any printed reference. A loosely formed group of several hundred unpaid active contributors keep order by screening out vandalism and chasing away miscreants. In an early 2006 study, the journal *Nature* declared that Wikipedia.org rivaled the venerable *Encyclopedia Britannica* in accuracy, even though it hosted four times the content.

Commercial efforts have also begun to organize bloggers into loosely structured teams. One is Corante, a company that aggregates the work of prominent bloggers on a single site. Another, called Gather, hosts blogs and floats the most popular content to the top using a community ratings system. Bloggers get paid based on the frequency and popularity of their contributions.

Pluck organizes leading bloggers into a network that it then syndicates out to newspaper publishers. Gawker and Weblogs, Inc. are collections of highly trafficked blogs that make money selling ads across a network. Some networks enforce or suggest written standards of disclosure and behavior.

A newer and more controversial player is digg.com. This enormously popular site allows users to vote for their favorite stories, with the most popular stories rising to the top. Digg attracts more than one million daily visitors and is the 24th most popular site on the Internet, according to Alexa.com.

Digg is a new twist on new media. Readers rate and comment on submitted articles, with a popular story or blog entry enjoying tens of thousands of visits as a result. It's a real-life application of the *Wisdom of Crowds* concept and it's enormously popular with young Web users, making it an important influence engine. Digg has its critics, though. Some people say a group of readers can never duplicate the judgment of a professional editor. If you don't like what shows up on Digg, there's no one to complain to. The community has spoken. There have been allegations of vote-manipulation. But there is no doubt that digg.com is increasingly a force to be reckoned with and probably a precursor of other community-editing ventures.

It's likely that many models will find a home in the blogosphere of the future. Many bloggers may align themselves with established media companies or blogger networks where the resources and pay are better. Some will achieve the visibility that makes it more lucrative to stay independent, while the vast majority of bloggers will plug away at individual labors of love. As we shall see in Chapter 4, however, some will be considerably more influential than others.

Emerging standards

Bloggers and podcasters want to avoid having their medium go the way of Usenet newsgroups and early discussion forums, which often degenerated into a cacophony of flame-mail and spam. Personal publishers have some significant advantages in that area, though. Bloggers each own their own space and can, to some extent, keep disruptors out. This is in sharp contrast to earlier forms of community media, which were basically open forums that were accessible to anybody. "Comment spam," or random messages posted by automated agents as blog comments, are an ongoing problem. Some bloggers have even had to shut down the comments function on their sites because of the volume of these annoyances. And opportunists quickly figured out ways to set up rogue blogs that have no original content but exist merely to drive traffic to advertisers. Nielsen BuzzMetrics, a firm that monitors blogging activity, estimates that these rogue sites constitute as much as 30 percent of all blogs.

However, the blogosphere is determined not to repeat the mistakes of earlier times. Blogs have a certain structural resilience to disruption because they are controlled by individuals. Many bloggers won't allow comments to be published without human review and about 20 percent of bloggers refuse to accept comments entirely (a controversial practice that is frowned upon by some purists). The blogosphere is also probably the largest decentralized community ever invented. As such, it resists coordinated attacks because each node in the community has its own set of operating principles. In that way, the blogosphere is like the Internet itself.

This characteristic is important to understanding why social media won't suffer from the spam attacks that have disrupted so many discussion boards. Think of Napster, the music-sharing service that was hugely popular among music-lovers in the 2001-2002 time frame. The recording industry hated Napster and successfully attacked, sued and ultimately shut it down. But when Napster died, a host of services sprung up that enabled users to exchange files directly between individual PCs. The music industry was powerless to stop these peer-to-peer services because it would have had to fight millions of enemies instead of just one. Five years later, the industry still hasn't come up with an effective means to fight peer-to-peer file sharing.[1]

Similarly, the highly decentralized structure of the blogosphere insulates it from coordinated attack. Services like Technorati and BlogPulse,

1. Though it's worth noting that the entertainment industry has been an innovative adopter of viral marketing, paid downloads and social networking tactics to promote its products. Services like Podshow Network and GarageBand have also created an extraordinary new means for small artists to showcase their talents and sell their music.

which are leading the effort to index and organize blog content, have developed sophisticated controls to screen out spam blogs. The battle between the legitimate bloggers and the spammers will continue far into the future, but today's bloggers are much better equipped to fight this battle than their predecessors in discussion groups.

As the model evolves, certain standards are being broadly embraced. This is happening without a vote, representation or governing committee. Instead, the movement is led by a cadre of visionary bloggers who are defining the operating standards for the followers. It's kind of a Five Commandments of social media. Let's look at some of them.

Thou shalt link—"Links are the currency of the blogosphere." That statement, sometimes attributed to podcasting innovator Adam Curry, defines the essence of how influence is derived in social media. Look at the blogs of the top writers as listed on Technorati, BlogPulse or IceRocket and you will see links everywhere. The more popular the blogger, it seems, the more links he or she has to other sources of information.

Links are a manifestation of the culture of attribution that pervades blogging. It's an unwritten rule that you never steal content. You can quote, elaborate upon, annotate and comment upon someone else's writings all you want, but you must always attribute and link to the source.

This unwritten rule provides much of the glue that holds social media together. Few bloggers post copyright notices but this understanding pervades the community: It's okay to copy and re-post my words on your blog—it's even a compliment—but you must attribute the source and link back to me so that I can enjoy some benefit of the traffic from your visitors.

Top bloggers understand their responsibility particularly well. A prominent blogger who liberates someone else's ideas or words without attribution is likely to be singled out in a barrage of comment and blog flames. That's one reason top bloggers are especially sensitive to this issue; they understand that they have a special responsibility to set the standards for their readers.

Links have a secondary advantage. Many lesser-known bloggers live for the beneficence of a link from an A-list player. Top bloggers know that the more links they bestow upon their fans, the more benefits accrue to the smaller players beneath them and the more gratitude they accumulate. Used judiciously, they reinforce the blogger's influence in the community without undermining it.

Links also define a healthy, friendly competition between bloggers for recognition. A blogger's ranking on industry popularity lists is a source of pride and bragging rights. Many blogs feature counters, link charts and other visual doodads that attest to their readership and level of influence. A few people achieve enough status to generate significant income from their writing. For most, however, it's enough just to have an impact. Asked what are the most important reasons they blog, respondents to my survey listed "influence market or discussion" as their third most important motivation, behind connecting with others and keeping track of their thoughts. Links are a broadly accepted measure of influence.

Thou shalt not diss—Blogs have a reputation of being crude, disrespectful and crass. And while some are pretty obnoxious, the reality is that the vast majority of influential bloggers practice an almost parliamentary civility.

This is a change from just a couple of years ago and it illustrates the determination of blogging enthusiasts not to let their neighborhood be invaded by vandals. "Attack of the Blogs," a November 2005 article in *Forbes* magazine, riveted the attention of the blogosphere. It states:

> *Weblogs are the prized platform of an online lynch mob spouting liberty but spewing lies, libel and invective. Their potent allies in this pursuit include Google and Yahoo...They are the ultimate vehicle for brand-bashing, personal attacks, political extremism and smear campaigns. It's not easy to fight back: Often a bashing victim can't even figure out who his attacker is..."Bloggers are more of a threat than people realize, and they are only going to get more toxic. This is the new reality," says Peter Blackshaw, chief marketing officer at Intelliseek.*

In fact, the dark future predicted by the *Forbes* article doesn't appear to be materializing. A-list bloggers were incensed by the story's conclusions and quickly rallied to defend the fort. Respected Silicon Valley columnist Dan Gillmor noted:

> *What a pile of trash from Forbes Magazine...it's worth reading to see how a normally solid business magazine can go astray with an alarmist and at times absurd broadside. Do bloggers sometimes go too far? Of course. But if the best-read bloggers typically did work of the*

lousy quality shown in the Forbes stories, they'd be pilloried — appropriately so.

Steve Rubel of the influential Micro Persuasion blog wrote:

Don't listen to Forbes. Take a look around the blogosphere for yourself and you will find real humans—good, bad and ugly…There are some who mean well, others who are more nefarious. And all want to be heard. Listen to them. Work with them.

While many bloggers may have dismissed the *Forbes* piece, it was a wake-up call. Devotees are committed to not let the vandalism and bad behavior that choked newsgroups in the Internet's early days affect their community. The ethics of blogging, as defined on thousands of blogs and in dozens of corporate blogging strategies today, is to defer to one's critics, engage with them in a conversation and respect their point of view. While there will always be flame wars and name-calling in the blogosphere, the A-list seems determined not to let things go that way.

Thou shalt be transparent—"Transparency" is a word bloggers use a lot. It's kind of a mashup of principles that include honesty, integrity, humility, open-mindedness and fairness. The idea is that blogs, like diaries, should lay bare the thoughts of the author and chronicle the development of his or her ideas over time without revising the process that got the person there.

This shows up in interesting ways. Blogging protocol dictates, for example, that you shouldn't revise a post once it's posted. Changes should be presented by striking through the original text and writing the revised text next to it. Major revisions may be presented as comments on one's own blog posting, kind of a public correction. Deleting a post is considered appropriate only when the author believes he or she might do harm or seriously mislead readers by leaving the words online. There's a deference to mainstream media here; newspapers can't retract stories they've written but must write follow-ups that correct or redefine the original content. Bloggers operate much the same way with the words they write. They may have second thoughts, but protocol says they can't disown their earlier comments.

This is an important point for marketers to understand. Good bloggers think carefully about what they write but they also possess the power to immediately correct their mistakes. And in fact, most bloggers are all too happy to revise published comments and opinions if they can be persuaded to think otherwise. My interviews with dozens of bloggers reinforced time and again that these people are more flexible, introspective and suggestible than their battle-hardened counterparts in the media. You are much more likely to persuade a blogger to rethink his or her opinion than you are a reporter.

I suspect one reason for this flexible attitude is that bloggers aren't bound by the cultural memory of conventional media. Once a statement is in print or on the air, it can't easily be retracted or corrected. Print journalists, therefore, put a premium on getting all the facts right before they publish.

Online publishers know that the record *can* be corrected. Even if you don't get it right the first time, the archive will at least be accurate. And since most bloggers aren't professional journalists, they don't have a journalist's aversion to going with speculative information. This isn't to pass judgment one way or the other. It's just the way a lot of bloggers think.

Transparency may be the most disruptive and far-reaching innovation to come out of social media. In the blogosphere, transparency is about a lot more than just not lying. It's about opening yourself to inspection, analysis, judgment, praise and ridicule. It's remarkable that a community of people with so little formal organization should embrace it as a core cultural value. Unfortunately, this value may also be the greatest obstacle to broader adoption of blogging in corporate America where openness is often punished. This issue will be explored in greater detail in Chapter 5.

Thou shalt comment—Commenting is core part of blogging protocol. In my survey of bloggers, 71 percent said they comment on four or more blogs at least monthly, and almost 30 percent comment on more than ten. Comments on their own blogs were also the second most important indicator of the blogs' performance, trailing only links from other blogs, respondents said.

A study by Gilad Mishne of the University of Amsterdam and Natalie Glance of Nielsen BuzzMetrics estimated that comments account for about 30 percent of total blogosphere content and that there is a direct correlation between commenting and a blog's overall popularity.[2] "Com-

2. To be fair, this is a bit of a chicken-and-egg phenomenon. Popular blogs tend to draw a lot of comments, which feeds back into their popularity. Mishne and Glance found that blog entries that had comments received, on average, 79 percent more page views and 300 percent more inbound links than entries without comments.

ments are regarded by most bloggers as vital to the interactive nature of weblogs," the researchers said.

In blog culture, commenting is considered an essential part of the conversation. Posting a comment on another person's blog is a way of inviting a direct interaction with that person. In contrast, commenting on and linking to another blogger's remarks in one's own blog is a way of recognizing the other person's opinion but adding, "no reply needed."

Experienced bloggers make commenting—and responding to comments—a part of their regimen, believing that regular engagement with others keeps them fresh and engaged. In my own survey, over 93 percent of bloggers said they respond to comments.

Comments can create new relationships that spark more blogging. Mike Kaltschnee, author of the influential HackingNetflix blog, tells of how one commenter on his site submitted so many observations that he encouraged her to start her own blog. The result, called NetflixFan, is now a fixture in the movie-lover community. In many cases, camaraderie and mutual support trumps competition.

The decision not to accept comments, even if for a good reason such as preventing comment spam, can be controversial. In early 2006, the *Washington Post* shut down comments on one of its blogs because they contained a large number of personal attacks on the paper's ombudsman, who had criticized Democratic legislators for taking campaign money from a convicted felon. Jim Brady, the *Post*'s executive editor, explained in a blog entry:

> *"There are things that we said we would not allow, including personal attacks, the use of profanity and hate speech. Because a significant number of folks who have posted in this blog have refused to follow any of those relatively simple rules, we've decided not to allow comments for the time being...[I]t's a disappointment to us that we have not been able to maintain a civil conversation, especially about issues that people feel strongly (and differently) about.*

Brady added that the task of screening out negative comments was occupying two *Post* staff members full-time.

The action provoked a storm of blogger protest. Writers accused the *Post* of arrogance and hypocrisy. "My beef is less with washington post.com's decision to shut down comments as it is with their unctuous tone, which appears to ooze contempt for the unwashed and serves to reinforce blogospheric mistrust of the establishment press," wrote veteran political speechwriter Bart Acocella on the Gadflyer blog.

Corporate marketers who are considering entering the blogosphere need to carefully consider the comments issue. Commenting is a great way of getting useful and free feedback from customers and prospects. But comments can be brutally honest and, in some cases, offensive. Businesses need to consider their willingness to absorb these blows and respond rationally and constructively.

"The blogger has to interact with the readers, welcoming comments and responding to them," wrote Bob Parsons, CEO of GoDaddy.com and owner of one of the top CEO blogs on the Internet, in an e-mail interview. "You have to have thick skin, and you have to like to write and communicate with a diverse group of people."[3]

"Even if you have Bill Gates' favorite product people will say bad things about it," wrote Robert Scoble in his "weblog manifesto." Don't try to write a corporate weblog unless you can answer all questions—good and bad—professionally, quickly, and nicely." In practice, few prominent bloggers answer all questions posed by commenters, but they make an effort to address the most common ones.

Thou shalt not blather—In the blogosphere, short and frequent trumps long and occasional. Most of the time. Many A-list bloggers rarely post entries of over five hundred words, believing that milestone to be the threshold of a reader's attention span. Some popular bloggers do a lot of link blogging, in which posts can consist of just a few words and a link. In fact, some bloggers see themselves as nodes on a network, pointing their visitors to items that interest them.

The subject of length is frequently debated by bloggers. The rule of thumb is that short is better than long. Even bloggers such as Lawrence Lessig and Nicholas Carr, who write books and long articles in professional journals, rarely blog over five hundred words. The key issue is that readers have less tolerance with words on a screen than they do with words on paper.

There are exceptions, though. Some writers have such an engaging style and enthusiastic audience that they can run on a bit. GoDaddy's Bob Parsons often posts more than a thousand words in his roughly once-

3. Parsons is profiled in more depth in the chapter on business blogging.

weekly entries. Parson's messages are so thoughtful and powerful, however, that he frequently receives hundreds of comments. And while his entries are less frequent than those of most A-list bloggers, he rarely goes more than a week without posting.[4]

Dave Taylor, an author and Web design guru, says he prefers longer, more thoughtful commentaries. He writes on Ask Dave Taylor, a popular question-and-answer site:

> *Personally, I don't subscribe to weblogs where the typical entry is less than about 250 words, because I'm not interested in* **discoverability**, *that is, what other pages on the Web I should be checking out, but in why the blogger thinks the page, article, site, entry, whatever, is worth my attention.*

Bloggers with strong personalities and loyal followings can get away with verbosity. The key measure of success, they say, is not to bore the audience. In fact, being boring is a crime in the blogosphere, punishable by loss of audience. The rule of thumb is to write (or speak, in the case of podcasts) as long as you have something to say.

The next level

In contrast to the virulent cesspool of trash talk and misinformation forecast by *Forbes*, the blogosphere is developing into an extraordinarily civil and deferential culture. This evolution is being led by a small cadre of influencers who are setting behavioral standards of which Disraeli would have approved. But as we shall see, these New Influencers aren't dictators so much as channelers. They exert influence by aggregating the thoughts and opinions of others whom they trust. This makes the blogosphere extraordinarily resilient to disruption. It also makes the task of determining influence devilishly difficult.

Social media influencers are defining a unique and enduring voice for themselves. This is needed before the medium can move forward to its next level of maturity. Increasingly, only the bloggers, vloggers and podcasters who adhere to these community norms will be taken seriously enough to achieve much influence in their community. That's an

4. Until GoDaddy filed for an initial public offering, at which time Parsons suddenly fell silent. Investor and regulator scrutiny are a strong argument against blogging by top executives and need to be carefully considered as a strategic issue. More in Chapter 6.

important fact for marketers to understand: the New Influencers take their craft seriously and understand the responsibility they have to their colleagues to uphold community standards. This is one reason that social media will be a force to be reckoned with for a long time to come. These cultural standards are turning an army of enthusiasts into a mover of markets.

Of Spaces and Tubes

Because this is a book about influence and not about tools and technologies, I intentionally chose not to devote a lot of space to the most popular social media sites in the world: MySpace and YouTube. These phenomenally popular sites have created models for Web 2.0 interaction and have spawned hundreds of imitators, but their influence is still limited to very specific markets, mostly those favored by teenagers.

Nevertheless, it would be a mistake not to acknowledge the contribution that MySpace, YouTube and other so-called social networking sites are making to the evolution of social media, if only because they are icons for a new generation of influencers. They are also creating a model for interaction that I believe will drive the next wave of social media: special interest communities.

MySpace is the 800-pound gorilla of social networks. With over 100 million members and 80 percent of the traffic to sites in its category, it has defined its market and spawned hundreds of other communities.

Practically every computer-savvy teenager in America has a MySpace account. MySpace has been called the online equivalent of a school lunchroom. The site's success is self-perpetuating in the peer pressure-driven world of teenagers: the more people who sign up, the more other teens need to be there. "I spend 99.9 percent of my [online] time on MySpace. I know one person out of all my friends who doesn't use it," said 17-year-old Steffie of Belmont, Calif., in a panel session at the O'Reilly Web 2.0 conference in 2005.

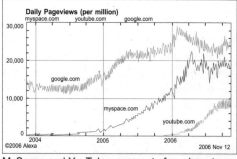

MySpace and YouTube came out of nowhere to approach Google traffic levels in less than two years. Source: Alexa.com

MySpace is built around the concept of "friends." Every member gets a basic set of Web 2.0 tools: a blog, photo- and video-sharing, e-mail and a personal profile. Members can seek each other out by browsing or searching or can discover other members though information that's shared publicly. "Friends" can give each other access to information that's hidden from public view. Given the demographics and tools, it's not surprising that MySpace is a major online dating destination.

In certain industries such as entertainment and beauty products, a MySpace account has become a must-have for marketers. When Twentieth Century Fox released *XMen: The Last Stand* in May 2003, it created a MySpace presence that included polls, contests, buddy icons, wallpaper downloads and shareable videos. MySpace members could add the film's trailer to their own sites with one click. The promotion garnered a record three million friends and the film grossed more than $230 million.

Music is the foundation of MySpace's popularity. If you're a music group targeting teens, you must have a MySpace presence, and some 2.2 million bands do, according to *Fortune* magazine. Some bands have hundreds of thousands of friends. Music-sharing is an important tool available to members, and MySpace has helped launch bands to stardom.

Interest has grown outside the entertainment world, too. Brands such as Nike, Honda, Motorola, Burger King and Starbucks have joined MySpace, offering downloads, giveaways and quirky characters as friends. Wendy's, Burger King and cable channel FX have created fictional characters and endowed them with interests and activities that resonate with teens.

One of the more notable commercial successes on MySpace is Wawa, an east-coast chain of convenience stores known for friendly customer service. Electronic word-of-mouth through sites like MySpace, Facebook and LiveJournal has spawned hundreds of fan clubs on social networking sites. The "I Love Wawa" group on MySpace has over 6,000 members, who share anecdotes and "claim" their favorite convenience stores.

MySpace's success has spawned many imitators. While no one takes on the gorilla directly, other services have applied the model to smaller communities. Facebook, with nine million members, targets the college audience with a format that's a little more buttoned-down and serious. Startup HeyLetsGo links young professionals in different geographic regions. DailyComedy gives aspiring comics a place to try out their routines with virtual audiences. Eons is a startup social networking site targeting seniors.

The MySpace model is a powerful force in social media and is likely to be the foundation for many similar sites in the future. Users each get their own little online kiosk and a set of tools for displaying digital information. They can then selectively share that information with other people. Businesses can have spaces for a fee and offer various promotional goodies. However, selling is strictly prohibited. Early indications are that this model transplants well to all kinds of other communities. In my view, MySpace will remain the leader in this market, but hundreds of special-interest clones will emerge targeting all kinds of topics and geographies.

YouTube is to video what MySpace is to personal publishing. The site, which sold to Google in late 2006 for $1.65 billion, is widely credited with kicking off the Web video craze.[1] Within a year after its December 2005 launch,

---

1. Actually, MySpace users watched 1.4 billion videos in July of 2006—or an average of 39 per member. That makes it the number one video source of the Internet ahead of YouTube, according to comScore Media Metrix.

YouTube was serving 70 million videos a day. Scores of competitors are now imitating the YouTube model, taking advantage of declines in storage and bandwidth costs and people's enthusiasm for video-sharing.

Although it lacks the mind-boggling membership numbers of MySpace, YouTube and its imitators present more interesting opportunities for marketers. TV commercials have historically had a short shelf life, but Internet video permits campaigns to run indefinitely, in some cases even exceeding their TV viewership over the long term.

For example, when GoDaddy.com was turned down thirteen times by ABC in its efforts to run a risqué series of ads on the Super Bowl, the company turned rejection into opportunity. The banned ads have logged more than two million viewings on Google Video and YouTube alone, and are a fixture on GoDaddy's popular site.

Perfetti Van Melle USA got a geyser of publicity when people learned that the company's Mentos mints produced an explosive reaction when dropped into bottles of cola. Thousands of people uploaded videos of their own Mentos experiments with various carbonated beverages. One video logged over 3.5 million views on Google Video alone. Perfetti jumped on the viral popularity of the experiments, posting a large link to YouTube on its home page and sponsoring a contest. Coca-Cola, which was perhaps concerned about potential safety issues and liability, largely ignored the phenomenon.

Blendtec, a Utah-based maker of powerful blenders, created a series of short videos featuring the company's CEO loading things like golf balls, marbles, Coke cans and rake handles into the company's high-end blender and pulverizing them. The first eight episodes of "Will it Blend?" drew over three million downloads in just one week.

Examples like these are still in short supply, however. As of late 2006, less than one-tenth of 1 percent of YouTube videos came from a professional marketer. That ratio seems likely to change, however, as the viral-marketing benefits of campaigns like Will it Blend? gain publicity.

To get visibility on video sites, you need to be witty, offbeat or intensely personal. Stunts like golf balls in a blender work, but so do serial dramas. Fantastic special effects and celebrity appearances are a plus. If you've got the stomach for it, you can even push the limits of good taste. The FCC doesn't regulate Internet video—at least not yet—and for the moment, anything goes.

Many people think video will be social media's killer application on the Web and will change TV viewing habits forever. "[Video-sharing] sites are not going to fade away," wrote Kathy Sharpe, CEO at digital-media agency Sharpe Partners in *OMMA* magazine. "Visitors will not suddenly go back to spending all of their online hours on espn.com. They may choose different sites, even different tools, but the behavior isn't a passing fad. It's part of who we are as human beings."

However, the market is still so young and volatile that it's impossible to predict how it will develop. Friendster, which was the first major social-networking site, caused a sensation when it debuted in 2002. However, it stumbled on execution and was quickly passed by MySpace. The rapid rise and fall of personal website communities like Geocities and Angelfire in the late 1990s leave lingering questions about the staying power of online communities.

There are also questions about demographic trends. MySpace hit the sweet spot of the teenage market, the most active online group in the country; 74 percent of 12 to 14-year-olds use the Internet regularly today. But the site's success has diluted its teenage audience. The percentage of MySpace visitors between the ages of 12 and 24 declined from 44 percent to 30 percent in just one year. The audience is rapidly getting older. If this trend continues, the MySpace audience will increasingly resemble that of any other mainstream website, making it a less appealing venue for reaching the teen demographic. A similar shift is going on at YouTube.

Then there is the potential for abuse. As site operators struggle to make a profit and marketers become more sophisticated at hiding their messages behind fictitious "friends," some people worry that there could be a consumer backlash, particularly when so many of the sites' visitors are children. "It can easily be deceptive because kids think they're interacting with an ordinary person, but they're really interacting with a shill," Gary Ruskin of consumer advocacy group Commercial Alert told CNET News. Kids don't have the analytical skills to differentiate a marketing pitch from a real friend and could easily be misled, sparking a consumer backlash.

That issue came to a head in the summer of 2006 when a popular series of Web videos about a 16-year-old girl named Bree turned out to be fake. The "lonelygirl15" incident raised ethical questions about whether the film makers who conceived of Bree should have disclosed their intentions, which were most likely to promote an upcoming movie. More than 15 million people had watched the videos, which offered intimate details of the young teen's tormented life, before the hoax was exposed.

In the fall of 2006, more than 300,000 Facebook users signed on as friends of "Brody Ruckus," purportedly a college student who claimed that his girlfriend would submit to a ménage a trois if he could sign up 100,000 friends. But Brody turned out to be Ruckus Network, Inc., a Herndon, Virginia-based file-sharing service. Ruckus got access to more than 300,000 e-mail addresses before the scam was exposed, according to the *Washington Post*.

Despite the controversies, social networking sites have clearly created a new model for online self-expression and a new avenue for marketers to reach their customers. It's a pretty wild scene at the moment but you can also get away with trying nearly anything.

CHAPTER 3
The Enthusiasts

When Alex Boese was a doctoral student at the University of California at San Diego in the mid 1990s, he discovered that the Web was a good place to store his research notes. Boese had an interesting dissertation topic: the impact of scientific hoaxes such as patent medicine and miracle remedies on the American public in the nineteenth century. But the insularity of the academic establishment was frustrating to this young student, who wanted to share his discoveries with the world.

"I'd do all this research and nobody would read it," he says from his San Diego home. "The process was that you'd beg some professor to give you feedback and it would take weeks or months. Whereas, if you posted on the Internet, you'd get feedback right away. I was tempted to spend more and more time on the Internet."

Posting research on the Web ate up valuable research time, but Boese was fascinated by the response he got. "It was a labor of love. I was risking never making any money because I was undercutting my dissertation research," he says.

A friend turned Boese on to RobotWisdom, the earliest blog on the Internet and an example of a link blog that spotlights offbeat and timely blog posts. The blog format was an immediate draw. New information could be quickly posted and commented upon. Readers could quickly chime in with their own opinions and ideas. And search engines would spread the content to wider audiences. "With a blog, it's easy to generate a lot of content," he says.

What started as a dissertation became a passion and now it's become a profession for Alex Boese. His Museum of Hoaxes blog is an engrossing compilation of trivia, oddities, and bizarre anecdotes about the human condition. It includes sections about the most famous April Fool's day hoaxes, gullibility tests, strange creatures, and many more. More than a million people visit the site every month, which has enabled Alex Boese to write two books and to turn a hobby into a career. His full-time job is Museum of Hoaxes. And he hopes to do it for many years.

Alex Boese is an enthusiast, the most quixotic and mysterious type of blogger. No one knows how many enthusiasts there are in blog space, but it is probably the largest category outside of politics. According to Technorati, there are 738 blogs about knitting, 794 about the Apple Macintosh, 12 about the Hummer SUV, 42 about pug dogs, 7,317 about travel, 796 about baseball and 98 about the Handspring Treo.

There are blogs about soccer, wine, cameras, Scrabble, fishing and playing the trombone. There are more than 3,000 blogs about blogging. Type "house painting" into BlogPulse and you get links to 1,200 messages. Many of them are not about house painting specifically, but it's a fair bet that most of the writers are painting or planning to paint in the near future.

Understanding enthusiasts

Enthusiasts are a vast and tantalizing opportunity for marketers, because they represent the cream of the crop of the company's customers. But they're also a difficult group to figure out. While some enthusiasts produce a stunning volume of output, their motivations are often driven more by the desire to share than to influence markets or make money. In a survey of 233 bloggers, the

More Blog to Share Experiences Than to Earn Money			
Please tell me if this is a reason you personally blog, or not:	Major reason	Minor reason	Not a reason
To express yourself creatively	52	25	23
To document your personal experiences or share them with others	50	26	24
To stay in touch with friends and family	37	22	40
To share practical knowledge or skills with others	34	30	35
To motivate other people to action	29	32	38
To entertain people	28	33	39
To store resources or information that is important to you	28	21	52
To influence the way other people think	27	24	49
To network or meet new people	16	34	50
To make money	7	8	85

Source: Pew Internet & American Life Project Blogger Callback Survey, July 2005-February 2006. N=233. Margin of error is ±7%.

Pew Internet & American Life Project found that three-quarters pursued their craft primarily to express themselves. Only 15 percent cited financial rewards as having any influence on their decision to blog.

This is a group, then, whose motivations can't be assumed. Unlike journalists, they don't write because they have to and they don't have "the man" looking over their shoulder. In my interviews, I also found surprisingly little competitive drive. In fact, enthusiasts were more likely to compliment their competitors than dismiss them. Contrast this to the intensively competitive environment in which newsrooms operate. Offering a blogger a "scoop" may have little effect.

But enthusiasts share one characteristic pretty universally: they know a lot. People who blog about a product, particularly if they do so regularly, are more likely to be knowledgeable and engaged than other customers. They are also more likely to influence other people around them, whether by word of mouth or through the medium of blogging. Ed Keller and Jon Berry documented this in their 2003 book *The Influentials*. Drawing on extensive research, they asserted that 10 percent of Americans determine what the other 90 percent buy. Influence the influentials, they advise, and your product or company can reach critical mass. They wrote:

> *Years before most people had heard of digital still cameras, Influentials were aware of them. By March 1997, two in three had heard of them, 1½ times the response of the public as a whole. They were well into the adoption curve. By early 2001, one in six Influentials owned a digital camera (double the rate of the public as a whole), and a comparable proportion were planning to buy one in the next year or two (more than double the public as a whole). Three in ten had viewed personal photos over a computer in the past month, about triple the rate of the total public. The net effect pointed to an increasingly digital future for photography. Good news for companies selling digital cameras and software to help people archive, edit, transmit, and tinker with their digital photo collections.*

Influentials, in short, are leading indicators of much bigger market trends. They're not the same as leading-edge adopters, who buy the latest and greatest technology but who don't necessarily tell anyone about it. Influentials are the people whom others consult to tell them what to do next.

The Influentials was published shortly before the blogging phenomenon caught fire. Its fundamental assumptions hold true, though, no matter what the medium. Blogs are simply another mechanism, and a very powerful one, for influentials to spread the word. It's no accident that word of mouth marketing has taken hold at the same time that blogging has caught the public's imagination.[1]

Enthusiasts are mysterious because their motivations are so elusive. Among the top reasons for blogging cited by respondents to my blogger survey were "Connect with people with similar interest," "Influence markets or discussions," and "It just feels good." In other words, a great many of these people practice their trade without common motivations like money or career development. As Pia Savage, author of the popular CourtingDestiny personal blog, told the *Long Island Press*, "Very truthfully, I don't understand my appeal."

Influencers can make themselves heard in unexpected ways. Museum of Hoaxes' mission is "to investigate dubious claims of all kinds. They can be hoaxes, urban legends, strange products, offers that people get in their e-mail, anything that makes people question whether it's real or fake," says Alex Boese. Because people trust Museum of Hoaxes, marketers with legitimate products besiege Boese to review their products and publications. And makers of patent medicines and other suspicious cure-alls have come to fear the Museum's investigations. "I get threats of lawsuits all the time," Boese said, though so far no one has followed through.

In our profiles of enthusiasts in this chapter, we'll see that many of them achieved influential positions in their markets without setting out to do so. And enthusiasts can be unpredictable. Some are adoring fans while others see themselves as objective commentators or even the conscience of their markets. There are also a few hate blogs, but they are relatively uncommon.[2]

Enthusiasts can be valuable resources to businesses and organizations. Most are knowledgeable, passionate and eager to influence the markets they care about. They can be, in effect, a global online focus group that works for free. All you need to do is listen to them.

1. Chapter 10 explores viral and word-of-mouth marketing in depth.
2. They're uncommon, but they shouldn't be ignored. Wal-Mart is a favorite target, with sites like Why I Hate Wal-Mart (http://www.davelippman.com/walmart/whyihatewalmart.html) and Sprawl Busters (http://www.sprawl-busters.com/) providing a forum for customers to vent about the company. Untied (http://www.untied.com/) does the same thing for United Airlines. Consumerist (http://www.consumerist.com/) is a popular blog where angry customers can write about their negative experiences with all kinds of companies.

Victoria's Secret did that when it introduced the Ipex bra in early 2005. The product was the result of two years of development and the company planned to spend heavily on focus groups to test response. But marketers were surprised to learn that hundreds of women were already blogging about their experiences with the bra, most of them positively. The savings on research was like found money.[3]

Hughes, a Saint Louis-based channel-marketing agency, used home-decorating bloggers to provide feedback for a client that was introducing a line of paint. Hughes staffers sifted through more than a thousand blog entries from twenty active decorating blogs that mentioned the client. The research revealed that many people knew of the client from its prime products but weren't aware that the company now made paint. The agency also learned that women were more influential in paint choice than they had anticipated and that women were the primary influencers of paint selection. The blogosphere "was a community of people who are very passionate about the subject," says Sarah Goodman, a Hughes brand manager. "If we had done a focus group, we'd never have been able to recreate that kind of value. Blogs are free, easy and accessible in real time."

Listening is the easiest part, but it's a critical first step toward engaging with social media. There are many tools you can use to listen,[4] but first you need to understand whom you're listening to. In the following pages, we'll meet enthusiasts from a variety of markets and learn how they started, what drives them and how they want to engage with the companies and industries that they cover.

HackingNetflix

Mike Kaltschnee didn't set out to influence an industry. He just really liked movies. The 41-year-old business development executive for a stock photo agency had been an early customer of Netflix, the pioneer in the DVD-by-mail industry. Kaltschnee was fascinated by opportunities on the Web, and by blogs in particular. "I knew blogging was going to be big," he says in an interview from his home in Danbury, Connecticut. He decided to follow the advice of blogging icon Dave Winer, who said, "If

3. This story was told by Doc Searls in an "On the Record...Online" podcast with Eric Schwartzman in January 2006.
4. Chapter 9 gives you a menu of free and inexpensive options you can tap to listen in on these conversations.

you want to learn about blogging, start a blog about something you're passionate about."

Mike Kaltschnee was passionate about Netflix and about the business model that made it possible for film buffs to rent movies from their living rooms. In November 2003, he started HackingNetflix.com, a blog dedicated to covering news about the DVD-by-mail business. He promised to use his privileged sources to give readers a peek at new Netflix releases, which the company kept secret. He'd also provide insight into such baffling questions as why Netflix's most active customers have the hardest time getting new titles.[5]

Kaltschnee caught a break when blogging icon Dave Winer linked to HackingNetflix and awareness spiked. It turned out there were a lot of DVD-by-mail enthusiasts out there. Mike Kaltschnee had the market for independent Netflix advice all to himself. By mid-2004, he estimated he had more than 20,000 readers every month. HackingNetflix was the second-highest result in a Google search on "Netflix."

The folks at Netflix weren't sure what to do about Mike Kaltschnee. He had repeatedly tried to contact the company to get on its press list. He wanted the same kind of access that was afforded to journalists and industry analysts. But Netflix wasn't buying that, at least not at first. Kaltschnee wasn't a conventional journalist and his motivations weren't entirely clear. Kaltschnee knew people at Netflix were reading his blog. He had the traffic logs to prove it. And Netflix employees were beginning to send him news and tips on the sly, bypassing the PR organization.

So, on June 23, 2004, a frustrated Kaltshnee posted the company's dismissive reply to his most recent plea for attention on his site. Netflix caved. A week later, a Netflix product manager called. As Kaltschnee said in a published interview with BloggerBusiness.com,

> "I thought, 'Oh great, they're going to sue me…I asked 'Are you going to shut me down? Are you sending me a cease and desist?' I mean, I use their name in my title. She said, 'No, you're our morning reading. Where else can we get customer feedback like this?"

In the years since, the relationship between the blog and the company has warmed. When a reader tipped off Kaltschnee about an unan-

---

5. It's true. The practice is called "throttling" and you can read about it at http://www.hackingnetflix.com/2005/06/throttling_revi.html

nounced Netflix download service, Netflix public relations verified the story. He's on the company's press list. Netflix representatives even asked him for help when the company was adding RSS feeds to its site. "They get it," Kaltschnee says.

Over at rival Blockbuster, Inc., the tone is quite different. As HackingNetflix's coverage expanded to include other DVD-by-mail services, Kaltschnee reached out to Blockbuster to begin a dialogue. More than two years later, there was still little response from Blockbuster's media relations department. "I tried several times to reach Blockbuster, and finally had one exchange with the PR people, but subsequent e-mails went unanswered," he told marketer Christina Kerley in an interview on her blog, ck-blog.com.

It's not like Blockbuster hadn't heard of HackingNetflix. Kaltschnee's July 2004 scoop on the imminent release of Blockbuster's rumored online service got 70,000 page views. Kaltschnee believes the anonymous tip came from a Blockbuster employee. He's published hundreds of items about Blockbuster. HackingNetflix is even a Blockbuster affiliate site. But officially, it isn't on the media relations radar.

A Blockbuster spokeswoman disputed Kaltschnee's claims. "To our knowledge, we have never been contacted by this site," she said. "We encourage Mr. Kaltshnee to contact us." In response, Kaltschnee points to a folder full of e-mail messages that went unanswered.

The differing approaches of Netflix and Blockbuster to this particular new influencer demonstrate the corporate world's confusion in deciding what to do about bloggers. Netflix engaged while Blockbuster avoided. Time will tell who made a better decision.

In the meantime, HackingNetflix has grown in popularity and prominence. The site has been mentioned in many mainstream publications and profiled on marketing websites and newsletters. It's ranked in the top 6,000 blogs by Technorati. The site is on track to draw two million unique visitors in 2006. Affiliate revenue is strong enough that Kaltschnee's wife was able to quit her job. Kaltschnee has launched two other blogs: TrackingTraderJoes.com about the specialty grocer and ABlogAboutBlogging.com, where he weighs in on lessons learned in the blogosphere.

Half of his tips come from readers. He gets inquiries and press releases from marketers all the time, but messages don't get attention unless they demonstrate knowledge of his market. His advice to marketers:

"At least understand what I'm writing about. Read the site for a day or two or subscribe to get a feel of what I'm trying to do. Your message has got to be interesting to my readers."

The Trader Joe's site is an experiment. Kaltshnee dreams of creating a network of sites that serve enthusiasts in different markets. The economics of blogging are making this possible as never before. "This is a totally different way of doing business," he says. "I have no sales staff, no marketing, no advertising, no search engine optimization. And yet I'm gong to have a couple of million unique visitors this year. The tools are all there to create your own media."

He's turned down offers to buy the site, hoping to build on the network idea. HackingNetflix remains, however, a labor of love. "When people send e-mail saying they've been reading the site for two years, that's what motivates me," he says.

Google Blogoscoped

Philipp Lenssen set out to write a blog that he wanted to read.

The 28-year-old German programmer built his first Web page at the age of 19. He's experimented with a variety of styles and gimmicks, including a blog that would uncover bad service in German businesses by featuring reviews and comments from frustrated patrons.

Not many ideas hit. But one hit big. "I used Google a lot and I wanted more tips and help," he says. "In early 2003, there was one Google blog that was posting once a week or so but there was not much there for me. I started to write the blog that I would want to read."

He called it Google Blogoscoped (blog.outer-court.com), and it's a blog about all things Google. It's about new products and rumors and financial news. It's about tips and tricks users were discovering and even games you could play with Google. It's about Google parodies and weird things you could do with Google Images and even fictional stories about people whose lives were changed by Google. It's about Google humor and offbeat ideas for Google logos. Google Blogoscoped has an incredible wealth of information about Google.

Lenssen posted daily and users came to read. Google would not launch its own blog until a year later. It was a year when Philipp Lenssen and a handful of others were the only independent influencers writing about Google.

But Philipp Lenssen was a little different. He blogged furiously about Google, posting daily and often many times a day. Lenssen blogged on topics that official Google channels ignored. He wrote about how Google employee Mark Jen got fired in early 2005 for comments he made on his blog about his employer. He wrote about undocumented features in Google search and tactics you could use to get search results Google didn't intend you to get. Google Blogoscoped became the complete unauthorized Google reference, with all the glory and warts the #1 search engine had to offer.

Google Blogoscoped has done very well. It's the 26th most popular blog on Technorati and the 22nd most popular on Blogpulse. Its influence has grown as Google's popularity has soared. According to the search engine Alexa, Google Blogoscoped has twice the online reach of *Time* magazine. It's running around four million page views a month, which doesn't account for the large number of readers who subscribe via RSS feeds and aren't measured in traffic reports.

Lenssen spends up to 12 hours a day blogging but manages to maintain a life despite the constant demands. "I often blog on and off throughout the day but go swimming, go out with my girlfriend, go to the library etc.," he wrote in an e-mail. "All the time, though, I'm finding new ideas that can be included in the blog. As the blogaholics blog put it, a blogger starts to 'filter' life into blog posts."

A protracted session may yield a dozen posts, ranging from an item uncovering bugs in Google's calendar to undocumented features in the Gmail e-mail service to rumors about Google financials. His tips come from all over. He reads sites like Search Engine Watch and blogs like Inside Google and John Battelle's Searchblog. But as with many enthusiasts, his best sources are his readers.

As the site has grown, other voices have contributed more and more of the content. An active forums section now generates hundreds of posts every day. Tips from readers have led him to some big stories, such as the launch of the Google Base classified ad site, where Google Blogoscoped scooped everyone. "A post like that will log 50,000 page views over two or three days," he muses.

Google is paying attention. Some Google employees participate in the Google Blogoscoped forums and the company keeps Lenssen on its press list. Other marketers are taking notice, too, courting Lenssen to write about their search sites.

Like many bloggers, Lenssen expects marketers to show him the same courtesy he shows others in the blogosphere. "Take the time to look up my first name in my blog. It only takes five seconds to know my name but these are five seconds that separate your e-mail from spam I don't even read."

Google Blogoscoped is an A-list site, which magnifies its influence. Public relations blogger Steve Rubel calls it a "great site" and has linked to it from his own blog more than thirty times. More than 4,700 other bloggers have linked, as well. Philipp Lenssen's position at the inner circle of the blog solar system is self-perpetuating. Top bloggers turn to him as a primary news source, which creates more links and more visibility.

Asked if such celebrity is ever a burden, Lenssen laughs, "I don't know if I'll do this for five years or fifty," he says. "I know that if I tried to shut down, people would riot."

Adrants

Let's state at the outset that Steve Hall is a very nice guy. I met him at a restaurant in his home town of Groton, Massachusetts, an upscale suburb about thirty miles from Boston. He was dressed in a casual white shirt and black pants, looking every bit like a guy you'd see coaching a soccer team on a Saturday afternoon. And the analogy is fitting; he admitted with some guilt that he was enjoying the reprieve from the chaos of his home, where his wife was hosting a clutch of kids from a local youth group.

Hall is, by all appearances, the kind of benign, unassuming, 44-year-old-father-of-two you'd expect to find in this unassuming town. Little would you suspect that he can strike terror into the heart of advertising executives. His Adrants blog has grown over four years to become one of the most influential voices in the advertising community. With a voice that combines nudge-nudge playfulness with wry impudence ("I owe a debt to whoever invented the word 'snarky,'" Hall says), Adrants has become the conscience of an industry that some people think has none.

Some ad industry insiders say a new campaign can't be considered really successful unless it gets the Adrants blessing. Ad industry professionals appreciate its bite and its honesty. "It's totally snarky," says a young, female copywriter at Slack Barshinger & Partners, Inc., in comments passed along to me by the firm's CEO. "Adrants injects clever commentary into the ad world, which totally takes itself too seriously."

Adds a media planner colleague: "It's got plenty of amusing, snarky commentary and it's that bite that makes me appreciate it." Snark is, indeed, a virtue.

Steve Hall's getting the last laugh and it feels good. After spending nearly twenty years at ad agencies in New England, he was laid off during the downturn of 2002.

With so many years in the agency business, the prospect of blowing off steam appealed to him. He started Adrants to pass the time while job hunting and found that, in the early days of the blogosphere, he had a green field to play in. Now it's become his career. "I've worked in the agencies. I have the grunt's perspective, which I find is very important," to the voice of the blog, Hall says.

AdRants' traffic—more than 25,000 visitors a day, on average—attests to its influence. The site is ranked in the top 300 blogs by Technorati, but given its narrow audience, its reach is far greater. It's assembled a bouquet of "best ad blog" awards from such influential media as AdvertisingAge, FastCompany and MarketingSherpa. Half its readers are ad agency people and some Madison Avenue insiders say you can't afford not to read it.

Hall posts several times a day, critiquing ads from around the world. He pulls no punches in his short commentaries, nearly every one of which includes a link to an image or video. Writing of one campaign for the Starz cable network that features a dorky enthusiastic customer, he comments, "Does it really require an idiot to sell everything? Are we so insecure we need to see dumb people just to make us feel better?"

Commenting on an ad for Oliver Stone's *World Trade Center* movie that appeared adjacent to a Yahoo! story about a foiled terrorist plot, he commented, "We feel it's our duty to point out contextual fuckery at its finest."

Hall, at one point, accepted an agency job, but his new employer's condescending attitude toward the Web convinced him that advertisers still didn't get it. The Internet "is not there yet and I don't think it's going to go too far very soon," he remembers his boss saying. At that time, Adrants was already getting over 10,000 visitors a day.

Steve Hall had the benefit of being early, but he also has a knack for words. Although he's never worked in New York, he frequently hears from Madison Avenue readers who think he works just up the street. The insider hipness is an image he cultivates through his wise-ass style. "I think it's more how I write than what I write," he says of Adrants' success.

Hall also has a knack for looking bigger than he is. Adrants is a slick site with lots of photos and videos, an e-mail newsletter and regular readership surveys. You could easily be misled into thinking there was a team of editors behind it. But there's just Steve Hall.

And now the evolution of the Web has made that image even easier to perpetuate. So much video and imagery is available free on Web that Hall sometimes feels like a kid in a candy store. "Social media has enabled me to be anywhere I want to be," he says, referring to the wealth of video content.

It's also been very good to Hall. He makes a six-figure income from selling ad space on the site and he doesn't have to work in ad agencies any more. There are now lots of ad blogs on the market but few bloggers have Hall's advantage of being able to tend to the blog full-time. "Adrants is a blog, but I think of it more as a website that happens to use blogging software to publish," he says. "It's cheap and efficient. Without any promotion, it's found its way out to people who want this kind of information."

The DisneyBlog

Few places on earth inspire the kind of rabid following that the Disney theme parks and resorts do. Their immersive fantasy environment, surreal cleanliness and relentlessly wholesome staff have spawned legions of competitors, but no one has ever come close to invoking the enthusiasm of the Disney devoted. People who post to the Disney message board on America Online frequently include a count of their total Disney visits in their e-mail signature lines. It's not unusual to see someone with a log of more than a hundred visits.

It's not surprising, then, that the Disney ecosystem has spawned a fair number of blogger enthusiasts. One is John Frost. The Portland, Oregon, native's grandfather, Vic Greene, was an Imagineer, the group of engineers that build Disneyland. Disney was part of Frost's life for as long as he can remember. For eighteen years, his family took annual trips to Disneyland in Anaheim, California. "Like a lot of other kids of that time, I was part of the Disney generation," says Frost.

Frost studied communications at Lewis & Clark College in Portland, was active in student government and even founded a magazine. He was on a communications career track. But his first love was always Disney.

Disney called to John Frost, with its promise of a temporary escape from the workaday world into a place of simple, wonderful things.

In a Disney theme park, you could lose yourself in a fantastical character. "Disneyland was maybe the first virtual reality game on the planet," Frost says, referring to the role-playing games favored by computer enthusiasts.

John Frost has never been far from Disney. In the early days of the Web, he helped organize a weekly meetup of fans who gathered at Disney every Sunday afternoon. They toured the park together, exploring its hidden treasures. He met his future wife at a Disney collectors' event. They married at the Grand Californian hotel at Disneyland.

In 2000, the couple moved to Las Vegas, but continued to visit Disneyland every few weeks. The previous year, John and a friend had launched LaughingPlace.com, a Disney fan site that persists to this day. When the post-9/11 recession hit, the Frosts decided to move. But they had few choices where to settle. They needed to be close to a Disney theme park.

They settled on Orlando. John had maintained a personal blog since 2000 and had been writing some travelogue-type articles for Laughing Place.com. Blogging was just coming online. Disney fan sites were springing up but they were mostly oriented toward travel planning. "Nobody was just blogging the news," Frost says. The Disney blog would be different. It would have news about the good and the bad of the Disney empire, wrapped up in a G-rated format. John Frost launched TheDisneyBlog.com in June 2004.

It's not like there's a shortage of Disney information online. There are scores of message boards and travel guides, even sites maintained by Disney haters. John Frost writes about the Disney ecosystem. He has news about Disney theme parks, competitors, films, the Disney company, the weather in Orlando, travel deals and anything else that interests him and, by extension, other Disney aficionados. Fans contribute trip reports and hidden treasures they discover at the theme parks. There's plenty of Disney information available elsewhere online but "most people don't want to read through 6,000 pages of a discussion board," Frost says. John Frost is their filter.

The Disney Blog quickly reached the next level of popularity. A few months after launch, two hurricanes swept through Orlando, closing the theme parks and wrecking homes and businesses. Frost blogged furiously. "I tried to be a news source for people who were in Orlando or coming there. I wanted to be a collector of all things about the hurricanes." His poignant stories about the devastation around him put The Disney Blog on the map. Before the hurricane, the Disney Blog was getting fewer than two hundred visitors a day. Afterwards, it got 1,000.

Other stories brought new loyalists. A spate of injuries and two deaths on Disney World rides prompted Frost to write long and eloquently about what Disney should do to make its attractions safer. Stories that got a few inches in newspapers were carried forth for days, with readers adding their own comments. The Disney Blog's coverage of the disasters was a living story with many authors.

Filtering is what John Frost does. "It's new journalism. It's about getting my voice, my particular opinion on the world of Disney out there in the conversation," he says. "The Disney Blog is for fans of Disney by a fan of Disney. I'm primarily an aggregator of information and then I add my own flair and opinion. I want the blog to be safe for the whole family. And that's it."

At this point, it's a three-hours-a-day pastime that could easily become an obsession. "I could do this fourteen hours a day," Frost says. He makes just enough money with the Disney Blog to harbor dreams of blogging full-time. By day, he's a philanthropy e-marketing specialist for a nonprofit organization in Orlando.

While Disney doesn't formally acknowledge the blog, Frost knows that Disney employees visit every day. And marketers in the Disney ecosystem have discovered the blog. They contact him asking for book and movie reviews or just to mention their products. John Frost's advice: "Hit me early and often. The earlier you can get me information, the better the chance I'll post it because I'll be a first mover. Don't try to shoot from the hip. Give me the straight news."

"I'd be interested in a little more promotional stuff," he adds. "Maybe contests for the readers, a chance for them to win something." For John Frost and many other enthusiasts, it's all about the readers.

Marketers, take note.

Courting the enthusiasts

I stated at the outset that enthusiasts are mysterious for many corporate marketers because they don't operate by the rules. Unlike the media, their chosen topics aren't a job but a passion. Unlike financial or

The Ombudsman
By Christina Kerley
ckEpiphany Marketing

Starting a blog with the goal of shutting it down may seem like an error in judgment, but not to Craig Silverman, a veritable aficionado of errors and the famed blogger behind RegretTheError.com. The blog has been monitoring media corrections, retractions and clarifications since 2004, with Silverman reviewing 125 media outlets and posting between three to fifteen items daily. Errors and regrets range from simple oversights to massive reporting failures. The goal, says Silverman, a Montreal-based freelance journalist is for there to be "so few errors and corrections that I would have nothing to write about."

So far, there's been no shortage of material: there was Reuters recalling beef "panties" instead of beef "patties," a local paper mislabeling two men as mobsters two days in a row and a Fox News pundit saying a home belonged to terrorists when the alleged terrorists actually lived there three years earlier (the current owners are still recovering from that one). Silverman views all errors equally. "The first point that I always make is that there are no small errors. Any time someone's name or title is spelled incorrectly, any time a wrong phone number or date is offered, it matters."

More change agent than media watchdog, Silverman says, "I felt there needed to be someone raising this issue. It's not about shaming or punishing the press; it's about cataloging and quantifying the problems and having a discussion about how things can get better. My interest is in making the press better, not tearing it down."

Minding the media proves popular: the site clocks 1,500 daily readers and 50,000 monthly page views from media, communications and marketing professionals, as well as general consumers. Further, the blog has helped establish Silverman as press critic; he's currently working on a book set for release in 2007.

Regret The Error's work has been cited by major media—including the *New York Times*, *Editor & Publisher*, the *San Francisco Chronicle*, the *Guardian* and National Public Radio—and by many other outlets from as far away as Israel and Vietnam. His work has prompted some organizations to upgrade their corrections policy, exposed plagiarism and called attention to significant errors that otherwise would have escaped notice. "A 27-year-old journalist in Montreal might just be leading a revolution in the way newspapers correct their mistakes," noted a May 2005 profile of him in *Editor & Publisher* magazine.

One might assume that the blog raises quills in the media community, but Silverman says quite the opposite is true. "The professional media have had an overwhelmingly positive response to the site. I have journalists sending in their own errors, and many others who draw my attention to competitors or other outlets. I think this says a lot about the commitment that journalists have to accuracy, and their understanding that correcting an error is of the utmost importance."

Especially popular are his annual best-of-the-worst roundups. Called "The Crunks"—a hip-hop term marrying "crazy" and "drunk"—the awards feature such categories as "Error Of The Year," "Correction Of The Year" and "Typo Of The Year." One of Silverman's favorite typos of 2005 came from the *Dallas Morning News*: "Norma Adams-Wade's June 15 column incorrectly called Mary Ann Thompson-Frenk a socialist. She is a socialite." You just can't make up stuff like that.

But there's a serious edge to what Craig Silverman does. By helping build awareness of the growing issue, the Crunks serve to generate publicity while drawing new people into the debate. "Stories now flash around the world in matter of seconds," says Silverman, "which means mistakes move faster than ever before. Yet fact-checking remains a luxury not afforded in most newsrooms."

As for Silverman's ultimate goal of shutting down the site? Readers hardly have cause for worry. Between the increase in the numbers of media outlets—and the speed of information delivery—there will be plenty more errors to correct for some time to come. For better or for worse.

---

industry analysts, they don't see their role as being influencers. Mainly, they want to share what they know and create relationships with others who share their enthusiasm.

Based on conversations and interviews with scores of enthusiasts, I've identified some characteristics of enthusiasts that you won't find in mainstream influencers:

They have great market knowledge—Enthusiasts are likely to understand your market, your product and your customers better than you, probably better than most of the people who work at your company. Chances are they've been enthusiastic about your product for a very long time.

They want to be involved—They are more likely than the media to want to get into the feedback loop, brainstorm with you and get in touch with the brain trust at your company. This is an important motivator for them.

They're meticulous about transparency—In my interviews, I found that a lot of enthusiasts had some writing or marketing background, but few would call themselves journalists. This means they didn't respond to the cat-and-mouse game that journalists and corporate marketers play with information. Business reporters learn to read between the lines of what marketers tell them and also how to trip up business executives in interviews. Enthusiasts find this approach distasteful. They want to ask straightforward questions and get direct answers. Anything less is unsatisfying.

They want a discussion—Perhaps the most common refrain I heard in speaking to enthusiasts is that they want marketers to know who they are, what's their voice and who is their audience. They mostly ignore blind pitches for this reason. Unlike mainstream reporters, who have a certain fiduciary duty to at least consider proposals that come in over the transom, enthusiasts have no one breathing down their neck to make sure they don't get scooped by their competition. Simply stated, if you demonstrate that you understand them and their audience and you have a relevant pitch, they'll listen to you. Otherwise, probably not.

They are passionate about their readers—Like it or not, most conventional media today face pressure on a variety of fronts, including their editors, publishers and business-side constituents. One of the reasons public trust in the media is so low, in fact, is because so many media outlets have allowed business factors to influence their editorial judgment. This just isn't the case with the New Influencers. Many have too little ad revenue to care. Those who do make money usually do it through affiliate or keyword ad programs. They don't worry about offending or catering to advertisers and so practice a much purer, more reader-focused form of journalism.

In my view, enthusiasts are a great untapped marketing resource. Not only are they a source of expert (and often free) advice, but they're usually wired into a network of other enthusiasts who read and comment on each other's blogs.

The enthusiasts I interviewed mostly have no preconceptions about marketers. They aren't jaded by years of business journalism and they don't get their hackles up when pitched on a story. What they do resent is ignorance. If you contact them without a clue about what they write or whom they reach, they're more likely than reporters to shut you down.

Professional journalists understand the PR pitch game. Enthusiasts want you to share their passion for a topic. Before contacting an enthusiast, spend some time learning about his or her specialty.

Tales from the field

Marketers are increasingly courting enthusiasts with innovative programs and seeing success.

When Nokia introduced the N90 video phone in 2005, the company wanted to do something different. The N90 was a new kind of device, designed from the ground up for use as a multimedia communications device. The company enlisted Andy Abramson, a longtime blogger and marketing/PR strategist who specializes in Internet marketing.

Nokia would target the usual journalists, but Abramson thought that a phone designed for enthusiasts should be reviewed by enthusiasts. Abramson looked at hundreds of blogs and scoured Google and Technorati to find out who were the respected voices in cell phone blogging. The process was time-consuming, but no more so than planning a traditional campaign, Abramson said.

Nokia selected fifty influential bloggers to get the $600 phone and a review package. There was no obligation and no pressure. Nokia committed to linking to each published review—good or bad—from its corporate blog. That step was important. Had Nokia chosen to spotlight only the positive reviews, its service would have been dismissed (or even trashed) in the blogosphere as self-promotional. Listing the good and the bad made it a valuable reference source.

In the end, more than forty bloggers reviewed the N90, most of them positively. The buzz was only part of the benefit. "Because of their passion, bloggers will give almost unlimited space to explaining how they used the product, not just what it does," Abramson explains. "They go into far greater depth than the traditional media reviewer."

Marketers can inexpensively spread their brand through the enthusiasts. If you maintain personal or company blogs, link to favorable coverage from as many of them possible. Links improve a blog's performance on influential sites like Technorati and BlogPulse. You can also tag positive reviews or articles on the enormously popular del.icio.us or vote for them on Digg to raise their visibility. Frequently tagged articles gain prominence in lists or "tag clouds," which define what people are talking about in the blogosphere. And bloggers love community-driven services like Digg or Bloglines.[6]

Abramson offers some key lessons he learned from working with bloggers:

Choose bloggers carefully—Nokia had hundreds of bloggers to choose from but narrowed the field by finding the most prolific writers who had the most links from the community. Calling this "more art than science," Abramson said the key is finding people who are passionate, prolific and popular with their peers.

Don't insult their intelligence—Enthusiasts know their stuff, so treating them like second-class journalists will blow up in your face. In fact, bloggers generally understand technology better than their counterparts at trade publications. Give them the equipment and the fact sheets and let them go to work.

Be transparent—Nokia's commitment to publish a summary and a link to every blog entry, whether good or bad, solidified the company's credibility in this project. Just be sure you keep your promise. Hand out the good news with the bad and your credibility grows. This is a difficult concept for some traditional marketers to swallow. Self-reporting bad news actually makes you more credible.

Be responsive—This is a near-real-time medium and bloggers expect to get quick answers to their questions. Your staff needs to be available nearly 24/7 to handle inquiries. You can't put people off for a day or two. They won't tolerate it. You can head off some of the more common questions by providing a rich library of screen shots and logos that bloggers can easily add to their sites. Make sure you include language authorizing this or post the content under a Creative Commons license.[7]

---

6. Don't be alarmed by all this terminology. Chapter 9 explains it in detail and (mostly) plain English!

7. Creative Commons (http://creativecommons.org/) is a nonprofit organization that's trying to create alternatives to current U.S. copyright laws that some people regard as too restrictive. The group offers a variety of alternative licenses that allow copyright holders to grant public rights to some material while retaining other rights. The group is highly regarded in the blogosphere.

The Five Things Marketers Just Don't Get
By Philipp Lenssen
Google Blogoscoped

It's about the product.

Maybe you've pitched the product, website, or tool well to the blogger, but positive reviews stand and fall with the quality of the product. Sometimes, the blogger doesn't like (or blog about) what she sees, but may get back to you with detailed criticism. Working with that criticism may help you improve the product, and if you did, why not tell the blogger about it again?

Beta logins and early previews don't equal exclusivity.

It's fashionable these days to call something "Beta" and make it invite-only. But even then, that doesn't mean the blogger deems the story "exclusive." After all, if a dozen other bloggers get the same Beta login to your site, chances are the blogger will not end up with any original content. Becoming just another echo chamber of the blogosphere is the one thing good bloggers try to avoid.

When the blogger posts something, that's just the beginning.

When I review any product, my blog post will just be the initial step. Usually, the first blog post is followed by insightful comments from readers that corrects the story, or expands it into new regions. (The "wisdom of crowds" beats even the most knowledgeable blogger.) Also, other blogs may point to my review and add their own bits and pieces. Only if you read the comment a blog post receives—or better yet, get involved in the discussion that unfolds—will you be able to see the whole story.

Your product is nice, but where's the hook?

Good websites offer something uniquely interesting to spark conversation. It can be a video, a song, a Flash game (make sure you allow free sharing of all that content), a live demo, a contest, something configurable you can play around with or a new approach to something old. Many bloggers aim not only to inform, but also entertain their readers. It's just much more entertaining to point to a product site that includes a game or video than one that includes a mere product description.

Bloggers aren't members of a holy cult; they're humans.

There's really no big secret to understanding bloggers; they're just humans. You don't need to e-mail an elaborate pitch. You can simply choose a descriptive subject, say "Hello John, here's a site your readers might like. It's about this and that," paste the URL, and hit send. Bloggers need content, you need exposure, and sometimes it's a match. Of course, it helps if you're a person already involved in the community that the blog targets. Take time to understand the spirit of the blog and people will spend more time listening to your own ideas.

Lest you think enthusiasts are a fan club waiting to happen, though, be aware that the culture and priorities of this group can be quite different from that of mainstream media. Jim Nail and Pat Fennessey of the word-of-mouth measurement firm Cymfony conducted a comparative study of coverage of retailer Wal-Mart in mainstream and social media and published the results in *Media* magazine in the summer of 2006.

Their analysis of 675 stories and posts about Wal-Mart found that mainstream media was much more likely to cover "issues" like the economy, financial performance, the environment and social responsibility. In contrast, the bloggers were more inclined to talk about the experience of shopping at Wal-Mart, sales, or items being out of stock. This would indicate that Wal-Mart would do better to engage with the mainstream media on big-picture while focusing on bloggers at a more personal level.

However, when the blogosphere weighed in on the big picture, they did so with a vengeance. Cymfony found that coverage of local issues, like a battle over a new Wal-Mart store, was much more likely to appear in mainstream media than on blogs. But the bloggers were likely to be far more negative than print and broadcast media. On the topic of Wal-Mart's impact on the economy, for example, mainstream media coverage was almost perfectly balanced while bloggers were three times as likely to be critical of Wal-Mart as supportive.

It doesn't take much spelunking through the blogosphere to see this trend play out again and again. Enthusiasts see their blogs as vehicles more for commentary than for original reporting. Since pain is a more powerful motivator than pleasure, it's not surprising that some prominent blogs aimed at businesses express indignation or anger. In fact, of the top ten results of a Google search on "Wal-Mart," four are anti-Wal-Mart websites. And it's not just Wal-Mart. Four of the top twenty results for McDonald's are hate sites. And the third Google result for Altria, parent company of tobacco company Phillip Morris, is an antismoking site.

Controversial companies know this, of course, and some have taken extraordinary steps to engage with bloggers. Last March, Wal-Mart and its PR agency, Edelman, took some body blows over a *New York Times* article that revealed that the retailer had been running a publicity campaign aimed at friendly bloggers. Critics charged that the campaign meant to seed the blogosphere with Wal-Mart-friendly messages without revealing their source. "...some bloggers have posted information from Wal-Mart, at times word for word, without revealing where it came from," the *Times* said.

The story caused a minor sensation in the blogosphere, with some bloggers lashing the company for deceptive tactics. However, what Wal-Mart did was really no different than what big companies typically do to influence local media. A campaign to bring a store into a small town, for example, is often preceded by vigorous lobbying of community newspapers and broadcast outlets about the economic benefits of the expansion. And resource-strapped local media are sometimes only too glad to publish that information verbatim.

"I think some newspaper ombudsmen should do PR audits of their papers," wrote A-list blogger and media critic Jeff Jarvis, in dismissing the Wal-Mart controversy. "How many stories come from flacks without disclosure? How much of the substance of stories comes from flacks without disclosure? How many benefits accrue from flacks and companies without disclosure?"

Wal-Mart has taken heat over other social-media initiatives. In the fall of 2006, the company terminated a blog written by two freelance writers about their experiences camping in Wal-Mart parking lots during a cross-country trip. Wal-Mart admitted to subsidizing the blog posts, which were almost uniformly positive about the retailer. The apparent deception was trashed both in the blogosphere and in maistream media.

In both cases, enthusiasts were among Wal-Mart's most vocal critics. Enthusiasts are to blogging what local newspapers are to journalism. They cover their markets in often exhaustive detail, going deep into topics that mainstream media ignores. They're short on time and money and have deadlines to meet. That makes them suggestible to businesses that can fulfill their need for information. They're less likely to be jaded or cynical than mainstream press but also less likely to feel the need to publish all the news that's fit to print.

Which doesn't make marketing to enthusiasts a slam dunk. The need to be transparent and credible is perhaps even more pronounced in the world of enthusiast bloggers than in big-city media. They don't necessarily understand how the game is played and will take any hint of deception as a sign of insincerity. You can curry a lot of favor with enthusiasts by catering to their needs. But you can ruin a relationship a lot faster with them than with the *Chicago Tribune.*

Nielsen BuzzMetrics vice president Max Kalehoff summed up the culture in an August 2006 column on the MediaPost website:

Disruptive, abundant, irrelevant, self-congratulatory, or exaggerated communications (or often gimmicks) may be tolerated in paid, one-way media, but the game changes with consumer-generated media (CGM). Becoming an active participant in CGM means entering into direct conversations with consumers, where there is a far greater expectation of humanness, honesty, and transparency. There is an expectation of conversation and social exchange, specifically not advertising. Respecting this core rule of most CGM venues is paramount... Whether in the context of media planning or active participation, media specialists must respect the consumer like never before.

Adrants' Steve Hall summarized the attitude voiced to me by many enthusiasts. "No one's looking over my shoulder. I'm not responsible to anyone but my readers," he says. That kind of fierce independence makes enthusiasts potentially the friend every marketer relishes and the enemy that they fear.

The Gadget King

No one has done more to legitimize blogging as a news medium than Peter Rojas and no one has profited more handsomely from it. It's an unexpected distinction for the 31-year-old California native, who holds a master's in critical theory from a British university and who was unemployed as recently as 2002.

Peter Rojas founded two of the most popular sites in the blogosphere: Gizmodo and Engadget. Both consistently rank in the top ten blogs on Technorati. Both serve a community of hard-core consumer electronics enthusiasts. Together, they are arguably the most important sources of news in their markets online or in print.

Engadget prides itself on being first with everything, with an edgy, attitudinal voice that can send shivers down the spine of electronics marketers. Engadget is so fast, so timely and so savvy about the market it covers that it's quickly become the gold standard for journalism in its field. Its traffic has soared past established publications and websites. Elite journalists like the *Wall Street Journal*'s Walt Mossberg admit that they read Engadget every day.

Peter Rojas was made for blogging. An engaging young man with piercing dark eyes that betray an intense intelligence, he seems unaffected by his sudden celebrity. "I just wanted to blog about gadgets and hopefully make a little money with it," he says. "The idea that you could make a million dollars was incomprehensible."

But that's what happens when you're one of the world's best and most prolific bloggers. Rojas was featured on the cover of *New York* magazine in February 2006. The story, titled "Blogs to Riches," was a coming-out party for the blogosphere, arriving just three months after *Forbes'* withering "Attack of the Blogs" indictment.

Wrote *New York* writer Clive Thompson:

> *To see just precisely how rich blogging can make you, it's worth visiting Peter Rojas, the cheerful, skate-punk-like editor of Engadget— and the best-compensated blogger in history. When I meet him one December evening in his apartment on the Lower East Side, he's sitting at an Ikea desk bedecked with three flat-panel screens and looking relatively fresh, considering he's just come off another eleven-hour blogging jag. Like most A-list bloggers, he hit his keyboard before dawn and posted straight through until dinner. "Anyone can start a blog, and anyone can make it grow," he says, sipping a glass of water. "But to keep it there? It's fucking hard work, man. I've never worked so hard in my life. Eighty-hour weeks since I started."*

Hard work clearly never bothered Peter Rojas. He sailed through Harvard, graduating magna cum laude with a degree in social studies in 1997. He completed a master's in English literature at the University of Sussex a year later. He loved his specialty—critical theory—but quickly realized there wasn't much of a market for it. "You get so specialized, it takes fifteen minutes to explain what you do," he says. By 2000, he was on the west coast, working as a media planner in an ad agency and trying to figure out what to do with his life.

Whatever that was, it wouldn't involve media planning, "the wrong job for me," he says. Rojas had no journalism experience, but that didn't matter much in the go-go late nineties, when Internet euphoria was filling magazines' coffers with venture-backed ad dollars. He got an interview at *Red Herring*, a magazine for investors, and got hired in June 1999. "They were desperate for people," he says.

Red Herring turned out to be an epiphany for Peter Rojas. He'd always been a tech geek. His father, a physician, had owned one of the first CD players sold in the U.S. As a child, Peter had owned an Atari 400, an early personal computer that failed to catch fire but ignited the imagination of enthusiasts. He was a musician in high school who dug playing with the latest audio equipment. Now, living in the Bay Area in the late nineties, where technology suddenly made anything seem possible, was like a fantasy. Rojas got to write extended pieces about the future of technology. "It was a perfect fit for me," he says.

Until 2001. That was when the Internet economy, erected on a bubble of inflated expectations, suddenly met reality. As venture capital drained out of the economy, magazines closed down or cut staff. Peter Rojas was laid off in May 2001, "a huge setback," he remembers. He spent days putting together portfolios of clips, only to be turned away or ignored. One magazine shut down two days after he interviewed there.

The Bay Area network did pay off, though. *Wired*'s Paul Boutin had become a good friend and began to feed Rojas some freelance work. Rojas had also befriended Nick Denton, a former *Financial Times* writer who had recently founded a news-aggregation service called Moreover.

Wired provided steady assignments, but there was no promise of a staff position. With the Bay Area in the throes of the worst tech recession in twenty years, Peter Rojas decided to go east to New York. It was 2002 and he was living mostly on savings. His income that year would total about $14,000.

Rojas had begun experimenting with a blog while in San Francisco. He didn't update it very often, but it had promise as a way to get feedback on story ideas. Not many people were blogging at the time, anyway.

It was Nick Denton who planted the idea that the blog could maybe make some money. Rojas demurred at first. "If I'm going to spend an afternoon writing, it might as well be a pitch" for a job or freelance assignment, he says.

"What if you could make a living with a blog?" Denton asked.

Preposterous. In 2002, no one was blogging for their bread and butter. But Peter Rojas was unemployed, so what the hell. He and Denton concocted the idea for a blog about consumer gadgets. They called it Gizmodo and Peter Rojas was the first and only writer.

It seemed an odd choice. The consumer electronics world wasn't hurting for information. There were several enthusiast magazines and many bloggers, even in 2002. But the mainstream publications mostly dealt with the topic the same way, delivering elaborate product reviews full of charts and graphs. A magazine's three-month production schedule precluded quick turnaround. The blogger enthusiasts mostly worked the same way. They delivered great substance, but not much immediacy.

Gizmodo filled a gap. Rojas and Denton understood the unique value of blogs: they could be updated quickly with the latest news, tips and rumors. Nobody was chronicling the hectic, day-to-day activity of a business that was set to explode in 2002. Gizmodo would be the fingers on the pulse of the industry.

For nearly two years, Peter Rojas was the voice of Gizmodo. He blogged furiously, often more than a dozen posts in a day, snatching tidbits of information and rumors from all over the Internet. The articles were brief, many less than 200 words, but they were timely and opinionated. "Stick to the topic, give an unvarnished opinion and style supports substance," says Rojas, summarizing his operating principles. "And never talk about yourself. Readers don't care."

Rojas always believed his readers knew more than he did. Gizmodo was an insider's guide with attitude. Rojas advocated feverishly for his readers. He wasn't afraid to poke a stick in the eye of the big electronics firms. What difference did it make? He was just one guy writing a blog.

But it did make a difference. People were noticing Gizmodo and the site's traffic was growing dramatically, reaching one million page views in a little over six months, then doubling that three months later. It was now part of a network called Gawker Media, run by Denton. Next to the namesake Gawker celebrity blog, Gizmodo was arguably the best known member of the family. Gadget freaks loved the constant stream of insider knowledge and electronics makers were beginning to notice.

So was Jason Calacanis. A Brooklyn native who had become famous in boom-time dot-com circles with an insider magazine called *Silicon Alley Reporter*, Calacanis was trying to build a business model around blogs. Like Gawker, he was recruiting individual bloggers to become part of a network, with advertising to be leveraged across the sites. Unlike Gawker, Calacanis's Weblogs, Inc. was going for massive scale: hundreds of blogs.

Calacanis needed Peter Rojas to build a franchise in consumer electronics, so much so that he offered equity in the company. In February, 2004, Rojas jumped. Speculation in the blogosphere was that Rojas and Denton had had a falling out, but Rojas dismisses the rumors. "It was just a better deal," he says. "It was a chance to blog full time."

With more time at his disposal, Rojas wasted none of it building Engadget's audience. The editorial model was similar to Gizmodo's, but the site emphasized even greater speed and volume. "Write it, find a photo, post it, move on to something else," Rojas says, summarizing the process. "I'd be on the phone with a PR person and they'd ask what my lead time was for publication. I'd tell them 'I posted as I was talking to you.'"

Engadget was a one-man show for a while, but added freelancers as the site grew. Its coming-out party was at the massive Consumer Electronics Show in January 2005. Rojas and a small staff posted more than 250 articles from the show, overwhelming competitors and putting Engadget squarely on the map. "We outhustled CNet and *PC Magazine*," he says. "We were covering the show in real time."

Engadget had some notable scoops, among them Microsoft's Xbox 360 game machine. In May, Microsoft's Bill Gates paid the site the ultimate compliment with a one-on-one interview. In true blogger fashion, the interview was published in its entirety, all 5,000 words of it. It wasn't long before Engadget surpassed Gizmodo on the technology rankings. Over the summer, its traffic passed *PC Magazine*'s, a fixture in the consumer technology industry since the late seventies.

In October, America Online bought Weblogs, Inc. for a price reported to be around $25 million. Peter Rojas' share wasn't revealed, but it was certainly in the millions. "I didn't intend to become a millionaire," he told *New York*. "But I wound up there anyway."

Marketers now beast a path to Engadget's door. But don't expect that door to open for a press release or product pitch. "If people ask how to get my product on Engadget," he says, "I tell them to start by creating a good product. Read the blog every day," he adds. "I can tell in an instant when somebody doesn't. Marketers can't control the news any more, but they can support the conversation that is part of the market."

Peter Rojas still blogs for Engadget but not with the intensity that he used to. A small staff of writers keeps the site humming, working from a six-page document articulating the site's distinctive voice. At 31 in the summer of 2006, Peter Rojas is rich, successful and has his whole life in front of him. That future may include blogging or it may not. "After 10,000 blog posts," he smiles, "I'm happy to step back."

CHAPTER 4
Measures of Influence

To understand influence in social media, you need to buy in to the power of small markets. This is difficult for people who were raised in the last half of the twentieth century, when "big" was synonymous with "important." People of my generation were taught that successful media companies had broad reach and big audiences. Big stories were those that interested a lot of people, even if they didn't affect many of those people very directly.

This mile-wide-inch-deep mentality dominated media for the last 150 years, but small markets have always had value of a different kind. The audience is highly engaged and often passionately interested. Often, it's because the topic relates to their work or a cause that concerns them. People are avid consumers of information in small markets, much more so than in large ones. But until recently, there were few cost-effective ways to address many small-market needs.

All that is changing, driven by the evolution of technology that enables networks of individuals or small groups to behave like big companies. Marketing guru Seth Godin writes in the introduction to his 2006 book, *Small Is the New Big*:

Small means that the founder [of an organization] is involved in a far greater percentage of customer interactions. Small means the founder is close to the decisions that matter and can make them quickly. Small is the new big because small gives you the flexibility to change your business

*model when your competition changes theirs. Small means you can tell
the truth on your blog. Small means that you can answer e-mail from
your customers. Small means that you will outsource the boring, low-
impact stuff like manufacturing and shipping and billing and packing to
others while you keep all the power because you invent something that's
remarkable and tell your story to people who want to hear it.*

Advertisers understand this, and that's why so many are shifting
their dollars online. Merrill Lynch estimated the size of the global online
advertising market was $11.6 billion in 2006, up 35 percent from the pre-
vious year. A survey by online ad network DirectoryM reported that more
than half of small and midsize businesses' advertising budgets were allocated to online media in 2006.

Influence online is a matter of small influencers affecting big
influencers. It's the small guys who are closest to their markets and who
are in the best position to say what should happen there. In the last half
of the twentieth century, marketers became fixated on big influencers:
national newspapers, broadcast TV networks and star radio personalities. Now the pendulum is swinging back. Small is cool. eBay can act like
a large company because there are 400,000 people who depend on it for
their living. But eBay is really quite small.

A personal anecdote

I learned about the power of small markets firsthand during six
years at a new-media company. Until 1999, I had worked for large publishing houses focused on information technology (IT) topics. With cir-
culations of more than 250,000, these publications treated their audience as a single group. They tried to address narrow interests through
sections and special reports, but it was hard to do, given the limitations
of print publishing.

My new employer, TechTarget, was publishing online, a fact that
gave the company a huge advantage in defining its audience differently.
TechTarget saw those 250,000 IT people as dozens of special-interest communities. It planned to build a portfolio of websites for them, each very
narrowly focused.

Conventional wisdom at the time was that there was no room for
new competitors. But as we began to build a network of what would
eventually number more than thirty websites, we found a welcoming

audience. When the tech market crashed in early 2000, TechTarget continued to grow, doubling revenues every year for five years while magazines and mass-market websites collapsed around us.

The experience taught me how hard it is for publishers and marketers to understand focused markets. During the first three years of TechTarget, we constantly looked over our shoulder, expecting some giant competitor to copy our model and stamp us out of existence. But that didn't happen. In fact, it was three years before the industry leaders did anything at all to respond, and even then their efforts were unremarkable.

I also learned about the economics of online publishing. At the weekly print publication where I worked for fifteen years, a staff of sixty editors was needed to produce each issue. Editorial production alone required a nine-person staff. Add in circulation, sales, marketing, administration and logistics, and you had more than two hundred people working full-time just to turn out one weekly journal. And that's not counting printers, shippers, mail handlers and other contractors.

At TechTarget, most websites had an editorial staff of two, a single sales person and access to a pool of back-end support. The company was producing thirty continuously updated media properties with a total staff of fewer than three hundred people. You do the math.

The rule of thumb in print publishing is that a new magazine with 50,000 subscribers costs at least $5 million to launch. Much of that is circulation development, a grossly inefficient discipline that usually involves dropping millions of pieces of direct mail. Most publications lose money on circulation. They must constantly hunt for new lists to keep their readership fresh.

Advertisers pay for all this. A display advertising page in even a modest trade publication often costs more than $10,000. It can run in the hundreds of thousands for major publications. Print publishing is inefficient. Online publishing is much better. But the economics of personal publishing put both of them to shame.

It's not new information that small markets can be profitable; newsletter publishers have known that for years. What's new is the power of the Internet to deliver these micro-markets with an efficiency that was previously unimaginable. The technology to enable advertisers to cost-effectively reach these focused markets is advancing rapidly.

The power of focus

Focused markets are more efficient than large ones. That's why TechTarget succeeded. Customers found that response rates to their messages were two to ten times higher than those from broad media. The targeted ad buy was much more efficient.

Social media takes small markets to another level. It obliterates the economic limitations of publishing that have defined the field for hundreds of years. In rewriting those rules, it has also changed the laws of influence.

Let's look at the economics. Blogging software is free or close to free. Many bloggers work for a pittance, though a few are making good money. Most bloggers and podcasters spend nothing on circulation development. In fact, most don't even seek advertising until their readership runs into the thousands every day. The blogger is writer, managing editor, production artist and often head salesman. Large blogs may support a full-time staff but most are solo affairs.

The influential BoingBoing.net blog grossed an estimated $1 million in 2006 with a staff of four, according to *Business 2.0* magazine. Fark.com is on its way to becoming a multi-million-dollar property with a full-time staff of one and two contractors. It gets 40 million page views a month. Google Blogoscoped generates four million page views a month, also with a single staff member. That puts it ahead of such venerable computer publications as *Infoworld* and *InformationWeek*, according to Alexa.com. As Mike Kaltschnee of HackingNetflix.com told me, "I'm not going to put my local newspaper out of business but they have forty or fifty employees. I'm one person and I have four times their traffic."

In short, there is no barrier to entry. A blogger's or podcaster's success is almost entirely dependent on his or her ability, ingenuity and hard work. New voices emerge all the time and they can gain traction and become influential very quickly. Whole industries are still almost untouched by social media, which means that influence has yet to be defined there.

This isn't a comfortable environment for marketers. Bloggers and podcasters can walk away from their business on a whim, leaving advertisers stranded. Rocketboom, which was one of the most popular video blogs on the Internet in the spring of 2006 with 300,000 daily visits, abruptly shut down in June 2006 when host Amanda Congdon and producer Andrew Baron had a falling-out. The site was down for more than a week while Baron scrambled to find an interim host.

In my interviews with bloggers for this book, several acknowledged that the daily grind of writing or podcasting was tiring at times and that the urge to throttle back or just quit was at times overpowering. And some prominent bloggers have actually logged off for a while. However, most have returned. Blogging, they've told me, is like a drug. Once you start, you have an insatiable urge to continue.

If money, circulation, brand recognition, corporate identity, list integrity and staff size have little or nothing to do with success in social media, how do you figure out influence? It's very different from anything marketers have ever seen, and it all starts with links.

Link culture

Hyperlinks are the most important metric of influence in social media. Links are the essence of the Worldwide Web, of course; the "http" that precedes Web addresses stands for "hypertext transfer protocol," which is the standard for links. Google's PageRank algorithm, which revolutionized search, is based on the assumption that a page's importance is defined by the number of other pages that link to it. Technorati and Nielsen BuzzMetrics, two of the leading companies that measure influence in the blogosphere, assign more weight to links than to any other factor.

Bloggers have developed a rich culture around links and they treat links with respect, even reverence. Links in blogging are equivalent to eBay's well-known feedback system. If you are a regular eBay user, you know how that works. Buyers and sellers are assigned positive and negative ratings by their commerce partners based on satisfaction with the transaction. The rating is expressed as a percentage, with 100 percent positive being perfect. Feedback is so important to the eBay ecosystem that members will engage in vigorous debates over the assignment of a single negative rating. The feedback system has been called one of the most important innovations eBay introduced to the Internet.

Linking is the blogosphere's version of feedback. Bloggers show appreciation and recognition of other bloggers by linking to them. A link is a way of saying, "I read this information, I found it interesting and useful, and I respect the author for creating it." Links are even be bestowed on content which with the blogger disagrees. The link is a sign of respect more than a sign of agreement.

Successful bloggers are link freaks. Look at a page in Instapundit or Micro Persuasion and you will see a dizzying number of links. In large part, this is recognition of those bloggers' understanding that they have a responsibility to the community to drive traffic elsewhere. In fact, the burden of being a top blogger is the knowledge that one influences the plight of lesser bloggers to a disproportionate degree. Small bloggers continually appeal to the most influential writers in hopes of gaining a link that may drive several thousand page views.

Statistical reference

The fact that linking is an important component of influence has been documented statistically. HP researchers Eytan Adar and Lada Adamic examined the phenomenon in a 2004 research study. They found that "blogs linking to one another have about a 45 percent chance of mentioning at least one common URL." But in addition, their model for "infection"—or the spread of information from one blog to another—"indicates that infection is six times more likely when this happened previously." In other words, bloggers who link to each other are more likely to talk about the same things.

If that sounds glaringly obvious, think about the consequences. When a prominent blogger writes about a topic, there is a high likelihood that it will be noticed and mentioned by other bloggers within that person's sphere of influence. The more bloggers who cite and comment upon a story, the more likely their comments will be noticed by someone else. The more popular a blogger becomes, the more people link to that person. More links create more influence, leading to still more links. The cycle is self-perpetuating, and it eventually leads to the emergence of a small number of highly influential bloggers, most of whom have practiced their craft long enough to accumulate a large number of inbound links.

PR blogger Steve Rubel calls these people "supernodes." The supernodes can create a swarm of activity and commentary about a topic almost at will. If they mention it, it's important. How do people come to acquire this kind of influence in such a democratic medium? Author and social media researcher Clay Shirky demonstrated in a 2003 study that it's almost inevitable that, in a vast audience of equals, power will come to be concentrated in the hands of a few people.

In "Power Laws, Weblogs, and Inequality," Shirky analyzed links in 433 blogs:

> ...the top two sites accounted for fully 5 percent of the inbound links between them The top dozen (less than 3 percent of the total)

accounted for 20 percent of the inbound links, and the top 50 blogs (not quite 12 percent) accounted for 50 percent of such links.

A second counter-intuitive aspect of power laws is that most elements in a power law system are below average, because the curve is so heavily weighted towards the top performers. [Of the 433 blogs analyzed,] the average number of inbound links (cumulative links divided by the number of blogs) is 31. The first blog below 31 links is 142nd on the list, meaning two-thirds of the listed blogs have a below average number of inbound links. We are so used to the evenness of the bell curve, where the median position has the average value, that the idea of two-thirds of a population being below average sounds strange. (The actual median, 217th of 433, has only 15 inbound links.)

A February 2006 article in *New York* magazine explained how this concentration of power occurs:

Imagine that 1,000 people were all picking their favorite ten blogs and posting lists of those links. Alice, the first person, would read a few, pick some favorites, and put up a list of links pointing to them. The next person, Bob, is thus incrementally more likely to pick Alice's favorites and include some of them on his own list. The third person, Carmen, is affected by the choices of the first two, and so on. This repeats until a feedback loop emerges. Those few sites lucky enough to acquire the first linkages grow rapidly off their early success, acquiring more and more visitors in a cascade of popularity. So even if the content among competitors is basically equal, there will still be a tiny few that rise up to form an elite.

So common sense would dictate that marketers should focus their efforts disproportionately on the most popular voices in social media, right? Well, not exactly.

Minor influencers

No one can be the all-seeing, all-knowing source of information about even a narrow subject. And top bloggers tend to write about big topics like global politics, major industries or the state of media. Most A-list bloggers actually select at least half the items they choose to highlight from tips sent in by their readers, many of whom are small-time players.

So the supernodes actually get their energy from satellites of much smaller influence who have their ear.

This is one reason influence is so difficult to measure; even small players in the blogosphere can exert an unusually high level of influence depending on who is reading them. It is a modern version of the six-degrees-of-separation model. The blogger without much influence may be a link between two bloggers who have significant influence.

If a blogger is following protocol, these sources would always be acknowledged. But that isn't necessarily the case. Some may mention a source without linking to it. Others will find their way back to the original source of information and link to it, bypassing the blogger who alerted them to the information in the first place. Over the long term, though, it's clear that bloggers in some markets continually serve as primary sources of information. If you can identify them, you can take your message to the influencers at the source.

The link economy

Nielsen BuzzMetrics monitors 30 million blogs yielding 500,000 to 1 million posts a day. The service provides marketers with insight into what's being discussed in the blogosphere, as well as what's being said about their products. Links are the best indication of a blog's influence, says Natalie Glance, Ph.D., a senior research scientist with BuzzMetrics, "Readership is a good proxy for influence," she says. "The more readers a person has, the greater their reach and the more likely they are to influence somebody in mainstream media and reach beyond the blogosphere."

Nielsen mainly looks at links. It crawls the blogosphere daily for new posts and harvests links to other blogs. Proprietary technology separates blog posts from, say, newspaper articles, and filters out disruptions like spam blogs and link farms.

Not all links are treated the same. Blogroll links (a blogroll is a list of weblogs that appears as a sidebar on the front page of most blogs), for example, aren't counted because they're persistent and most bloggers don't scour their blogrolls every day. The correlation between links and readership is elusive but measurable. To establish the relationship, Nielsen BuzzMetrics found sites that list traffic meters and then correlated link activity to those sites. The truth: The more active links a site has, the more traffic it gets.

While links are important indicators of influence, they can be situational, Glance says. Entertainment and celebrity sites, for example, don't generate much cross-linking activity, while tech sites are notable for having a copious number of links. That's where comments are figured into the equation. Sites that don't generate many links often spark a lot of comment activity. Gadget blogs have a lot of both.

Influence in different markets is, therefore, different. Link counts are relative to the overall link activity in a market. In other words, a site that doesn't generate links or comments may still be influential if its competitors don't either. That also factors into the BuzzMetrics equation.

Glance acknowledges that influence measurement in the blogosphere is still primitive, and Nielsen BuzzMetrics, like other measurement firms, is refining its craft. One idea is to categorize blogs by topic and measure their metrics against each other on the assumption that overall activity is relative to the topic being discussed. Another is to weight different blogs differently, so that a link from an A-list blog is assigned more importance than one from a lesser-known outlet. Mainstream media is also not currently figured into the equation. The service measures links from blogs to newspaper articles, but not the reverse.

Two things are clear, Glance says. One is that the blogosphere would be a very different place without mainstream media. "There's more linking to mainstream media in the blogosphere than there is to other blogs," she says. Mainstream media is the principal source of information upon which bloggers comment. Another truism is that blogs about sex, movie stars and Paris Hilton get a disproportionate amount of traffic. "The most popular stories in the blogosphere aren't necessarily the most important ones," she says.

Nielson BuzzMetrics' BlogPulse is an excellent window on the blogosphere with a lot of interesting metrics and search tools. If you're a Technorati fan, check it out because you will find new and interesting resources there.

Hidden influence

Digital Influence Group, a social media marketing agency, is combining input from most of the major search services to create an index of influencers. "We try to identify the ten or fifteen influencers that relate to our client's business and not as they relate to Internet rankings," says Cinny Little, executive vice president at the Waltham, Massachusetts-

The Power of the A-List

While I was writing *The New Influencers*, I got a first-person introduction to influence.

At my publisher's suggestion, I posted draft chapters of this book on my blog beginning in late July 2006 and invited comments. I e-mailed a few prominent bloggers and notified some friends and colleagues. For the next two months, traffic to the chapters was light, averaging about forty page views a day.

Then, on Friday, September 8, Steve Rubel posted a summary of the book and a link to the chapters on his influential Micro Persuasion blog. The day before Rubel's comments appeared, there were eighteen page views from twelve visitors. On September 8, there were 1,119 page views from 505 visitors.

That was just the beginning. After a weekend slowdown, traffic resumed at a new level the following week, averaging 400 page views a day. What's more, other bloggers began to take notice. Over the next two weeks, more than forty other bloggers posted links to the chapters. My blog's ranking on Technorati shot up from 55,000 to 30,000. Traffic eventually stabilized, but at an average of 200 page views a day, or five times previous levels. All because of one link from the right blogger.

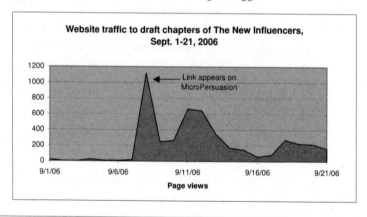

based firm. "Influencers could be your competitors or someone within your organization. They could be people with very little visibility in the grand scheme but huge visibility in the niche you're trying to reach."

Digital Influence Group subscribes to most of the major influence ranking services and then combs through the results looking for patterns. Influence is about much more than Technorati or Alexa rankings, Little says. For one thing, influencers may participate in multiple media and multiple venues. In the travel industry, for example, prominent forums include BootsNAll and America Online discussion boards, as well as hundreds of individual blogs. In the technology market, ITToolbox maintains scores of e-mail lists, called listservs, that function as virtual discussion groups. All wield influence. The influencers might also include analysts whose reports are never published on the Internet but who have credibility with a small number of important paying clients. These small-market experts don't get quoted in the national media because their research is so focused, but to the communities they serve, their opinions move markets.

Other factors may affect influence without creating a link ranking:

- Is the influencer frequently quoted in mainstream media?
- What's the competitive environment? How many other influencers are targeting this topic?
- How many comments does the influencer get for each blog post? An infrequent blogger who doesn't draw many links may still be well respected whenever he or she does draw comment on a topic.
- Does the influencer work in multiple media? Someone who maintains multiple blogs, podcasts and writings in other venues may have inbound links spread out over multiple properties.

The bottom line is that influence is hard to measure and doesn't lend itself to a single number. "The biggest misconception a lot of companies have is that some engine will provide you with one definitive "ranking" of a blogger, a community site, or an area in a social network," Little says. "At the end of the day, you have to consider both quantitative and qualitative measures, and you still have to build relationships. You have to learn who the influencers are and understand what's relevant to them."

So many variables are involved in measuring influence that even the most astute measurement firms can't give definitive guidelines. The good news is that corporate marketers who are wrestling with this problem aren't alone; no one has figured it out. The bad news is that any effort to influence the influencers is almost necessarily haphazard and error-prone.

Blog swarms

A single reference from a top blogger is sometimes all it takes to kick off a "blog swarm," which is one of several terms used to describe a massing of blogger activity around one topic. Kevin Whalen, a public relations professional who hosts a weekly political radio program in the Boston area, was a catalyst for one swarm involving Michael Yon, a military blogger and former Green Beret.

Yon had paid his own way to Iraq to write about and photograph the war, building a large audience of readers following his blog in the process. One photo he took of a soldier cradling a dying young girl in his arms was selected as one of the top ten photos of 2005 by *Time* magazine.

The U.S. Army thought the photo was powerful, too, and distributed it without Yon's permission. Yon sought compensation but the Army refused, saying he had abrogated some rights as an embedded blogger. A couple of newspapers picked up on the story but the situation wasn't resolved until Whalen offered to rally bloggers to the cause.

"The post was picked up by major traffic bloggers like Glenn Reynolds, Michelle Malkin, Wizbang, Mudville Gazette and dozens of others," Whalen wrote in an e-mail interview. "General [Vincent] Brooks [the officer in a position to resolve the issue] received several hundred e-mails in a matter of hours and contacted Michael. The seven-month long dispute with the U.S. Army was over within 24 hours. Absolutely amazing."

Philipp Lenssen, the 28-year-old programmer who built Google Blogoscoped to one of the top thirty blogs on the Internet, explains the phenomenon this way:

> *A major blogger won't find all the news bits, whereas someone who finds the news bit might not have a regular blog. Often it works like this: Peter snoops around someplace, finds an interesting bit on Company X and blogs it. David is Peter's friend and reads his blog. He sees the news and passes it on to popular blogger Frank, who covers Company X. Frank posts the news in his blog (linking to Peter), exposing it to many readers who like to hear Company X news. Some of the readers get active and send around e-mails. Some employees of Company X hear the news and spread it inside the company. The blog post is submitted to highly trafficked sites like Digg, Slashdot, BoingBoing, Waxy, Metafilter and such. Mainstream news sources pick up the chatter on Company X as well, further escalating things.*

Major blog swarms are still rare, but they are happening with increasing frequency. AOL had the dubious distinction of being the victim of two of them almost simultaneously. Shortly after the Vincent Ferrari customer service incident detailed in Chapter 1, AOL mistakenly released data on more than 20 million search terms entered by 650,000 members.

Michael Arrington of the influential TechCrunch was the first major blogger to jump on the story. "AOL is hitting bottom when it comes to brand image," he wrote. Actually, the bottom was still to come. Technorati recorded more than six hundred daily posts in the blogosphere on the subject each of the next three days. The story quickly jumped to the mainstream media, where it made headlines for days. Again, the first news of the embarrassing privacy breach came from a blogger. Other bloggers fanned the flames before the first mainstream media (which was, interestingly enough, OhMyNews, a Korean venture in community journalism) caught wind and turned the story into a blockbuster. More than 1,000 articles have been published in the mainstream press about the incident, to go along with 13,000 blog posts.

Blog swarms can strike terror into the hearts of marketers because they appear to come from nowhere and can reach momentum that is seemingly out of proportion to the actual importance of the story. They can also just be flat wrong.

"If blogging is journalism, then some of its practitioners seem to have learned the trade from [disgraced former *New York Times* reporter] Jayson Blair," wrote Daniel Lyons in "Attack of the Blogs" in the November 14, 2005, issue of *Forbes*. "Many repeat things without bothering to check on whether they are true, a penchant political operatives have been quick to exploit. 'Campaigns understand that there are some stories that regular reporters won't print. So they'll give those stories to the blogs,' says Christian Grantham, a Democratic consultant in Washington who also blogs."

Fact checking

There's no question that character assassination or the profit motive play a role in some blog swarms and that people and businesses have been hurt. This is where the role of the A-list bloggers becomes more important. In my interviews with top bloggers, many admitted that they will publish information based on speculative sources. The benefit of this approach, they say, is that it allows them to get the story first. They rely on their readers to fact-check the information. It is, essentially, a public draft-and-revise process, but it makes many people distinctly uneasy.

However, there may be no turning back. "Blogs are the future of journalism," says Larry Weber, a leading public relations executive. "Journalists don't like to hear that. They say nobody validates blogs. I say what do you mean? Two million people are doing the fact checking that newspapers aren't doing any more because they can't afford the people to do it."

In an analysis of the Dell Hell incident, in which A-list blogger Jeff Jarvis' frustrations with Dell Computer customer service became an international incident (see Chapter 2), a U.K. research firm stated that misinformation and poor fact-checking on the part of bloggers contributed to a negative and unfair image of Dell in the media.

> *Bloggers do operate in packs which predominantly reference one another. However, by conventional journalistic standards bloggers have characteristics that weaken their individual influence: They single source stories and are themselves referenced by stakeholders who single source stories. Bloggers gain prominence and link volume by being outspoken and partisan, but this prominence comes at a price. As they lose balance, they weaken their credibility with key authorities (i.e. do not cite more than one source)*
>
> *It is clear that one person's perception of a brand, if it chimes with that of others, can materially damage that brand. Dell's customer services now have a somewhat negative perception. This may not be the result of Jeff Jarvis's blogging, but he is viewed as an authoritative source on it. Any attempt to redress the public perception of their customer services by Dell will have to pass via Jeff Jarvis's influence.[1]*

Mainstream media also has an important role to play in addressing the accuracy issue. Once a newspaper or broadcast outlet picks up the story, the information acquires a level of legitimacy that gives it new momentum. For this reason, blog swarms that stay in the blogosphere generally stay small. Once they jump to the press, however, the news can spread with alarming speed.

Experts advise marketers to monitor developing blogger conversations carefully but to stay out of the discussion until the mainstream media picks it up. Use the insights gained while the story is still small, though, to have your response ready when the first newspaper story runs.

1. "Measuring the influence of bloggers on corporate reputation," *Market Sentinel*, Onalytica and Immediate Future, Ltd., Dec. 2005

"Ignore [the story] initially unless it starts gaining credence," says Bill Comcowich, whose CyberAlert service monitors a variety of news and consumer sources, including blogs. "Answer only if it is gaining credence and answer openly, not surreptitiously. Answer only where the information has appeared. You don't have to respond in the *New York Times* because Joe's blog tweaked your president."

A new breed of community websites is also coming to exert great influence. Slashdot.org is a site for

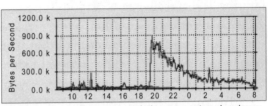

Graph from a web server statistics generator showing a moderate slashdot effect in action.

computer techies that was one of the earliest group blogs. Slashdot has huge clout in a community of software developers who read and comment enthusiastically on the stories it posts. It can drive tens of thousands of page views to a site with a single mention. In fact, "the Slashdot effect" even has an entry in the Wikipedia encyclopedia describing the trouble website operators can experience when Slashdot sends an unmanageable amount of traffic to their sites.

More recently, Digg and Fark have joined Slashdot as key influencers. Both sites give their readers a say in choosing which articles are deemed to be the most important and readers debate these choices in active forums. If your blog post is mentioned on Digg or Fark, you can not only see a huge increase in traffic, but scores of other blog posts may be created linking back to your comments. Slashdot, Digg and Fark don't play favorites. They claim to make their decisions based solely on the quality of the content. Thus, a small blogger can become a bigshot in cyberspace just because he or she has a big idea or something interesting to say.[2]

For all the statistical analysis and academic studies that have been performed on the early stages of social media, there is no one metric, formula or service that can reliably measure influence. Nor do any of the experts I spoke to believe that there will be a reliable metric in the near future. The best strategy is to gather together as many tools as you can, so that you can make informed decisions about how to engage when the

2. Digg was embroiled in controversy in the fall of 2006 over allegations that a small group of members colluded to promote their favorite stories to top positions on the site. The incident highlighted the limitations of the community model when it comes to deciding the value of information.

time comes. "The first step in any strategy is to be aware," says CyberAlert's Comcowich. "The major use [of monitoring services] is to spot trends."

In Chapter 9, we'll talk in more detail about the tools that are available. In general, though, the best strategy is to narrow the range of influencers that really matter to you. The analytical tools will do a pretty good job of getting you started. At the very least, they can tune you into what is being said in the conversation. But at some point, you need to put your head down, start reading and come to some conclusions about what motivates those influencers that matter to you.

The rules of thumb apply no matter who the influencers are. You must engage with people at their own level.

CHAPTER 5
Corporate Conversations

On May 31, 2006, the *New York Times* published a column by world affairs columnist Thomas Friedman that contained some pointed criticisms of General Motors. Friedman charged that GM's promotion of SUVs, and the Hummer SUV in particular, were feeding America's addiction to oil. Comparing GM to a "crack dealer" for oil dependency, he said the corporation is "more dangerous to America's future" than any other company.

GM officials were livid. They drafted a letter to the editor, which has typically been the only tool available to public figures who believe they've been wronged by the print media. But they also took their case to the Web.

The day after the Friedman column appeared, GM's global communications vice president, Steven Harris, posted a 1,000-word entry on GM's Fastlane blog refuting the Friedman column in detail. Titled "Hyperbole and Defamation in *The New York Times*," Harris' essay pulled few punches. "Either Mr. Friedman is being a propagandist, or he's woefully misinformed," Harris wrote. The posting went on to highlight GM's achievements in improving fuel economy while disparaging rival Toyota, whom Friedman had praised in his column.

At the same time, GM began discussions with *New York Times* editorial page editors, hoping to place a letter to the editor. The discussions broke down after a week when the sides were unable to agree on length and terminology. In the end, GM's response to the Friedman column never appeared in the *Times*. What it did online, though, was much more powerful.

A week after the Harris post ignited the firestorm, GM upped the ante. Brian Akre, a GM publicist who had been charged with placing a letter in the *Times*, wrote with a voice mixing passion and disgust of his experiences with the Old Gray Lady of journalism.

> *Our letter opened with a paragraph that accurately summarized the most bizarre elements of Mr. Friedman's attack, then reacted with this one-word sentence: "Rubbish."*
>
> *That word accurately portrays how we felt about the column. Personally, I felt a stronger word referring to male bovine excrement would have been more appropriate, but my boss tends to express himself more politely than I in these situations.*
>
> *The* Times *suggested "rubbish" be changed first to, "We beg to differ." We objected. The* Times *then suggested it be changed to, "Not so." We stood our ground. In the end, the* Times *refused to let us call the column "rubbish."*
>
> *Why? "It's not the tone we use in Letters," wrote Mary Drohan, a letters editor.*
>
> *What rubbish.*
>
> *How arrogant.*

Friedman fired back with a 1,200-word opus in the *Times*, restating his position and accusing GM of using lobbyists to defeat tighter federal fuel economy standards. GM blogged. In a June 15 post, Harris was more conciliatory, highlighting GM's fuel conservation efforts and inviting Friedman to visit GM.

At that point, the back-and-forth between GM and the *Times* abated, but the storm in the blogosphere was just beginning. In the month of June, bloggers posted more than one hundred articles about the spat. Mainstream media picked up on the story. *BusinessWeek* blogger Stephen Baker wrote that the controversy was a microcosm of the struggle going on in U.S. corporations today, with the old-line spinmeisters jostling with the new breed of marketers who believe conciliation and humility win more friends.

Readers flooded the GM Fastlane blog, posting hundreds of comments about the dispute, most complimentary to GM. A month after the original column appeared, newspapers, magazines and websites were still writing about the dustup. GM, whose letter to the editor had never even appeared in the *Times*, had generated far more publicity and awareness about its fuel-economy initiatives by blogging than it ever would have created with a letter in print.

Corporate soapboxes

GM's experience exemplifies the best of what corporate blogs can accomplish. As online soapboxes, they offer an unprecedented opportunity to deliver a business's slant on topical issues. Used wisely, they can galvanize customer opinion, humanize executives and boost employee morale.

However, corporate America is still distinctly uncomfortable with the idea of enabling, much less encouraging, that kind of openness. Although blogs are easy to set up and use, fewer than 10 percent of CEOs in Fortune 500 companies maintain them, and most of those executives are in the high-tech field, where blogging is common. Surveys show that more than two-thirds of corporations still have no blogging policies in place.

Only 5 percent of 150 executives polled by Harris Interactive in early 2006 said they were convinced "to a great extent" that corporate blogging is growing in credibility. Even fewer thought blogs were effective at building brands. Podcasting, which has already demonstrated a track record of success for corporate outreach and publicity, is being tested by only a few large companies outside of the tech sphere.

Why is big business so slow to catch on to social media? And do they know something that the rest of us don't?

Changes in attitude

The answer to the second question is "probably not." Corporate reticence is more likely a by-product of cultural conservatism and paranoia about a raft of regulatory restrictions imposed by Congress and the FTC during the late 1990s than a thoughtful strategy of avoidance. In fact, the evidence is that attitudes are changing quickly.

In a survey of 250 companies conducted in the spring of 2006, JupiterResearch found that 32 percent of corporate marketing executives had used blogs to generate word-of-mouth marketing opportunities. More important, the researcher reported that the number of mid-sized or large

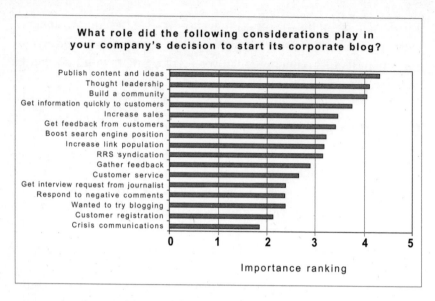

What role did the following considerations play in your company's decision to start its corporate blog?

Importance ranking

companies that are blogging would double in 2006.[1] "By engaging prospective customers in active dialogue, companies can showcase their expertise and domain knowledge [and] generate buzz around their products or services, while eliciting feedback as well as collaboration from product evangelists," the report said.

A mid-2006 survey by market intelligence firm Cymfony and PR agency Porter Novelli reported that 76 percent of corporate blog owners said that media attention and/or website traffic grew as a result of their blogs. Most thought their brands had benefited from exposure in the blogosphere.

Jupiter's estimate that over a third of large corporations were already blogging is much higher than most others, but there's no question that the growth trend is there. Storied franchises like Benetton, Southwest Airlines, Guinness, and Dell Computer all launched blogs in 2006. They're joining an exploding number of small businesses that are finding that blogs and podcasts are a cheap and easy way to grow business and create an online voice.

The motivations for small and large businesses to blog are very different, and so are the rewards. Talk to a small business blogger and he or she will tell you about sales leads and orders that came in as a result of the blog. Big businesses don't see such ROI, or at least they don't measure it.

1. Jupiter's forecasts were optimistic. There's no evidence that that doubling actually happened.

For them, the appeal is in creating new communication channels to customers, exposing the quality of their human capital or just looking hip. The ROI is easier to measure than many people think, as we'll discuss later in this chapter, but the cost can be so small that it almost doesn't matter.

Corporations have a lot of built-in biases against the transparency and openness that the blogosphere demands. Some of these fears are irrational but some aren't. Not every big public company should let a hundred flowers bloom and not every CEO should be a blogger. In fact, it's probably a bad idea for many of them.

Small firms, on the other hand, have a lot less to lose. If they're lucky enough to have a culture that encourages individual expression and customer engagement, there's no reason not to work with social media. And increasingly they are. You'll meet some of them in the next chapter.

For now, we'll turn our attention to how to become an influencer. The rewards of doing it right are substantial and the costs are low. But the issues are quite different for large public companies than they are for entrepreneurs. That's why we'll deal with business blogging in two parts. In this chapter, we'll talk about the issues surrounding corporate and large-business blogs. They can be tricky. Chapter 6 is about small businesses, which have far fewer barriers to entry.

We'll also touch on podcasting, which is quite a different form of expression. Businesses that are apprehensive about blogging may still get great value from podcasting. But it's a different medium.[2]

Joining the Conversation

If you think your corporate blog is going to make your customers love you, the media go easy on you and your investors buy your stock, you're wrong. Blogs are public meeting places and public meeting places can be used for executions just as easily as celebrations.

If you join the blogosphere, be ready to play by the rules (see Chapter 2). If you don't, you'll be ignored or vilified, particularly if you're a corporation. Bloggers are not very tolerant, so expect your mistakes to be pointed out to you. On the other hand, bloggers can be very forgiving, so don't take their criticisms too hard.

Blogging isn't going to make you cool and you shouldn't do it for that reason. In fact, there's no correlation I can find between hipness and

2. Chapter 8 has more detail about how businesses can leverage podcasting.

blogginess. General Motors, Microsoft, Wal-Mart and the Air Conditioning Contractors of America aren't hip, but they have blogs. Apple Computer is hipness personified and doesn't blog at all. In fact, it has sued bloggers. Google owns the most popular blog-hosting site on the Internet but has a tame corporate blog presence, hosting a single corporate blog and links to a few employee blogs. In fact, Google doesn't accept comments on its corporate blog, which is considered kind of a party foul in blogspace. Nike's the hippest shoe company in the world but in blogging, it's all but absent. There is no Harley Hog Blog.

Which leads to a point: corporations shouldn't blog unless they know why they're doing it. As much upside as there is in social media, a poorly conceived, lightly maintained and boring blog will do you more harm than good. You'll be pasted in the blogosphere, and the bigger you are, the more enmity you'll incur. Blogging requires a goal, a plan and a lot of ongoing work. If you don't have a reason to do it, don't bother.

That said, there are a lot of reasons a blog might make sense to a corporation:

Customer relations—Blogs, discussion boards and other forms of interactive media are the most cost-effective customer feedback mechanism ever invented. You won't get a representative sampling of customers but you will get your most passionate customers. The number-one best reason in the world to blog is to engage in a conversation with people who care about your company and products.

GM revived the Chevrolet Camaro in August 2006 driven, in part, by more than 900 requests posted on the Fastlane blog. "Ever since we launched this blog over a year and a half ago, a few recurring themes have peppered your comments...For a while there, it seemed like Fastlane would turn into 'All Camaro, All the Time,'" wrote GM vice chairman Bob Lutz in a blog entry. "I'm not going to tell you that Camaro is happening because the blogosphere demanded it...but I will tell you that the enthusiasm shown for Camaro in this forum is a shining and prominent example of the passion that exists for this automobile."

This can be a mixed bag and you should be careful you don't end up getting more than you bargained for. Dell Computer waded tentatively into the blogosphere in July 2006 with its first corporate blog. You could understand Dell's trepidation. A year earlier, the company had been the target of a withering blog swarm over deficiencies in its customer service.[3] It was a year before Dell healed enough to enter hostile territory.

And the critics had been waiting. Dell made the mistake of launching its blog with some initial entries that looked like they'd been created by the advertising department. The messages were promotional, boring, and disappointing. The blogosphere was quick to respond. Jeff Jarvis ridiculed the effort as too self-promotional. Steve Rubel of Micro Persuasion said he was disappointed and invited Dell to join the conversation, not just talk at people. Both bloggers got plenty of comments from Dell-haters, of whom there were apparently still many.

Fortunately, Dell was listening. A week after launching the blog, a Dell spokesman posted a defense again the criticism. The same day, a customer support manager posted a rather remarkable confession about Dell's support woes. And on Friday, another essay elucidated the blog's commenting policy, which had also come under ridicule.

All in all, it was a baptism of fire, but Dell came through okay. It adjusted quickly to criticism, showed openness and contrition and demonstrated determination to do better. Even its most determined critics acknowledged that the company was trying. Dell has kept its tone humble and receptive. It's going to do fine in the blogosphere.

Chances are you don't face a contentious situation like that, but you should know what to expect before launching a company blog and it's worth taking time to learn the lingo and the culture.

There have been plenty of bad experiences. One friend of mine related the story of a marketing VP at her employer's company who launched a blog and used it to savage his competition, the media and other market influencers. He didn't last long in his job. Another client complained to me that his company had lost interest in blogging after an early experience failed to generate any interest. Looking at the blog, though, it was easy to see why. The entries were long, jargon-filled marketing promotions that said nothing. There were no links and comments were turned off.

"As corporate blogs flood the market under the guise of authenticity and as every department within the corporation sees value in entering the conversation, we risk not only deceiving ourselves about what's truly real or authentic but, more important, confusing or alienating our

3. As noted in Chapter 1, this was one of the most notable blog swarms to target a business. Jeff Jarvis, the blogger who started it all, has an archive of the affair at http://buzzmachine.com/archives/cat_dell.html.

consumers," wrote Peter Blackshaw, chief marketing officer of Nielsen BuzzMetrics, in a column on the ClickZ Network.

It's easy to stub your toe. If you have critics, they will use the forum to make their opinions known. You can't stop them from complaining (nor should you try), but you can anticipate their issues and prepare to respond to them. Silence is not an option. Acceptance, tolerance and humility will serve you much better.

Media relations—If you launch a corporate blog, you will automatically go on the reading list of every journalist who covers you. And if you do it right, they will actually want to read you. Contrast this with press releases, 90 percent of which go into the trash, unread, in my experience. A mid-2006 study by influence-measurement firm Cymfony and PR agency Porter Novelli found that 76 percent of corporate blog owners said company Web traffic and media attention increased as a result of the blogs. If you follow the advice presented later in this chapter, reporters will actually seek you out.

CEO bloggers see a lot of value in this. Sun Microsystems CEO Jonathan Schwartz has said that his blog is far more efficient than the gauntlet of media interviews he used to run, saying the same thing over and over to different reporters.

When GoDaddy.com tussled with ABC over the network's objections to its Super Bowl ads in 2006, CEO Bob Parsons blogged frequently to tell his company's side of the story. "I was constantly posting new entries," he said in an interview. "We made that our central point for any updates for employees, customers, and the media. The blog was great for increasing the company's profile and feeding the publicity machine."

The GM/*New York Times* flap described at the beginning of this chapter is perhaps the best example of a corporation using a blog to take its message to the public and, indirectly, to the media. Many news organizations that covered the dispute excerpted statements from GM Fastlane in their stories.

"The great thing about new media is that you are no longer dependent on a third-party outlet to get the message to the target," says Eric Schwartzman, founder of iPressroom and an active blogger and podcaster. "When you have a novel way of looking at things, it can be very difficult to communicate to the public. [By going direct], you don't

Blogging at Benetton

One of the more distinctive corporate blogs is written by Benetton, the Italy-based global clothing powerhouse. The Benetton blog (benettontalk.com) regularly comments on issues of the environment, AIDS, social activism and sex. The site was created by Fabrica, the Benetton research center on communication. Renzo Di Renzo, Fabrica's artistic director, told me about it in an interview.

What was Benetton's business objective in launching the blog?

I do not think we can talk about business objective; it is just a matter of "communication." Benetton has shown that it wants to pay attention and create a long-term relationship with people, rather than sell one more product. Benetton has built this image by showing that a company can have a conscience. The blog is a place to ponder global themes and is a two-way communication.

Your blog is much more issues-oriented than most and is quite outspoken. How did you arrive at this activist tone?

We believe that a company has a social responsibility and should use its power of communication to raise social awareness about global issues. The "activist" tone may be just the result of the blog being directed to young people and that most of it is written by young people.

How do you select which topics to write about?

Our mission says we want to ponder "global themes and stuff we think we all should care about. The goal is to highlight what is too often silenced by the media noise." Sometimes we are inspired by what is happening in the world; other times it is more a personal concern that we want to share.

Who writes regularly for the blog? What guidance or feedback, if any, do you get from Benetton?

At Fabrica, we have a writing department with five or six young creative people. The blog is mainly their responsibility. They have the freedom to propose and write what they consider interesting, having shared in advance the editorial line. We want to talk to young people around the world and the best way to reach them is to let them speak in person.

What kind of response have you had from readers?

The response has been very good. Of course, this takes time, especially for people to understand that they can really participate. But the figures have been growing every month.

Have you seen any measurable business benefits, or have the benefits been mostly intangible (corporate reputation, brand enhancement)?

The benefit is added value to the brand. The blog is the natural evolution of our attention to the social issues that Benetton has always pursued.

Have you had any objections from people who do not agree with the blog's politics?

There is always someone who disagrees or considers us pretentious. But this is good. We launched the blog to listen to this criticism as well as praise. The dialogue is much more interesting when people have different opinions.

Does Benetton have a policy on employee blogs?

It is impossible to have a "policy" on this matter. The net is the place of freedom with the good and the bad that comes with that. You cannot put rules on that. You can just play or not play.

have to worry about an editor not understanding you or getting it wrong."[4]

There are several good reasons to consider a corporate blog:[5]

Tell your story—One of the reasons GM has been so active in social media is that it is under so much pressure. Facing charges that it's bloated, inefficient, wasteful and slow to market, it has taken its case to the Web with some notable results. GM has also engendered some scorn for the sometimes promotional or defensive nature of its blog statements. You can't please everyone. The important thing is that people are reading the

---

4. Schwartzman's success using podcasts to promote his own business is covered in detail in Chapter 7.
5. I list my six top choices here. In *The Corporate Blogging Book*, Debbie Weil expands that to 13 including community building, advocacy, and branding.

blog and reporters are reporting on it. GM is bypassing the media to take its message to the public and, ironically, is actually getting more press coverage as a result.

Telling your story can take many forms. At its most basic level, a blog or podcast is a chance for your executives to speak directly to their constituents, almost as if the media isn't listening. GM has used the Fastlane blog effectively in this way. Chrysler has a site, TheFirehouse.biz, that it uses to criticize the oil industry, a favorite target for auto makers. The tactics can also be more nuanced. Microsoft used Channel 9, a behind-the-scenes video series, to give its developer audience a peek at its programming operation. The effort helped humanize the company at a time when it was widely regarded as arrogant and impenetrable. Channel 9 was widely considered a success (see the accompanying profile of Robert Scoble for more).

On the other hand, Ford Motor Company's Bold Moves campaign, which was launched in June 2006 as a daring experiment in corporate openness, encountered mixed reviews. Ford promised to throw open its doors to an independent film crew that would document its efforts to rescue its tattered image. It sounded bold, but some bloggers thought it was a little too contrived, particularly since Ford said it was spending $50 million on the effort.

"It's sure to impress the Ford employees who've yet to be laid off and its increasingly irrelevant dealers, but you won't find a link from the company's main website or in its print or TV ads," wrote prominent blogger B. L. Ochman. "Like a lot of big companies, they swim in new waters kind of like my puppy, Benny—refusing to get completely immersed." Other bloggers weighed in with similar reservations.

Ford responded in the best Web 2.0 fashion, linking to Ochman's criticisms on its Bold Moves blog and promising to address the sincerity issue.

Wal-Mart and its public relations firm, Edelman, drew widespread scorn in the blogosphere for using blogs to simulate grassroots support for the retailer's employment practices. The blogs were the work of working Families for Wal-Mart (WFWM), an advocacy group that turned out to be a company-sponsored endeavor. A WFWM blog called PaidCritics.com talks about alleged links between Wal-Mart critics and all kinds of special interests. As of this writing, it is still in operation. The practice of using blogs to create the illusion of grassroots activism—sometimes called "astroturfing"—is condemned in the blogosphere but will probably become more common as blogs go mainstream.

The lesson is clear: when it comes to transparency, a certain amount of open-wound honesty is important. GM's campaign against *Times* columnist Thomas Friedman campaign was effective precisely because it was so raw: two GM employees bared their frustrations in personal terms, without the benefit of a corporate marketing parade. Ford's Bold Moves may ultimately prove successful, but at first blush, it was so slick and scripted that it almost undermined its own message. Such Madison Avenue gimmickry is antithetical to bloggers and can submarine even the most well-intentioned efforts.

The bottom line on telling the story, as in almost anything in the blogosphere, is to be passionate. The community will forgive a lot if you have that going for you.

Tackle an issue—A small number of corporations have used blogging not to market themselves so much as to take a stand on controversial issues or just to define a political agenda. In most cases, there's a marketing agenda at stake, but the payoff can be substantial if the company's target audience has a clear political slant.

Stonyfield Farms maintains two blogs devoted to child-care and cattle-care issues, respectively. The tone is crunchy granola and the politics clearly liberal. Stonyfield, which sells $200 million in organic products each year, knows its audience.

Benetton's new blog, Benetton Talk, is edgier and more controversial. It tackles problems ranging from war in the Mideast to AIDS and has a racy side as well. "This is a blog, a place to ponder global themes and stuff we think we all should care about: Environment, rights, diversity, local communities, development," the disclaimer says. "The goal is to highlight what is too often silenced by the media noise. This blog is sponsored by Benetton, but does not necessarily reflect its corporate view." Benetton explains its reasoning for this approach in an accompanying sidebar.

If you don't want to take on an issue directly, you can use a proxy. The National Association of Manufacturers' ShopFloor.org blog takes a blunt, sometimes pugnacious approach to defending the interests of its 14,000 mostly small-business members. Pat Cleary, senior VP of communications at the organization, calls his uppity style "New Jersey wise guy."

The ebullient Cleary blogs daily, three posts a day for the last two years. The blog is a hit with the group's members but does its best work influencing Congress. "We had about twenty visitors a day at the beginning in November 2004 and now get a couple of thousand visitors a day, seven days a week," Cleary says. "We have readers all over Capitol Hill, the press and influential people. I've got Capitol Hill staffers writing to call my attention to something their Congressman is doing. That's fantastic."

Cleary pulls no punches with his pro-business agenda, taking on organized labor, environmentalists, the Democratic Party, the *Washington Post*, and his favorite whipping boy, Lou Dobbs ("One-note Louie" to Cleary).

"This is about advocacy. We want to get people to click on a button to let members of Congress know what they think," he says. Cleary credits NAM president John Engler with giving the green light to the blog and thereby transforming the organization's profile. "Without the blog, we'd be posting press releases that no one would be reading," he says. "This has grown beyond our wildest expectations."

Feed a frenzy—If you're fortunate enough to have a rabid customer base, a blog is a cheap and effective way to stoke the fires of that passion. Southwest Airlines takes that approach with Nuts about Southwest, a frothy, upbeat journal reinforcing that a great group of folks work at the airline. Guinness & Co. maintains a blog that tells stout-lovers where they can go to meet the Guinness marketing crew. GM's most-trafficked blog entry was an interview with the chief architect of the Chevy Corvette.

If you think this is a slam-dunk decision, though, you'd be wrong. A surprising number of companies with passionate customers are silent in the blogosphere. Why that's the case is a mystery. This seems like a natural way to connect with the best field-level sales force a company could ask for.

Promote a product—A trickier but by no means off-limits reason to blog is to promote a product or service. A few corporations have tried this using proxies or fictitious characters. For example, Owens Corning has an energy blog hosted by its Pink Panther mascot. Arc-Zone, a welding company, has a fictitious female blogger named Carmen Electrode. And distiller Diageo North America ran but later discarded a Captain Morgan blog named after the eponymous pirate mascot for its rum. (The captain was replaced by a video bartender.)

Marketing-driven efforts like this should be approached very carefully. The blogosphere reacts suspiciously to marketing messages in general and to pseudonymous blogs in particular. Prepare for your effort to be scrutinized in detail and for blunt criticism. News Blog called the Captain Morgan effort "a stunning example of what not to do in blogging." The Marketing Shift blog said "The Craptain's [sic] blog sucks! I give it two swords down!" In both cases, the reviewers cited language, topic selection and lack of originality in their negative reviews.

Both of those reviews, by the way, show up in the top ten Google search results for Captain Morgan blog. So arguably, the effort was a net minus for Diageo. The lesson: if you're going to launch a character blog, choose a character and a voice that your audience will relate to.

The inevitable ROI question

It's the most common issue corporate marketers raise when the subject of social media comes up: what's the ROI?

To some extent, the question is irrelevant. A Typepad account costs fifteen dollars a month, plus staff time, and if even a few customers are kept aware of what's going on in your development or service organization as a result, the cost is cheap. Look first at the "I" factor in ROI, because it may make the decision moot.

The support team at Intuit's QuickBooks Online Edition is a good example of an inexpensive blog plugging a hole in customer support. Aware that customers were increasingly frustrated by support staff shortages, the team took matters into its own hands in July 2004 and launched a skunkworks blog on Typepad. The site is still active and, while it's currently updated less than once a month, gets a healthy number of customer support questions. Intuit is thus spending next to nothing on a blogging initiative but getting payback that well justifies the cost. You don't even have to provide questions and answers on your blog to address support concerns. You can simply use it to update customers on your ongoing efforts to fix those problems.

Many smaller initiatives can easily measure the return through click-throughs and purchases on a company site. A theatre company or specialty retailer that blogs, for example, can easily determine who goes to its site from the blog and, once there, actually buys something. Figuring ROI in those cases is easy.

For more ambitious projects involving multiple blogs and/or podcasts, the ROI equation is more difficult to unravel. Katie Paine is the queen of blog ROI. A veteran public relations executive in the technology industry, she's spent the last fifteen years researching, writing and speaking on the topic of measuring the value of public relations and social media investments. She believes nearly everything online is measurable; it's just a matter of choosing what to measure.

At its most basic level, Paine sees the blogging question as being a choice between competitive necessity and competitive advantage. If you're in an industry where a lot of people are already active in social media—entertainment, high tech or politics, for example—nearly everyone is online and you probably need to be there, too, with a voice that's distinctive and original. Chances are others already talking about you and your silence is conspicuous. "In some markets, if you're not visible, you're invisible," she says. That's competitive necessity.

Conversely, a lot of markets have almost no social media presence. This is true of business-to-business markets, in particular. First movers there can gain a quick advantage for little money. The Air Conditioning Contractors of America has been blogging since early 2004 and seems to like the results, given the activity level on its blog. In businesses like that, an early entrant can have the market almost to itself. Vast swaths of the b-to-b landscape are still untouched by blogs. There could be competitive advantage by being the first to plant your flag there.

For her own consulting business, Paine counts click-throughs from her blog to her website that result in requests for information. She also monitors her performance on Google for key search terms, using the blog to boost her standing when necessary. Good search performance is like money in the bank for consultants.

But what works for a small consultancy won't necessarily work for a big corporation, where broad issues like feedback on new products is important. In that case, other metrics are available.

There needs to be an objective in order to measure a return. A company that has a reputation problem can measure customer perception over time to see if a blog is having an effect. Media measurement will give even more immediate feedback. Paine suggests these criteria:

- Is traffic growing over time and is there a corresponding increase in click-throughs to your corporate site?
- What paths are visitors taking once they reach your site? Standard web-tracking metrics should tell you where customers are going.
- Are visitors to your blog spending more time there and on your corporate site? Again, web-tracking metrics will tell you this.

- Is your search-engine ranking improving on certain keywords with which you want to be identified?
- Is your blog generating comments from visitors and is the number of comments growing over time? Is the general tone of the comments critical or supportive and is that metric changing? This will give you a good idea of what generates discussion.
- Are certain referral URLs generating a disproportionately large amount of traffic to your blog or corporate site? These may be the influencers you want to influence.
- Have media citations increased since you launched the blog and are the media citing blog posts in their articles? If so, you're probably having an impact.
- Has overall media coverage of your company changed versus your competition? If you measure positive and negative media mentions over time for you and your competitors, and you filter out other factors like a new product launch or advertising campaign, you should be able to determine whether your social media activities are moving the needle.

Tracking the competition is a key element that's often overlooked, Paine says. Media coverage will fluctuate depending on the topic, so you can't get an accurate reading of the effectiveness of your blog unless you're measuring against another data point. Conversely, if a blogging competitor is moving ahead of you in press coverage, that's probably a message you should listen to.

And consider the value of search, a source of free exposure that many marketers still discount. Internet users conduct more than 500 million searches every day. Search engines love frequently updated information, and that's one reason blogs do so well on them. Blogs are a particularly effective tool to establish presence in new markets, where there isn't a lot of content already on the Internet. You can quickly build credibility and move up the search ranks, branding yourself as an opinion leader in a new space. "The more frequent your updates, the more you move up in the search results," Paine says. And the more you use the keywords that are important to your market, the better you'll do in search.

The business imperative

The worst reason I hear for launching a corporate blog—and, ironically, the reason most often cited—is that it's the thing to do. Competitors are doing it, customers expect it and the "cool" factor is too overwhelming to deny.

These are bad reasons to blog. As noted earlier, there's nothing inherently cool about this medium. And if you go out there with a weak message or a me-too angle, you'll just look foolish.

A lot of corporations use blogs to address problems in the business. The General Motors story cited at the top of this chapter is part of an aggressive push by the troubled company to tell its story through social media.

GM is a company in crisis. Its cost structure is bloated, its products have a reputation for being uncompetitive and slow to market and it has relied for too long on gas-guzzling trucks and SUVs for its profits.

Companies like GM typically don't lead the charge into new technologies. But it was one of the first major corporations to enter the blogosphere. Its strategy was guided by Michael Wiley, a PR guy who understood social media from the early days and saw it as a low-cost means to connect with customers. GM's Small Block Engine blog, was launched in 2004, "basically as an anniversary blog for the 50th anniversary of small engines," Wiley says. "It served us well because it allowed us to dip our toes into blogging. It was safe because we were basically dealing with a fan club."

Response was strong enough that Fastlane was launched in early 2005. "This blog came to fruition in about two hours," Wiley says. "We had the idea, we took it to a couple of senior PR people, they liked it, we asked Bob [Lutz, head of GM's North American operations] if he wanted to do it and he said yes." Although ROI has been hard to measure, Wiley says there's no doubt the effort has modified GM's "dinosaur" reputation. "It gave us a fresh image. It's humanized us."[6]

GM's decision wasn't driven by a hard ROI but the company did have a goal in mind: to talk to customers and the media during a very tough time for the business. Customers have responded with more than 10,000 comments in the first eighteen months. Lutz told Debbie Weil, author of *The Corporate Blogging Book,* that the unvarnished customer feedback has been exhilarating. Whether it contributes to the auto maker's turnaround is still in questions, but it has clearly become part of the company's culture.

---

6. It also worked out well for Michael Wiley. In August 2006, he was lured away to an executive position at Edelman, the world's largest public relations firm.

Port 25

Microsoft had a different goal in mind when it launched Port 25, a blog named after a computer gateway used to transmit e-mail. It was aimed at developers of so-called open source software. Microsoft and the open-source community had been at war for years. These were ugly, name-calling battles with no sign of a resolution. This made Microsoft's outreach effort remarkable to begin with. Even more remarkable was that Microsoft decided to allow visitor comments on the site, a decision it must have known would lead to an outpouring of hostility.

The director of Microsoft's open source group, Bill Hilf, posted an introduction on March 28, 2006, explaining what the blog was about and that Microsoft was a supporter of open source. He invited comments. And that's what he got: over four hundred of them in two weeks. Most were nasty, some were vulgar. "MS is pathetic, Port 25 is a waste of time," read one of the printable ones.

Microsoft was ready for the onslaught. As the venom poured in, staffers responded thoughtfully and courteously. The obscenities were deleted, but not the criticism or the passion. Microsoft later instituted a registration system to screen out the vulgarities, but it didn't edit anyone.

Over the next few weeks, a shift became apparent. The vitriol subsided and the comments became more constructive. Some people even complimented Microsoft for taking the plunge and not losing its cool. By June, the conversation had turned largely positive. While a few visitors still took their shots, they were increasingly shouted down by the community.

Microsoft's experiment was a bold breakthrough. A few years ago, it would have been unthinkable for a corporation to invite such blunt criticism in a forum of its own making. That Microsoft did so indicates that corporate attitudes are beginning to shift away from blasting a message to engaging in a conversation. Microsoft declared Port 25 a success and if its objective was to break the logjam with the growing open source community, then it achieved that goal.

Your own business objective need be no more specific than that. Perhaps your company wants to make a case for alternative energy or health care reform or a return to basic values. Maybe you've got a customer service problem that you need to acknowledge and address. Or maybe there's a public policy issue that gets you fired up. The point is that an objective will keep you focused and focus is what will make you successful. You need to keep your commentary relevant and interesting.

A business goal gives you a single guideline against which you can measure what you say.

Who should blog?

A lot of people wonder why more CEOs don't blog. I believe the answer is simple: Unless they want to, they probably shouldn't. Public-company CEOs are under enormous pressure these days from federal and financial regulators, the media and shareholders. For most of them, blogging probably isn't a good idea.

It's very difficult to thread the needle of being interesting and provocative while at the same time avoiding the risk of running afoul of constituents. Take the safe route and you risk being boring. Take a stand and you may offend board members or regulators. Thanks to the corporate excesses of the late 1990s, CEOs can now go to jail for things they say. For many, blogs probably aren't worth the effort.

Nevertheless, there are exceptions. GoDaddy.com's Bob Parsons is one of the blogosphere's most prolific executives. His fiery, passionate essays took on Internet regulators and federal agencies. That is, until GoDaddy filed for an initial public offering. In May 2006, BobParsons.com strangely fell silent. When I asked a GoDaddy publicist the following month why Parsons had suddenly hit the mute button, she said, "He's dying to blog but we're in a quiet period."[7]

It's a good point. Public companies have at least four quiet periods every year—just before earnings announcements—and more under extraordinary circumstances. In the blogosphere, you can't go silent for two weeks without losing momentum. But the stakes are high. Google had to delay its IPO for a week in 2004 just because its founders had earlier given an interview to *Playboy*.

Another prominent CEO blogger is Jonathan Schwartz, CEO of Sun Microsystems. Schwartz is a good writer who has credibility in the technical community. But his blog is hardly a rant. He is a relentless Sun cheerleader whose writings are full of boosterism. That works fine for the rabid audience of Sun users, but could be seen as shallow in a more critical market.

Schwartz sees his blog as crucial to his role as communicator. "A CEO's number one job is to communicate," he told the audience at the

---

7. Parsons got at least that wish. Two months later, the company pulled its IPO, citing adverse market conditions, and Bob Parsons reentered the blogosphere.

Supernova conference in June 2005. "Blogs are a very efficient mechanism to our customers, our shareholders and our business partners."

Federico Minoli, the CEO of Ducati Motor Holding S.p.A., launched a blog in early 2006. It chronicles his travels and insights as he promotes the company's high-performance motorcycles around the world. Written in Italian and English, it portrays an executive who's highly engaged in his company's business and who's also got a little of his customers' thrill-seeker spirit in him.

The blog was Minoli's idea. "Federico feels free to write what he has in mind," says Valentina Tolomelli, a spokesman for the Italian company. "It was another instrument to get in touch with the Ducati community."

The site gets about sixteen hundred visitors daily and logs dozens of comments for each post. A surprise has been the number of U.S. visitors, Tolomelli says. Through the first six months, Minoli has maintained a regular update schedule, even writing while on vacation.

"You have to have something interesting to say," Tolomelli says. "You have to be motivated and avoid becoming boring. You have to be honest in what you write and you cannot censure critics."

Bottom line: if you're going to launch a corporate blog, consider letting your employees do the talking. There's good reason for that. Employees have more credibility than executives. The Edelman Trust Barometer, a survey of nearly two thousand opinion leaders in eleven countries, found that U.S. respondents said their trust in "a person like me" increased from 20 percent in 2003 to 68 percent in 2006. My own experience with readership studies in publishing is that "peer advice" is identified as the most valuable source of trusted information year after year.

Launching a corporate blog

Before blogging or podcasting, take your time and learn the cultural nuances.[8] Don't rush in with an undifferentiated strategy or underprepared employees, because you'll fall down and look foolish very quickly. As we've noted, the blogosphere is not very forgiving of foolishness. Have a strategy and also an approach that makes sense for the people and the culture you already have. Don't try to be someone you aren't

---

8. Chapter 2 will get you started. See also *Naked Conversations* by Robert Scoble and Shel Israel and *The Weblog Handbook* by Rebecca Blood.

because other bloggers will sniff that out quickly. Launch internally about four weeks before you create your public presence and give people a chance to work out the kinks. Outsiders can give you a take on how you're going to measure up against your competition.

The safest route for most corporations is a **company blog**. Good examples are Nuts about Southwest (blogsouthwest.com), the official Google blog (googleblog.blogspot.com), Dell Computer's One2One (direct2dell.com) and the Taylor Made blog (taylormadeblogs.com) by the golf equipment company. These are topical blogs where the topic is the company. They permit you a fair amount of showboating because readers understand that the purpose is mainly promotional. Company blogs are a great way to tell existing customers about new initiatives and to celebrate successes. In my opinion, Google does the best job of publishing a company blog, with Yahoo!'s more recent effort, launched in mid-2006, also leading the way. The Google site is disciplined, usually with only one new post a day. Google employees have to apply to get on the schedule, which means the blog consistently has good material. For Google fans, it's the number one place to go. And not surprisingly, it's in the top ten in the Technorati ranking.

A company blog is like a bulletin board for your customers and business partners: a good place to tell people what's going on. It's not very personal, though, and developing a distinctive voice is difficult. Contributors must be coached or edited to make sure they have the right tone to their writing. It helps to have an editor to lightly edit posts to even the tone. It's also tougher for individuals to engage in conversations with customers when the lineup of contributors is always changing. If someone does strike a nerve and unleashes a lot of comments, you may have to let that person have the stage for a while to continue the conversation.

On the other hand, there's a lot to like about this approach. Company blogs are easier to maintain and update because several cooks are stirring the soup. The variety of voices can be a plus if your employees have a lot to say. It's a good place to float ideas and seek feedback. And a company blog is a great way to take a company-wide stand on an issue, even a very controversial one. Frankly, I don't understand why more corporations don't do this.

A somewhat more complex and controversial option is to start **executive blogs**. These are journals written by senior managers in the company and you may have one or several, depending on how engaged and chatty your executives are. Hewlett-Packard and Edelman do this, and there are elements of executive blogging at many sites that openly encourage this kind of expression, including IBM, O'Reilly Media, and Thomas Nelson Publishers.

I'm not a big fan of this approach. Executives are busy people and the blog often falls low on their list of priorities. Also, executives tend to be excessively cautious. That's not surprising, given that they are subject to some of the same legislative and regulatory restrictions as the top officers in the company. But caution can create boredom and boredom is death in the blogosphere. I also think executives have a hard time connecting with customers. People in the trenches are more likely to know the customers personally, and everyone wants to know what the CEO is thinking, but the VP of customer support, for example, may be in a netherworld where no one really knows her or wants to hear from her.

The approach that's emerging as the most successful is a **company-wide blog platform**, in which employees are allowed or encouraged to speak to their constituents through multiple personal blogs with little or no company oversight. This is different from a company blog in that each contributor has his or her own space. Many tech companies take this approach, including Microsoft, Borland and IBM. An increasing number of non-tech companies are following suit.

This inclusive approach to social media requires more time and money than the alternatives but also provides more customer interaction and greater employee involvement. It's a particularly good tactic for companies that have difficulty getting feedback from customers or that have layers of resellers between themselves and their customers.

A company-wide blog platform usually requires an investment in hardware and software to host the blogs and administrative time in setting them up, training writers, and establishing policies. Nevertheless, it's debatable how much cost one has to incur. Most people who have done it say the burden isn't onerous. Some companies like to host all their employees' communications directly while others are content simply to point to content on popular blog-hosting services. It doesn't really matter, as long as you link equally to the writings of all employees who want to be listed.

There are many benefits to this company-wide approach. Everyone gets to speak, which means that all aspects of the business can be fairly represented. There is usually plenty of content, which keeps readers engaged and coming back. And the feedback from customers when you have fifty or more people blogging is fantastic.

Downsides? Well, give up on controlling the message. You can't possibly monitor the writings of dozens or hundreds of people, so you shouldn't even try. Put a set of guidelines in place and let people go. Deal with the problem-makers when they come up, but if you already have good policies in place regarding employee behavior, you'll probably have few problems.

Among the companies that freely encourage employees to blog are Microsoft, Borland International, Thomas Nelson Publishers, Google, IBM and iUpload. Some, like Microsoft and Borland, maintain company-controlled websites where all employee blogs appear. Others, like IBM and Google, don't particularly care what software or hosting service their employees use. They simply point to the employee blogs that they think are worthy of notice.

The podcast companion

Blogs and podcasts go together like peanut butter and jelly. In fact, most podcasts have accompanying "show notes" that are basically blogs. Once you get people comfortable with the idea of publishing online, it's a small step to add audio to the mix.

Many corporations are using podcasts to show off the hidden talent in their organizations or to place a stake in a market they covet. "IBM and the Future of…," which is produced by IBM's investor relations organization, demonstrates the company's visionary perspective. Hewlett-Packard podcasts about new products, consumer electronics tips and how its channel partners can make more money.

Disney podcasts travelogues for its resorts. Whirlpool's American Family podcast is an extraordinarily useful and successful resource for families. Contact lens maker Acuvue supports a podcast hosted by two teenage girls. GM's Fastlane blog sports an accompanying podcast that features interviews with key designers and marketers as well as features like reports from the floor of major auto shows. GM's Michael Wiley said the programs cost next to nothing to produce but can draw tens of thousands of downloads from, say, Corvette enthusiasts.

We'll look at some of these examples and examine podcasting in more detail in Chapter 8.

Standards and procedures

The culture of the blogosphere is freewheeling, opinionated and fast. Readers respond to writers who have a lot to say, especially if it's edgy or controversial. Unfortunately, edgy and controversial are the not the way most corporations approach communications. Typically, marketing organizations tone down messages to a bland monotone that varies little from company to company. If you write a blog in that tone, no one will read it. Don't bother.

Corporations should blog to become influencers and that means adopting the cultural norms of the community: transparency, discussion, personality and the like. It's important to have a good set of guidelines for business conduct before you put any blog-specific policies in place. Your blogging policies should complement, not replace, your standards for business conduct.

Dozens of organizations and companies post their blogging policies online, including IBM, Yahoo!, Harvard Law School and Sun Microsystems. They range from ninety-two words (at the *Herald-Tribune* newspaper in South Florida) to more than 1,200 (Harvard Law). Forrester Research analyst Charlene Li[9] has assembled an excellent catalog of these policies. Rather than go into depth here, we'll provide a list of sample policies on the NewInfluencers.com website.

As a rule, you don't have to go overboard writing policies. Most companies that have created them have simply specified that employees are responsible for what they say, should adhere to the standards and norms of the community and should use common sense. Some policies, like IBM's and Yahoo!'s, are even lighthearted and a little playful, quite a contrast to the ponderous HR manuals that typify large companies.

Whatever you do, don't institute an approval process. It will douse whatever expressive spirit your social media initiative may have kindled. Approvals can also suck the personality out of what is a very personal medium. It's a good idea to have blog entries examined for spelling and usage errors. It's a terrible idea to have them reviewed for political correctness. A light touch, simple guidelines and an emphasis on common sense seem to work best.

9. Li's list is at forrester.typepad.com/charleneli/2004/11/blogging_policy.html.

The Corporate Renegade

In early 2003, Microsoft found itself at a turning point.

The company sat atop the personal computer industry. It had been legally classified as a monopoly in operating systems. It had already achieved more milestones than any 28-year-old business in history. A decade earlier, it had vanquished a rival—IBM, more than thirty times its size—in a sequence of moves that many people regard as the most brilliant act of business sleight-of-hand in the past century. Microsoft owned 90 percent of the market for desktop operating systems, a position from which it could dictate much of what customers could and couldn't do with their personal computers and, by association, corporate networks. Its Office suite of business applications was its largest and most profitable business, throwing off margins that rivals could only dream of from a customer base that had no choice but march in lock step to Microsoft's upgrade cycles.

Microsoft had just finished a bruising five-year antitrust battle with the U.S. Department of Justice while at the same time fighting upstart rivals in a war to dominate the Internet. By most accounts, it had done very well. The government penalties in the antitrust case had amounted to little more than a slap on the wrist while Microsoft had steamrolled its most serious Internet rival, Netscape, by undercutting prices and driving Netscape's business model into the ground. In early 2003, there were very few apparent threats to Microsoft's dominance.

And that made it the most hated company in the computer industry.

Winning isn't enough

There was good reason rivals despised Microsoft. The company had destroyed its competition in spectacular fashion. Companies like Novell, WordPerfect, Borland and Netscape, which once employed thousands of employees, were either demolished or left on life support after a fight with Microsoft. The company's take-no-prisoners style drove it to excess; Microsoft was never satisfied just to win, its competitors also had to lose.

That style had earned Microsoft respect from investors but increasingly was causing friction with customers and independent software vendors (ISVs), two groups whom Microsoft couldn't afford to alienate. In fact, the company's traditional stronghold had always been ISVs, who valued Microsoft's generous programs to encourage them to write software for the Windows platform. Microsoft understood small developers as no other large software company did. But ISVs were losing faith. Microsoft was so powerful and aggressive that it seemed that any market, no matter how small, was fair game for its growth ambitions. Indeed, Microsoft had recently bought two small companies—Great Plains Software and Navision—in its first real foray into back-office business applications.

The government antitrust case had sensitized Microsoft to its growing image problem. Media coverage was relentlessly negative; Microsoft's foes used the government's case to air their grievances to a receptive press. Although by most accounts, Microsoft had gotten the best of the Justice Department in the case (it still faced government prosecution in Europe) its reputation had suffered. Increasingly, the computer industry and the technology-buying public saw Microsoft as a ruthless predator, eager to profit at any cost. ISVs were eyeing the free Linux operating system, which had no corporate parent and thus couldn't turn on them. Business customers had no choice but to deal with Microsoft, but they were increasingly airing their gripes in public. Microsoft had an image crisis.

Historically, companies that have been under antitrust prosecution have behaved predictably: they clam up. IBM and AT&T, two behemoths of the early technology industry who were simultaneously prosecuted by the government in the 1970s, became black holes of information as a result. Years after those cases were settled, both companies exhibited extraordinary suspicion and paranoia.[1]

It would have been understandable if the post-antitrust Microsoft had cloaked itself in a veil of secrecy. But that's not what it did. Not by a long shot.

---

1. Early in my career as a technology reporter, I had several amusing demonstrations of this behavior. On one visit to IBM's mainframe production facility in Poughkeepsie, New York, an IBM public relations official insisted on accompanying me to the men's room and standing next to me while I urinated. Another time, I spent more than an hour on the phone with a PR person debating the definition of the word "announce."

Experiment in openness

Instead, Microsoft blogged. In 2003, the company launched what would become the most far-reaching and aggressive corporate openness initiative the business world had ever seen. The company created a corporate site, blogs.technet.com, and invited its employees to begin writing. Its formal blogging policy consisted of two words: "Be smart." And it took one employee, Robert Scoble, and elevated him to the most visible position in the company.

Scoble had been online long before he joined Microsoft. As a former software developer and marketer, he had answered customer questions in online forums since the 1980s. He launched his blog in 2000, when the entire blogosphere consisted of about 200 souls.

Scoble believed that openness was good for business. As a camera store clerk in his teen years, he often referred customers to other merchants when he honestly believed the competitors could better meet their needs. And a strange thing happened. Those customers came back to his camera store because they believe that any merchant who would refer them to a competitor had to be a credible source of information.

Robert Scoble had plenty of opinions, and he liked to share them. Blogging was a natural extension of his personality and he reveled in the opportunity to tell the big guys just where to go. As both a competitor and business partner with Microsoft when he worked at NEC, he had some strong opinions about Microsoft's relationship with its third party developers and its customers. He had never held back about sharing them. So he was surprised, to say the least, when he got a call from Vic Gondotra, the visionary behind Microsoft's evangelism program.

"Vic told me, 'You're doing something interesting and we want to try it out here. But we're not sure if it's going to work,'" Scoble says.

Scoble was hired as a developer evangelist to go out and sing the praises of Microsoft programmers, but it quickly became clear that his blog could be a potent force for Microsoft's tattered image. Top executives at the company knew that during the long antitrust trial, Microsoft had begun to lose contact with third party software developers, which were its strongest constituency. Blogging could help that effort, but Microsoft had to accept the bad with the good. An employee like Scoble would stir things up internally but he wouldn't succeed without stepping on some toes. In a prior job at a technology publisher, in fact, Scoble had almost been fired for writing positively about a competitor.

Microsoft took a gamble. Scoble was told to continue to blog about whatever he thought important with no corporate restrictions or approvals, other than the caveat that he couldn't discuss the company's finances. "Their attitude was that as long as I was saying thoughtful things, then I was helping them to get better," Scoble says.

Creating disruption

Scoble did mix things up. Early on, he wrote that a marketer in the company's MSN online division should be fired for not using a new technology called RSS on his own blog. The executive complained over Scoble's head. The situation got pretty heated, in the end Scoble wasn't fired. And pretty soon, RSS started turning up all over Microsoft.

Scoble didn't evangelize for long. One evening, he and some developers were brainstorming ideas for connecting with the third-party development community. They got on the idea of taking a video camera into the cubicle farms and talking with individual developers. "We had no clue what we were doing," Scoble laughs. The goal was to humanize development at Microsoft, to make the company's developers more approachable and accessible. The team named the venture Channel 9 after the audio channel some airlines make available for passengers to listen to cockpit conversations.

Whether by luck or insight, the team chose a perfect candidate for its first video interview. Bill Hill is a burly, bearded Scotsman who was known to wear kilts into the office. He worked on Cleartype, a technology that controls the display of text on a screen. Hill spoke passionately about typography and punctuation and reading as the foundation of human prosperity.

People loved him. Channel 9 got 100,000 unique visitors its first day. The two short interviews with Hill were downloaded more than 160,000 times. Channel 9 was a hit and transparency was a new Microsoft value.

The Channel 9 team recorded more than four hundred video segments in the next year. Most logged several thousand downloads, with a few bell-ringers clocking stratospheric numbers: more than 350,000 for a tour of MSN Virtual Earth and 250,000 for a tour of Microsoft Office 12.

As Channel 9 grew, Scoble blogged incessantly. Microsoft had given him a travel budget that enabled him to attend all the top industry conferences. Emboldened by his early success, he increasingly spoke out about industry issues, tweaking competitors like Google and business partners like Apple. He even occasionally criticized Microsoft, although hardly with the harshness reserved for the company's foes.

Many people couldn't believe Scoble was getting away with this. Microsoft, a company that appeared to have everything to gain by withholding information, was openly setting up as its most visible spokesman a mid-level techie who occasionally poked a stick in its eye. It was about the most counterintuitive thing people had ever seen. And it was working.

"He has...succeeded where small armies of more conventional public-relations types have been failing abjectly for years: he has made Microsoft, with its history of monopolistic bullying, appear marginally but noticeably less evil to the outside world," wrote the *Economist* in a February 2005 profile.

And that was the key. By opening up and acknowledging its critics, Microsoft was actually making itself more human and accessible. Even likeable. Back home in Redmond, Washington, the message got through.

Blogging took off at Microsoft. As the company threw open the doors and invited employees to write, Scoble demonstrated that they wouldn't get fired for doing so.

Unlikely stars

The company built a simple home page that listed the most recent blog entries from all its bloggers. Anyone who wanted to blog was encouraged to do so. No approvals, no legalities, just Be Smart. Microsoft employees joined by the thousands. Mostly they were developers blogging about technical topics, standards, new products they were working on. They asked for feedback and advice and they got it. But increasingly, more than just developers joined the party. People in marketing, sales, human resources and information systems got involved. They blogged with different levels of ferocity but they kept at it. Blogging was so popular at Microsoft that the peer pressure kept them in the game.

And new stars began to emerge from unlikely places. Heather Hamilton is a marketing recruiter. She looks for talented marketers who want to make a career at Microsoft, which means that they have to mesh with the company culture.

The staffing department "is generally perceived as the black hole where resumes go," she says, "especially with a large company that gets thousands a day. Creating a blog helped removed some of that stigma and reluctance."

Hamilton sweats the basics. She writes about three hours a week and spends an hour a day reading and commenting on other blogs. She writes about all kinds of things: technology, online courtesy, travel, food and working for a corporation. She doesn't pull many punches. "I'd be hard-pressed to find a corporate blogging policy longer than a sentence or 2 that doesn't totally stink," she wrote recently.

Blessed with an engaging personality and good writing skills, Heather Hamilton has turned her forum into an effective recruiting tool. Technorati.com lists "Heather's 'Marketing at Microsoft' Blog'" (blogs.msdn.com/heatherleigh/) in the top 13,000 of the more than 50 million blogs it indexes. Her monthly traffic is in the hundreds of thousands of page views. She estimates that at least ten people have come to work at Microsoft after meeting her through her blog. New hires whom she's never met frequently tell her that they're fans.

The Microsoft blogging initiative and the visibility of bloggers like Scoble have emboldened employees to start writing, she says. "Bloggers need to create content without fear of getting in trouble. That's not everybody's corporate culture," she says.

"Happy employees make great bloggers. I'm a happy employee."

Humanizing Microsoft

By the middle of 2006, Microsoft had some three thousand employee blogs, or a remarkable 5 percent of the total work force. Microsoft's blog directory listed more than two hundred fifty topics, including every manner of product, vertical market and customer type, not to mention hobbies and interests. Many employees were also podcasting or video blogging, demonstrating that inside a company perceived by many people as a corporate raptor lived a creative, energetic and even playful spirit.

More important than humanizing the company, the initiative was changing the culture. Developers, marketers, sales people and support representatives were buying into the idea that customer relations was a conversation, not an obligation. And they were treating their freedom to blog as a company perc.

"As a Microsoft employee, I have always regarded my ability to blog in public as a supreme privilege," wrote Korby Parnell, a Microsoft

A Blogger's Manifesto
Adapted from a blog post by Robert Scoble

1. Tell the truth. The whole truth. Nothing but the truth. If your competitor has a product that's better than yours, link to it. You might as well. We'll find it anyway.

2. Post fast on good news or bad. Someone say something bad about your product? Link to it—before the second or third site does—and answer its claims as best you can. Same if something good comes out about you. It's all about building long-term trust. The trick to building trust is to show up!

3. Use a human voice. Don't get corporate lawyers and PR professionals to cleanse your speech. We can tell, believe me. Plus, you'll be too slow.

4. Make sure you support the latest software/Web/human standards. If you don't know what the W3C is, find out. If you don't know what RSS feeds are, find out.

5. Have a thick skin. Even if you have Bill Gates' favorite product, people will say bad things about it. That's part of the process. Don't try to write a corporate blog unless you can answer all questions—good and bad—professionally, quickly, and nicely.

6. Don't ignore Slashdot. [Editor's note: Slashdot is a hugely influential website that caters to Linux and open-source techies.]

7. If you screw up, acknowledge it. Fast. And give us a plan for how you'll unscrew things. Then deliver on your promises.

8. Under-promise and over-deliver. Look at Disneyland. When you're standing in line you trust their signs because the line always goes faster than the sign says it will.

9. If Doc Searls (doc.weblogs.com) says it or writes it, believe it. Enough said.

10. Know the information gatekeepers. If you don't realize that [consultant and author] Sue Mosher reaches more Outlook users than nearly everyone else, you shouldn't be on the PR team for Outlook. If you can't call on the gatekeepers during a crisis, you shouldn't try to keep a corporate blog.

11. Never change the URL of your blog. I've done it once and I lost much of my readership. It took several months to build up the same reader patterns and trust.

12. If your life is in turmoil and/or you're unhappy, don't write. When I was going through my divorce, it affected my writing in subtle

ways. Lately I've been feeling a lot better, and I notice my writing and readership quality has been improving, too.

13. If you don't have the answers, say so. Then get them and exceed expectations. If you say you'll know by tomorrow afternoon, make sure you know in the morning.

14. Never lie. You'll get caught and you'll lose credibility that you'll never get back.

15. Never hide information. The information will get out and you'll lose credibility.

16. If you have information that might get you in a lawsuit, see a lawyer before posting, but do it fast. Speed is key. If it takes you two weeks to address what's going on in the marketplace because you're scared of legal liability, your competitors will figure it out and outmaneuver you.

17. Link to your competitors and say nice things about them. Remember, you're part of an industry and if the entire industry gets bigger, you'll probably win more than your fair share of business and you'll get bigger, too. Remember how Bill Gates got DOS? He sent IBM to Digital Research. They weren't all that helpful, so IBM came back to Gates.

18. BOGU. This means "Bend Over and Grease Up." It means that when a big fish comes over (like IBM, or Bill Gates) you do whatever you have to do to keep him happy. Personally, I believe in BOGU'ing for everyone. You never know when the janitor will go to school, get an MBA, and start a company.

19. Be the authority on your product/company. If you're writing a blog about a product, you should know more about it than anyone else. If there's someone else who knows more, you better link to them.

developer, in a May 2005 entry entitled "A Brief [and Subjective] History of Corporate Blogging at Microsoft." "The fact that I was allowed to blog in 2002 and am encouraged to blog in 2005 by my managers is a clear indication that Microsoft thinks of and treats its employees as partners, not peons."

Customers were noticing the difference, too. Developer Nick Bradbury of FeedDemon posted an angry blog entry on June 9, 2006, complaining about a bug in Windows. Within twenty-four hours, developers at Microsoft had noticed the entry and fixed the problem. "Microsoft is on the ball," Bradbury wrote. "They jumped in, asked for more information, and deactivated the bug after being able to reproduce it… Microsoft's reaction was impressive."

Within Microsoft, the new spirit of openness had to be causing some heartburn. In June 2006, a Microsoft blogger named Philip Su posted a scathing entry attributing persistent delays in the delivery of the Windows Vista operating system to organizational complexity and management politics. The post was taken down for reasons that weren't revealed but was later restored, not because of any pressure from Microsoft management, Su said. The company has also had to endure rogue bloggers like Mini-Microsoft, a blog allegedly written by a Microsoft employee who relentlessly criticized the company and became a virtual water cooler for Microsoft employees.

As Microsoft's prominence in the blogosphere grew, Scoble's visibility grew with it. In 2006, he teamed with marketer Shel Israel to release *Naked Conversations*, a shamelessly enthusiastic manifesto about the benefits of blogging. It quickly became the best-selling book in the short history of the medium.

Robert Scoble had become almost larger than life. He was arguably the best-known Microsoft employee outside of chairman Bill Gates and CEO Steve Ballmer. He was a constant presence at trade shows and elite industry events. Not surprisingly, the job offers were pouring in. Tech companies saw his blog as an irresistible marketing asset. In June 2006, Scoble relented and joined PodTech.net, a startup that was creating a channel for podcasts. In perhaps the ultimate tribute to the arrival of blogs, the news of his departure was carried by more than one hundred thirty newspapers.

Speculation ran rampant that Scoble was unhappy at Microsoft. He had complained on his blog that he was underpaid (less than $100,000) and spent a lot of time in meetings. Some bloggers theorized that the Microsoft bureaucracy had finally gotten to him.

Scoble took umbrage at the critics. "I love Microsoft and Microsoft did not lose me—at least as a supporter and friend," he wrote. "Career decisions are personal and opportunity and growth require thinking about a lot of different things…I've turned down quite a few offers for more money than I'm now making." The Podtech job, he told me in an interview, was simply a great opportunity to combine his passion for multimedia and social media and to get some equity in a growth company.

He sees the opportunity to create massive libraries of podcasts on all kinds of subjects. Visitors to Paris, for example, could listen to a French language course on the plane, download a guide to French cooking by a local chef and take a tour of the Louvre narrated by an art expert—all supported by advertising. The low costs of podcasting make these kinds of services feasible, he says.

Scoble left a lasting legacy at Microsoft. By sticking out his neck, he established a precedent for employee openness that jump-started Microsoft's blog experiment. By not cutting off his head, Microsoft blazed a trail in corporate tolerance and transparency. It's an example that will no doubt be followed by many other businesses in years to come.

CHAPTER 6
Small Is Beautiful

Stephen Powers isn't an Internet guy. Stephen Powers is an automotive guy. He opened his first auto reconditioning shop when he was 17. That was 1983 and Powers has been passionate about auto reconditioning ever since.

Stephen Powers is smart about technology, though, and when he first used the Internet a decade ago, he realized it was going to be an asset to his business. That's because Powers' business, Rightlook.com, Inc., isn't the kind you'd find in the phone book. San Diego-based Rightlook helps people get started in the auto reconditioning business. Rightlook provides education, training and materials to help them market, manage and grow a real company.

The problem with marketing a business like Rightlook is that it doesn't fit into any conventional "bucket." People don't go to the phone book looking for help getting into auto reconditioning. They might look for books or magazines in the library about entrepreneurship, but they're probably going to hit on auto reconditioning only by accident.

But people might open up Google and type "automotive reconditioning" and up pops Rightlook. That's because Stephen Powers is a marketer at heart and has used Internet savvy to build Rightlook's visibility and make it a leader in its niche. Rightlook's website is about as polished as you'll ever see for a company of its size. There are only twenty employees in the company, but one of them works full-time on the website.

In the summer of 2005, Powers bought an iPod. He began to poke around the Internet, looking for podcasts about his interests, like photography and marketing. "It didn't take long to realize that this would be big," he says.

Powers invested $5,000 in equipment, a princely sum in the low-rent world of podcasting. But he wanted to do it right. Rightlook has succeeded, in part, because it always looked bigger online than it was in real life. The company was in the business of creating training materials. It couldn't afford to put out a shoddy educational product.

Rightlook radio would be no different. Launched in early 2006, Rightlook radio is a talk-show format and new shows are posted every three weeks or so. Powers and cohost Mel Craig bring customers into the studio to talk about their success and extol the benefits of auto reconditioning as a career. The show isn't about selling Rightlook. It's about spotlighting success. It just happens that Rightlook's services relate very directly to that goal.

Stephen Powers is having a blast. He's got an engaging, friendly style and he's a natural for radio. A female staffer conducts field interviews, a subtle message that auto detailing is a good business for women, too. In fact, one of the shows spotlighted a reconditioning business run by women.

Powers is putting every ounce of his marketing experience behind Rightlook radio. It has promoted the podcast in full page trade magazine ads, sent out press releases and made t-shirts. When clients come to visit, they get a tour of the professional-looking studio. Rightlook looks hip and in tune with technology.

Powers doesn't have any hard statistics on the podcast's success, but says downloads have been in the thousands. It doesn't really matter. The whole program paid for itself after one customer signed a $24,000 deal after listening to a podcast. Another show about ozone machines led to multiple machine sales in the days after the podcast launched.

Operational costs are next to nothing, and the buzz that the program generates in its industry is well worth the effort, Powers says. "Without question, we're going to continue to do this for a long time," he says. And with each episode, Rightlook puts more distance between itself and its competitors.

Just do it

Stephen Powers is a prototypical New Influencer. He cares deeply about a very specific discipline. He has plenty of expertise and the gift of communication. He's in a position to influence a lot of other people who care about his specialty. The only difference between Powers and the enthusiasts profiled in Chapter 3 is that Powers has a product to sell.

In the last chapter, we talked about the tightrope that corporations walk in venturing into social media. Small and medium-sized businesses have none of those issues, though. Regulatory pressures are minimal, everyone in the company is in contact with customers and the owner probably is an expert in a very specific discipline. Corporations must answer questions about why they should be in the blogosphere. Small businesses need to answer questions about why they shouldn't.

Here are some reasons that social media is so well-tuned to smaller businesses:

It's all about search—Google and its competitors are the best thing that ever happened to small business. Companies that can't afford to advertise can achieve international visibility in vertical disciplines through search performance. As we noted earlier, blogs do exceptionally well on Google because of the search engine's fondness for frequent updates and relevant page titles. A focused blog, podcast or videocast that stakes out an unclaimed niche in the market can come to dominate search results in a short time. The more you write, the faster you'll move.[1]

Get personal—One of the main reasons people do business with a small company is to get personal service. Blogs and podcasts are all about personality. If you bring a distinctive voice, a sense of humor and a hint of passion to your commentaries, people will feel like they know you. And that will make it easier for them to do business with you.

The voice of authority—Let's suppose you're a small business that specializes in scuba diving equipment, training and excursions. You decide to specialize in the new technology of closed-circuit rebreathers.

1. On the other hand, one doesn't want to become too beholden to Google. In *The Search*, John Battelle tells the hair-raising story of Neil Moncrief, an online shoe retailer who nearly went bankrupt when Google changed its search algorithm and pushed his site from the top 10 to 300th in search results.

Launching a blog that helps people to understand the technology and its benefits will get you quick results. People searching on that term are likely to find your helpful, educational articles on rebreathers ahead of the catalog entries of the equipment companies because, remember, Google favors content over commerce. You won't get anywhere near that kind of cost-efficiency from advertising.

You can't beat the cost—At monthly prices that top out at fifteen dollars, the cost of a blog is a non-issue. You can produce a decent podcast with less than three hundred dollars' worth of equipment. Your real investment is time, so you have to ask how much of your new-business investment you're willing to channel into this effort.

Several tales of small-business blogging success are almost legendary at this point.

EnglishCut.com is a blog by Thomas Mahon, a Saville Row tailor who was frustrated that more people didn't appreciate the distinction between off-the-rack suits and the work of a professional custom tailor. His blog, launched in early 2005, talks about the fine points of fine tailoring. Because Mahon was one of the first tailors to start a blog, he got lots of attention from other bloggers and the media. And the recognition translated directly into business.

As detailed by Robert Scoble and Shel Israel in their book *Naked Conversations*, "When Mahon was in New York in December 2004, he sold only two [suits]. When he returned 10 weeks after starting a blog, he sold 20 suits and eight sport coats, more than he had sold before in an entire year."

Mahon's blog has become such a must-read phenomenon that he speculates that he could make a trip to any city a success by simply posting on his blog that he plans to be there on certain days. Marketer Hugh McLeod, who dreamed up English Cut, said Mahon's business tripled in six months because of it.

Stormhoek, a startup South African wine maker, entered the U.K. market by sending free bottles of wine to 150 bloggers—no strings attached. Instead of a commerce website, the company channeled all its marketing through a blog. Sales doubled to 100,000 cases in the year after the experiment was launched and the company went from 0 percent to 20 percent market share in its category in the U.K. For its U.S. entry, Stormhoek invited bloggers to organize local dinners. As long as they supplied the people, Stormhoek would provide the wine. Bloggers came up with creative ideas like a Father's Day theme in Santa Maria, California, a hot dog-eating contest in Bellevue, Washington; and a GPS treasure hunt in Burlington, Vermont. The campaign was organized by David Parmet, a public relations professional and blogger.

SignsNeverSleep—This frequently updated blog by the owner of a small sign maker in Lincoln, New Hampshire, is a testament to the power of social media as a way for craftspeople to share their expertise. Owner J. D. Iles details the loving attention that master sign makers pay to their craft in his posts and copious photos of Lincoln Sign Company's latest creations.

Iles spends only about fifteen minutes a day on the blog, but he writes nearly every day. He told Radiant Marketing Group: "The weblog shows my customers what we are: a small business that is approachable, fun, and hopefully they like the work we do." Websites and weblogs are great tools, but you can use a tool well, or badly. A "web-presence" should show off your company as it is, and highlight the strengths you have because of "how your business is." Iles attributes about a 10 percent increase in business to the blog.

A Painting a Day—Duane Keiser, a Richmond, Virginia-based painter, creates a small painting every day and posts a image of it on his blog, along with an invitation to buy. He originally sold them for $100 each, but demand got so strong that he started taking bids on eBay, according to a *USA Today* profile. He was soon getting $400 to $800 per painting and without the 50 percent commissions typically charged by galleries. Keiser, who used to sell a couple of paintings a year, is now able to make a good living selling his art.

Nancy Boy—The San Francisco-based toiletries maker owes its success, in part, to a blog. The company, which targets gay men, did about $100,000 in business in 2001, when it launched. Then it became a favorite of Shaveblog.com, a blog dedicated to shaving. As favorable references to Nancy Boy continued to appear on Shaveblog, business grew to $4 million in 2006. Nancy Boy cofounder Eric Roos also maintains a popular blog on the company site detailing his experiences as a gay man.

Here are some more recent examples of how small/midsized businesses are becoming influencers and having fun at the same time.

The tin man

Some of the best small-business blogs are in some of the most prosaic industries. The Tinbasher blog was started by Paul Woodhouse in May 2004 to help out his brother, who runs Butler Sheetmetal, a U.K.-based metalworking company. "Initially it was nothing other than an experiment. There was very little to lose and my expectations were simply to be able to open the company up," says Woodhouse.

The site was lightly trafficked until it was mentioned in an article in the *Times* of London that fall. That's when traffic started to build and Woodhouse began to blog more aggressively. He's developed a style that's uniquely Tinbasher: a friendly insider with a puckish twist. "I try to convey what we'd be like if you actually came round to the workshop for a brew," he says. "It's informal, parochial and colloquial."

It's also amassed quite a following: about two thousand visitors a day for a website about sheet metal. Tinbasher Blog has already paid for itself many times over. According to a profile in the *Guardian*, Butler's annual sales rose from £60,000 to £80,000 a year before the blog was launched to £130,000 in 2005. "Probably 30 percent to 40 percent of that comes through the website," including around 90 percent of new business, Woodhouse told the paper. "When we just had the website, we would get a very general enquiry. When people have read the blog, they invariably refer to an individual post—it's a lot chattier e-mail you receive."

Customers have quoted from blog posts when placing orders and products featured on the blog frequently see a spike in sales. Then there's the boost in search engine results that the blog has stimulated and the media calls. Tinbasher has been profiled at length in the press.

The unanticipated payoff for Tinbasher has been the boost it's given to employee morale. Sheet metal work isn't exactly a glamour profession, but Butler's long-serving employees are proud of their craft and their expertise. The blog has become a way to show off their achievements.

"At first they called it a 'blob,' but now they love it," says Woodhouse. "They regularly tell me tales that have happened during the week with the proviso that they'd be good blog material."

Girl power

AskPatty.com is a new business that helps auto dealerships and automotive retailers tap the female audience. Women buy more than half the new cars in the U.S. and influence 85 percent of new auto and truck purchases, says Jody DeVere, president of the company.

The male-dominated auto business is notoriously weak at addressing female customers. Sales outlets tend to be owned by individuals, more than 90 percent of whom are male, and sales tactics are handed down through generations. With women increasingly flexing their economic muscles, AskPatty is addressing dealers' and retailers' needs to better serve that audience. The business model is to provide a comprehensive training and certification program for sales and service organizations, who can then display the AskPatty logo in the showrooms and on their websites.

A blog is a key part of AskPatty's business plan. The company could have built a standard FAQ or question-and-answer section on its website, but the founders felt the user experience would be too sterile. A blog was more personal and provocative. Voice was important.

AskPatty's blog celebrates women. Its articles not only offer advice but showcase the accomplishments of female drivers, encourage women to get into the automotive business and trumpet the power of female buyers. It features profiles of and guest columns from women who have been successful in the male-dominated industry. The site defines Patty as

> ...a Mom, Daughter, Wife, Niece, Grandmother and Auntie; Patty is young, old, married, single, an experienced driver, a new driver, a race car driver, a hot rod driver, a classic car driver, a mini van driver, a truck driver, a luxury car driver, an SUV driver, a disabled driver, a carpool driver, a stay at home Mom, a female executive, is gay, straight and comes in all the sizes, shapes and colors of the rainbow...Patty is YOU, ME and US: Women Consumers.

AskPatty struck a chord with its audience. It also got lucky. Shortly after its May 2006 launch, the site was spotlighted on the home page of Typepad, a leading provider of blog hosting software. Traffic soared to more than a half million visitors a week over the next two months. Visitors were submitting so many questions that the site struggled to meet its commitment to a twenty-four-hour turnaround on answers.

DeVere says the blog offers capabilities for connecting with readers that a website can't match. The authors of the AskPatty blog are clearly women and their style belies a sympathetic voice. Asked what works in running a business blog, she writes, "Pick a theme and stick to it. Don't be afraid to use all the tools and means available to publicize your blog. Stay committed to providing interesting content at least three to four times a week. Serious business blogging takes a big commitment of time, energy and brain power."

Becoming an influencer

The factors that constrain small/medium businesses from leveraging social media are completely different from those that limit corporations. It's mainly an issue of time. Small business owners and employees are generally more resource-constrained and time-strapped than their corporate counterparts and the frequency with which you need to update a blog—ideally at least once a week—can be a hardship. Smaller businesses owners also don't necessarily have strong writing or speaking skills or access to people with those talents.

But you can be effective enough with a modest investment of time to make the effort worthwhile. Here are some tricks to consider:

Specialize—If your topic is very specific, you can get away with a less-frequent publishing schedule and still see good impact in search engine results and links. The dive shop that specializes in closed-circuit rebreathers is one example. Tinbasher is another. If no one else is writing about your topic, you can afford to be a little less rigorous about maintaining a strict writing schedule.

Choosing the right topic can be tricky, though. If you're too specific, no one will come at all. Or you may run out of things to say. Try homing in on a new practice or technology that's affecting your business. Or you can take a tips-and-tricks approach, posting a new idea every week. Several highly trafficked blogs take this approach; take a look at 43folders.com and Lifehacker.com for ideas.

Be offbeat—Cater to readers' sense of humor or the bizarre by featuring nuggets of trivia that relate to your business. If you're an insurance broker, for example, spotlight the strangest claim of the week. If you own a pet store, feature an interesting cat fact or new pet idea.

Start a diary—Blog software is the perfect format for recording a sequence of events because it's organized chronologically. Many of the most popular personal blogs on the Web are nothing more than personal diaries of people who have a knack for finding humor or meaning in ordinary events. Would other people be interested in knowing about what you do? Don't sell yourself short; there's a little voyeur in most of us and peeking into the day-to-day life of others is intriguing.

If you run a local theatre company, blog about the process of getting a performance ready. If you're a hairdresser, talk about the stories your customers tell you. If you install air conditioning, write about what's involved in ducting an old house. In fact, take a video camera along on your next job and record some of the tricks you use. Then post the video on YouTube or Google Video or another free service and link to it from your blog. This is reality TV writ large and you're the star, if you can just get across to your readers the passion you feel for your work.

Use audio and images—All blog software supports images and a fifty dollar digital camera can take pretty nice snapshots these days. Illustrate the topics you write about. If you're a hairdresser, show some new styles you've come up with. If you own an auto body shop, snap some before-and-afters. Be sure to tag your images (we explain that in Chapter 9) so they get picked up by the search engines.

In the same vein, podcasting is a golden opportunity for small businesses. You can get acceptable quality with a couple of hundred dollars' worth of equipment, free editing software like Audacity and cheap or free hosting services. Try Q&A interviews with your staff or sit down with a steady customer and talk about a problem she solved. How-to podcasts are also a good bet. If you're a floor refinisher, tell people how to remove wood spots or identify different kinds of hardwoods. If you're a recruiter, share resume and interview tips. A painter? Help customers make perfect corners. Call it "tip in a minute" and really keep your length to sixty seconds and you'll have a winner.

Celebrate others—Small business owners enjoy a level of collegiality with others in their markets that doesn't exist in the hyper-competitive corporate world. If there are others in your business who blog or podcast, point to their sites and compliment their good work. Send them an e-mail and post a trackback, so they know you were there. You'll get reciprocal links and everyone's traffic will grow.

As you can see, there is no shortage of ideas for small business people who want to build an online presence. However, one group, more than any other, has led the way in using social media to raise their visibility and promote their expertise. They're the public relations professionals, and many people think social media is their chance to shine.

CHAPTER 7

Putting "Public" Back Into Public Relations

The holidays are typically a slow time in the public relations business, but David Meerman Scott isn't the type of guy to take it easy. Scott, a former bond trader and content marketing specialist who launched his own marketing consulting company in 2002, took advantage of the 2005-2006 holiday season to write down some ideas that had been kicking around in his head for some time.

What Scott did over those three weeks would change his career and his life. It would launch his business in a new direction and make him an internationally recognized authority on content marketing. And it started with a blog.

David Meerman Scott had a beef with the PR business. He had long believed that the public relations profession was too focused on the media. His epiphany came in 1995, when Yahoo! made the decision to start including press releases along with mainstream media coverage on its financial news wires. When you searched on a company name, a press release was just as likely to appear in the search results as a Reuters story. Anyone could now read a press release. So why were PR agencies so focused on the media? And why did they call them "press" releases in the first place?

On December 20, 2005, Scott began to write down his thoughts. He came up with the idea for an electronic book called *The New Rules of PR: How to create a press release strategy for reaching buyers directly*. In it, he proposed to blow up the old rules of PR. Stop writing press releases only when news happened. Find reasons to send them all the time. Stop writing just for the media. Address the public directly. Make releases rich with searchable keywords and URLs that lead to landing pages on your website. Optimize them for searching and browsing.

It was very Web 2.0 and Scott's timing was impeccable. He invested a couple of thousand dollars in professional design and, on January 16, 2006, posted the twenty-one-page document on his website. Then he fired off e-mails to about thirty friends and waited to see what happened.

"I was hoping for a couple of thousand downloads and maybe three or four mentions from bloggers," he says. He didn't have to wait very long.

Viral traffic got news of the book out to a few bloggers, who posted links. Downloads jumped immediately to over a thousand a day. Then marketing guru Seth Godin posted a link on his blog, praising Scott's ideas. So did PR super-blogger Steve Rubel, only Rubel was critical of the proposal. It didn't matter. Traffic skyrocketed.

Between January 19 and 22, more than 15,000 people downloaded the e-book. The blogosphere was swarming. Dozens of bloggers were now commenting on and linking to Scott's book. The media picked up on the thread. The *Toronto Globe and Mail* called. Then the Associated Press and Reuters. The Marketing Profs website asked for a bylined article, then an online seminar. Speaking invitations started coming in.

Six months after publication of *New Rules,* the e-book had been downloaded more than 75,000 times. A Google search on "new rules of PR," which had returned only one result in January 2006, yielded 42,000 hits. Scott was under contract with Wiley to turn the e-book into a bound book. And his business was increasingly about advising clients on how to rethink their press releases.

Drinking the Kool-Aid

No profession stands to influence social media more than public relations. And while most corporate marketers remain leery of the new frontier, some PR people are diving in with bold viral marketing campaigns and using the tools of social media to advance their own businesses. David Meerman Scott's success was almost accidental, though he worked the basics very well. But as marketers come to understand the fundamentals of social media marketing, they're turning the new forum to their clients' advantage and to their own.

PR people intuitively understand the value of relationship marketing, with social media simply being another way to build relationships. PR pros have flocked to social media because it plays so naturally to their strengths as relationship managers. PR has long been the neglected stepchild of corporate marketing departments hooked on lead generation and advertising metrics. Social media is PR's turn to shine.

"The irony of the New PR is that it's not anything new, it's just the industry adapting to new forms of communications—which is something that our industry has always been able to do," wrote Jeremy Pepper, a prominent PR blogger, in a *Global PR Blog Week* article in late 2005. "PR firms out there do get it, there is an understanding of blogs, and an understanding that PR needs to be involved with blogs—whether tracking, pitching or blogging."

There are hundreds of PR blogs and quite a few compelling podcasts. Blogger Constantin Basturea maintains a list of PR bloggers that numbered more than 500 by mid-2006.[1] It includes writers from twenty-nine countries and is growing by about a hundred listings every six months.

In late 2004, Basturea started the New PR Wiki, an exhaustive resource of interviews, articles, blogs, and discussions devoted to the evolution of public relations. At the time of this writing, it already had more than sixty contributors.

PR professionals see social media as both an opportunity and a threat. The opportunity is to raise the profession's visibility at a time when market trends are clearly headed their way. The threat is that no one really knows how to deal with all these new influencers.

Consider how complex the public relations profession has become. In 1990, the number of media outlets that were important to any given business probably numbered in the double digits. If you got a hit in the *Wall Street Journal*, you could take the rest of the month off.

By the late nineties, the Internet had perhaps doubled the size of that list to include a number of special interest websites and a few new syndication services.

Social media has completely disrupted this model. With mainstream media losing readers, listeners and viewers, the growth areas have shifted

---

1. It's at blog.basturea.com/pr-blogs-list/.

to special-interest electronic media, including cable channels, satellite radio, and personal blogs. Some product categories, such as consumer electronics, support literally hundreds of bloggers.

Not only has the list of influencers grown, but the dynamics by which they are influenced has changed. In the old days, a company got media coverage by courting a reporter. Today, a news story in a major newspaper may begin as a blog discussion or a viral e-mail thread that takes on a life of its own.

Corporate and agency PR professionals are scrambling to get out in front of this trend and leaders in their field are trying to show the way. So far, it's largely been a matter of the blind leading the blind. But patterns are emerging that are spawning new companies and taking existing firms in new directions.

The corporation as publisher

Larry Weber struck gold once and is digging hard again. In 1987, he founded the Weber Group, a technology public relations agency. The company got some lucky breaks: An unknown startup called America Online was an early client, and a contact at MIT got Weber a contract with an obscure scientist named Tim Berners-Lee to promote an idea called the World Wide Web. Mainly, though, the Weber Group thrived because of its remarkable creativity, a laser focus on high-tech and an appreciation of the power of new media.

Weber sold the Weber Group to Interpublic Group and stayed on as an executive for several years, but left to start his own venture in 2004. "The media is going through the biggest change in 200 years, so we need to understand where it's going, " he says of the waves of change sweeping the industry.

The new venture, W2Group, Inc., is an integrated marketing services company for the social media age. "Influence opportunities are no longer centralized within a few widely read publications or from podiums at industry…events," says the company's website. "In a web-driven economy, the spheres of influence are infinite."

Larry Weber believes this deeply. He was preaching the value of marketing via social networks when few PR types even understood the concept. The Web went off-course during the first ten years of its existence, "hijacked by marketers," he says. Its potential to serve as a medium for conversation was sabotaged by the people trying to make it a vehicle for commerce. Basically, the only interactivity was placing an order.

All that is about to change dramatically, Weber believes. The response rate-driven, lead generation-focused mentality is going away. In the future, "Marketers' sole job will be the aggregation of customers and potential customers through content and interfacing with other customers—what I call enterprise-generated content," he says. "The question will become how to create a branded website where people want to come and talk to you."

What? Enterprise-generated content? Get people to come to your site to talk to you? That's just not what marketing does! But Weber believes the old style of marketing is dead. People have too many choices, too many channels and low tolerance for listening to messages. The only way you will even be able to get a message across to a customer in the future, he believes, is by becoming a content provider.

"Why can't a company website produce content that's as good as the *Wall Street Journal*?" he asks. "In fact, why can't a *Journal* reporter write for a company website?"

Talk like that is heresy in journalism circles, but Larry Weber isn't about conventional wisdom. He believes the media world is at a turning point, one in which businesses have the opportunity to break out of their traditional role as message-makers and become legitimate publishers.

And he's doing that for clients. For Genzyme, Weber's agency is creating a website about rare diseases that includes a blog written by the family of a young girl suffering from a debilitating illness. The agency is building a social network about travel for Visa International. The idea is to get travel enthusiasts to come and share tips and advice in an community environment.

In Weber's view, the future of the Web is in communities. People will belong to dozens of them, some more important than others, but all receiving a slice of their attention. There is no reason those communities can't be operated by corporations. Some may even be gated and limited to customers. The opportunity, he believes, is for businesses to provide content that is every bit as good as the information customers would get from mainstream media.

The company's social media arm, Digital Influence Group, is trying to redefine public relations through a focus on New Influencers. To promote *Technology Review* magazine, the agency sent advance copies of the publication's articles to bloggers who were writing about those topics. Online subscriptions doubled in six months.

To promote a search engine company, the agency created a humorous video aimed at the college market. Students passed it around enough that the video eventually made its way onto a number of top college-oriented websites.

"What's different now is that it's no longer about the selling products and services," says Cinny Little, executive vice president at Digital Influence. "It's about how you pull together the client's resources and intellectual capital and shape it based on what the influencers want."

The press release is not dead, Little believes, but it is slowly being replaced. What is replacing it is useful information delivered to influencers in any form that suits their needs. These people have an insatiable need to publish information, and they care little about where it originated as long as it meets their standards for quality and relevance—standards that are probably different from those a company uses when crafting its press releases.

The power of peers

Weber's thinking mirrors, in many ways, the ideas of Richard Edelman, CEO of the 2,000-person PR company that bears his name. Edelman has been harshly critical of the practices that brand the profession as "flacks" and "spin doctors." The profession stands on the doorstep of a revolution as mainstream media, its credibility in tatters, gives way to new sources of information. In accepting the National Public Relations Achievement Award in April 2006, he said:

> The media, communications, and marketing landscape in which the public relations industry was developed is being knocked down...In this model, a small group of elites are briefed in advance with messages that are too often tightly scripted...The message is then simplified and communicated to a mass audience via advertising or as "earned" editorial. This model is premised on the audience being passive receptors for the message.

Citing his annual Trust Barometer survey which illustrates the evolution taking place, Edleman continued:

> This increased trust in peers has advanced steadily over the past three years. It correlates with the rapid growth in peer-to-peer media

we have witnessed over this same stretch of time. In the U.S., for example, a "person like yourself or your peer" was trusted by 22 percent of respondents as recently as 2003, while in this year's study, 68 percent of respondents said they trusted a peer…[C]ompanies and organizations should be willing to yield control of the message in favor of a rich dialogue, in which you learn by listening… [R]ank-and-file employees should be seen as a new credible source for information about a company … [T]he consumer will be a cocreator, demanding transparency on decisions from sourcing to new-product positioning… Historically, companies keep all information close to the vest until the last minute…It is better to reveal what you know when you know, and to commit to updating as you learn more.

Edelman practices what he preaches. His PR firm includes more than a dozen bloggers, including Edelman himself, who has been writing since 2004. In 2006, the company launched a practice called me2revolution to identify communications opportunities through new channels. It also staged a coup with the hiring of A-list blogger Steve Rubel as head of the practice.[2] In May 2006, Edelman teamed with Technorati to launch international versions of the search service in five languages.

Icons like Weber and Edelman are leading the charge in a broad transformation of the public relations profession, but the real activity is going on in small agencies. It's the little guys, like U.K. blogging pro Hugh McLeod of Stormhoek (see Chapter 6), who have had some of the most notable early successes. A lot of PR people find that blogging and podcasting are natural outlets for their communications gifts.

PR pro as blogger

Andy Abramson is a PR professional who understands the blogosphere well because he's been successful there. His VOIP Watch blog (andyabramson.blogs.com/voipwatch), which covers technology that transmits voice calls over Internet lines, averages more than 12,000 page views a day. And that's not his only social media activity. Abramson, who runs Comunicano, a PR agency in Del Mar, California, also cohosts a daily technology podcast (kenradio.com) and a blog dedicated to wine (winescene.com/wineblog.html).

---

2. Rubel's work is examined in "The Marketer," a profile accompanying this chapter.

The visibility has paid off for the PR business. "I have more clients asking us to consider working for them than I have time to handle," he says. Holding down a dual role as both influencer and publicist keeps him in tune with the culture of the blogosphere. Abramson's innovative campaigns to promote Nokia phones through blogger enthusiasts has been written up in mainstream media worldwide[3] and is widely viewed as a seminal campaign in blogger relations.

As a blogger, Abramson sees four basic benefits to his business: being quoted in the media, making new contacts, generating speaking engagements and bringing in business. The strategy has worked on all fronts "I get asked to do hundreds of briefings a month [as a journalist]," he says. "At trade shows and conferences, I get the same number of pitches as any journalist."

As a PR professional, he sees his job becoming more complex. For the Nokia NSeries campaign, he had to search through hundreds of blog postings. Personalized pitches are key, he says, and that means understanding the author. While the number of influencers has grown significantly, the job of influencing them hasn't changed.

In effect, each blogger requires a custom pitch and vigorous follow-up. "It takes the same amount of effort today to get a story on a website or blog for one day as it used to take to get a feature story in a monthly magazine," he says. That means PR people need to change their tactics and the expectations they set for their clients. "Leverage your skills and relationships beyond being a story planter," Abramson says. "Don't sell PR by the pound."

Renee Blodgett has never been the type to do that. She's a relationship person who has leveraged blogging to showcase her friends and extend her social circle. In the process, she's become one of the top bloggers in the profession.

Blodgett has been blogging since 2004, making her one of the first PR bloggers—and perhaps the first woman PR blogger—on the Internet. Her Down the Avenue blog is must reading for the Silicon Valley cognoscenti. Tom Foremski, a former *Financial Times* journalist who writes the popular Silicon Valley Watcher blog, calls Blodgett "probably the best known woman blogger in tech today."

Down the Avenue is smart, savvy, hip and very in tune with the culture of the Valley. Blodgett is everywhere. An independent PR coun-

3. Including in this book. See the account of the Nokia campaign in Chapter 3.

sel, she spends half her time on the road and counts as friends scores of the most influential journalists, CEOs, venture capitalists, entertainers, authors, academics and other opinion leaders in tech. Her blog is a mix of professional insight, personal experience and even fiction. It's full of photos and anecdotes of her encounters with leading journalists, technologists and visionaries. It's a kaleidoscopic window on a person of many dimensions that clearly communicates that the author is plugged into the tech industry.

Yet Blodgett isn't smitten by the new PR culture of social media. She's skeptical about the vaunted transition from messages to conversations. "You mean we're moving from message to conversations, Cluetrain Manifesto stuff?" she says, wrinkling her nose. "Don't get me wrong; I'm all for conversations. But you need to have a message. Otherwise, what are you doing this for?"

Blodgett sees the whole focus on conversation marketing as jargony and overly simplistic. Conversations don't replace messages and marketers need to have a message, she says. Whether it's blasted out through e-mail or conveyed subtly through a blog, the message still has to get through. It's not like she couldn't play the game.

Although ranked a respectable 10,000 on Technorati, Down the Avenue could be a more popular and more lucrative venture if Blodgett wanted it that way. "If I was more focused and practical about PR and marketing, I could quickly double my traffic," she says. But that's not what Down the Avenue is all about. In many ways, it's a classic weblog, detailing the multidimensional life of one person for whom relationships are the essence of marketing.

Blodgett says Down the Avenue isn't an ad for the business, but the site is commercially effective in an indirect way. The copious photo albums from top industry events belie a person who is in touch with the Valley. It says that Renee Blodgett knows who makes things happen in the tech industry. And in PR, that's a pretty powerful image. Blodgett is turning away at least one business opportunity a week these days. That's probably not a coincidence.

Podcast pioneer

Eric Schwartzman jumped on the trend early and has turned podcasting into a PR bonanza. The Los Angeles-based publicist launched an audio interview series on a whim in the spring of 2005. The effort helped catapult him into the elite of social media PR specialists just as the field was about to take off.

For Schwartzman, the epiphany came when he was working in the entertainment PR field. It was at the Grammy Awards, with its mammoth, 20,000-square-foot press room and schedule police that moved celebrities through the press gauntlet in twenty minutes. It was an assembly line of stardom.

In 1999, the online media were allowed to cover the Grammys for the first time. "It was an 'ah-hah!' moment," he remembers. "For years, the PR organization had been turning journalists away because of fire rules. And now we had the ability to put all this information on the Internet so people could time-shift and place-shift. I knew I had to go in this direction."

Shortly thereafter, Eric Schwartzman opened Schwartzman PR with the express goal of helping clients merge PR with the Internet. The dot-com meltdown hit at about the same time, but the timing was actually good for Schwartzman. "Everyone was looking to save money," he says. "I had the big agency pedigree but not the overhead. So I got some great accounts like the Salt Lake City Olympics and Cirque du Soleil. But I didn't have the manpower."

Looking for ideas to do more with less, Schwartzman hit on the idea of creating a tool that would enable businesses to put their PR activities online. He thought corporations spent too much time distributing content to the media. Why not put press releases, audio clips, video streams and other communications on a website? It would save Schwartzman time and the clients money.

The idea seems like a no-brainer today, but in 2000 it was visionary. The first iteration of what would become iPressroom was ready in time for the Winter Olympics and it was a hit. Client companies saved on the drudge work that was previously necessary to pull together press materials. And once they loaded up a lot of content on iPressroom, they tended to stay with the service, even when budgets were cut. It was an annuity stream.

That's not why Eric Schwartzman is a New Influencer, though. The big idea came at an annual conference organized by Bulldog Reporter, an information service for PR professionals, in early 2005. The buzz was all about podcasting, a new form of consumer-generated media that had potential PR applications. iPressroom was going to announce support for podcasts at the event. "So I said why don't we do a podcast ourselves?" Schwartzman remembers. "We figured it'd attract attention on the floor."

His team hit on the idea of inviting media influencers who were attending the show to stop by the booth to talk about how they used the Internet in their work. A bunch of journalists agreed, including senior reporters from the *Wall Street Journal, USA Today, Wired* and *Time* magazine.

The experiment was a success but it was never intended to be more than a one-event affair. "We put the podcasts online and forgot about them," Schwartzman said.

That was in April. Two months later, someone checked the traffic numbers. The eleven recordings had drawn more than 15,000 downloads. Schwartzman had a hit on his hands.

Today, On the Record…Online is a franchise. In the first year, Schwartzman recorded almost fifty more interviews, broadening the scope to include prominent figures from the PR world. Schwartzman studies up for each podcast and tunes his questions to the issues unique to the subject's area of expertise. For PR professionals, they're a gold mine.[4]

For iPressroom and Eric Schwartzman, the podcasts are a signature part of the business. The library averages more than 20,000 downloads a month and the series has heaped credibility on iPressroom. "When the salespeople call on a prospect, typically they've heard of us," Schwartzman says.

There have been other benefits to the business. On the Record…Online has been a door-opener with prominent media figures. iPressroom has also generated leads by coordinating e-mail campaigns with new podcasts. CEOs from prominent vendors have registered for downloads.

And Eric Schwartzman has become quite an influencer in his own right. He gets a steady stream of requests to speak at conferences and seminars, boosting iPressroom's visibility. "We are invited to bid on projects because people have heard our podcasts. I'd say that happens once a month," he says. Schwartzman understands social media's potential to address niche audiences and the podcasts have become core to the business.

"When it comes to reaching a wide audience, mainstream media may still be the way to go," he says. "But to reach an underserved niche audience, social media really has something to offer."

---

4. They're also pretty useful if you're writing a book on social media. I listened to dozens of Schwartzman's podcasts in the process of researching this book.

Influencer profile
The Marketer

Steve Rubel wasn't the first public relations professional to enter the blogosphere, but he is unquestionably the most successful.

For the 36-year-old Long Island native, blogging has been more than a soapbox; it's been a launch pad for his career. His Micro Persuasion blog is consistently in the Technorati top 100. It's must reading for public relations professionals worldwide, with its timely and pointed observations about developments in social media, geeked-out Web tools and even an assortment of family photos. Micro Persuasion works because it's hip, current and relentlessly enthusiastic. It's also in a constant state of change. Steve Rubel is easily one of the most prolific bloggers on the Internet.

His story is a case study in how to apply sound public relations principles to self-promotion. A Hofstra journalism major who was bitten by the tech bug while working for publisher CMP in the mid nineties, Rubel hit on the idea for Micro Persuasion while working at a small PR firm, CooperKatz, in 2004. "I always spent a ton of time online," he says. And when he first started reading blogs, "I realized something big was going on."

Rubel had already helped launch some CooperKatz clients into the blogosphere but hadn't made the leap himself. "One Sunday morning I sat down and decided I was going to start blogging about how blogs and RSS are changing the PR business," he recalls. "I really had no expectations."

It was April 2004 and not the greatest time to launch a top-tier blog. Bloggers already numbered in the millions. Other PR pros had been blogging for years and the category was crowded. Steve Rubel took a different approach. He set out to promote his own blog in the same way he'd promoted his clients for years.

The name Micro Persuasion reflected Rubel's belief that social media was about individuals extending influence beyond their immediate circle of friends. His first post stated the mission: "…to serve as an open forum where all PR pros can learn how micro media outlets persuade audiences and how to communicate key messages through the blogosphere in this new age." Micro Persuasion's focus has remained pretty much the same ever since.

What has changed is that the site has itself become an icon of influence. How that happened is Rubel's secret sauce and it's an instruction manual for anyone who wants to build online mass.

His first smart move was to send e-mails to a few prominent bloggers announcing the launch of Micro Persuasion. Robert Scoble, Microsoft's preeminent blogger, responded immediately, resulting in a Q&A interview on Rubel's site. Traffic came from Scoble's own blog, which caught the notice of other bloggers, leading to interviews with icons like Weblogs, Inc. CEO Jason Calacanis. Links begat links and traffic grew steadily. As it did, Steve Rubel kept talking. He made it a point to tell people of influence what he was writing about. They came to read and they linked to Micro Persuasion.

Smart move number two was to never let up. Blogging is more than a passion to Steve Rubel. It's a way of life. "You can probably count on two hands the number of days I haven't blogged in the past two years," he says.

While many corporate executives shun blogs as too time-consuming, Steve Rubel pours an average of twenty hours per week into Micro Persuasion. His desk is a control panel of blog activity. He is always updating, and frequent updates are what keep readers coming back.

He posts on the road, at two in the morning and on weekends. Even if he doesn't have a great idea, he posts a table of links to interesting articles. He posts photos, screen shots, tags and news clips. He subscribes to more than two hundred fifty RSS feeds and leverages a variety of online tools to update his blog automatically. "It'd be nice to go out after work for a beer but often I can't because I blog," he says. "That's a trade-off you choose."

But it's not just frequency. Rubel has applied the same PR principles that worked for clients to his own brand. In 2004, for example, he went on an all-blog diet, swearing off conventional media for a week. As a flourish, he convinced an acquaintance at the respected Poynter Institute, a journalism think tank, to administer a current events quiz. (He got twelve of the twenty questions correct). Was it showmanship? Absolutely. But it got attention. That was smart move number three.

The media called. National Public Radio's "Talk of the Nation" featured the all-blog diet in a broadcast in June 2004. Other reporters began to follow Micro Persuasion and write about what Steve Rubel was saying. Rubel was in a perfect position: he knew how to speak to the media and his blog was helping to demystify a world that journalists knew they needed to understand but didn't.

Then, *Business Week* called. It was early 2005, and the magazine was about to recognize the blogging phenomenon in a cover package. Rubel had kept a key BW reporter up to speed on Micro Persuasion. When she got the assignment, she called him first.

When the issue arrived the following spring, there was Steve Rubel in a full-page photo leading off the cover story. "That piece," he says, "changed everything."

What followed were more interviews, more news articles and more speaking engagements. Rubel gave five speeches in 2005 alone. And with each hit in mainstream media, Micro Persuasion's influence grew.

In fact, Rubel's influence was outgrowing the firm where he worked. The phone began to ring with calls from headhunters and other PR agencies. "I wanted to do something big," Rubel says. That's when Richard Edelman called.

Edelman's namesake company is the world's largest independent PR firm.[1] More important for Rubel, Edelman has a track record of innovation (it invented the media tour) and was serious about social media. In fact, its payroll includes Phil Gomes, considered to have launched the first PR blog in 2001, and about a dozen other PR bloggers.

Rubel and Edelman met. "It was total kumbaya from day one," Rubel remembers. The deal was done quickly. In February 2006, Rubel joined the firm as a senior vice president of me2revolution, a new practice focused in integrating new media into client programs. In May, he brokered a deal with Technorati to speed the launch of localized versions of the service in different languages. That month, he also started writing

1. For more detail on Edelman, see Chapter 6.

a weekly online column for AdAge Digital. In August, he hired Michael Wiley, the driving force behind General Motors' social media activities. He's trying to make Edelman synonymous with the new PR.

   With his global following, rich corporate parent and market momentum, he'll probably succeed.

CHAPTER 8
The Talkers

In January 2005, Paige Heninger and Gretchen Vogelzang (left and right, respectively, in the photo on this page) were living the rather chaotic lives of two suburban mothers in northern Virginia. Heninger attended to the needs of her four children, ranging in age from 11 to 2. A fifth was on the way. Vogelzang, a mother of two, ran a dance studio. The two moms kept in touch by phone and frequently got together to laugh, commiserate and share the joys and trials of motherhood.

Vogelzang's husband, Paul, held a high-powered job with a Washington-area public relations firm. The PR profession was undergoing a lot of change. Social media was growing quickly and smart PR people were trying to keep pace with new developments. Paul Vogelzang is a bit of a gadget freak, and one new innovation called podcasting had caught his attention.

A podcast is basically an offline radio show. Podcasters create their programs on a computer and upload them to a server for distribution over the Internet. Listeners download the programs to their portable audio devices and listen to them in the car, on the beach, mowing the lawn or whenever time permits. Not many people were podcasting in January 2005, but Paul Vogelzang saw the potential in the medium.

Gretchen Vogelzang didn't know podcasts from anything. But when Paul came home one evening talking excitedly about the technology, she thought it would be fun to try. "Paul thought this was perfect for moms," she says. "It's mobile, flexible, and you can listen anywhere. He thought Paige and I would be great at it."

Paige liked the idea, too. It took the pair less than two days to come up with a slogan for the show they christened Mommycast: "Holding the world together, one child at a time." They didn't do a lot of scripting, they just set up a computer and a couple of microphones in Gretchen's bedroom and recorded the kind of show they thought their families would like. They talked about their kids and their husbands and silly things you encounter in everyday life. Paige went off on tangents and laughed a lot. Gretchen kept the conversation on track. A college student developed the website. The first Mommycast was posted in March and submitted to Podcast Alley and Podcast Directory, two online listing services.

On the west coast, Adam Curry was meeting with venture capitalists. Curry, a former MTV video jockey who had made a killing in interactive marketing in the early days of the Web, was trying to raise money for a new idea. He wanted to build a network that would syndicate podcasts created by individuals. Curry thought this was the biggest thing since radio.

During the meeting, one of the VCs, who happened to be a mother, asked what Curry had for her. Curry skimmed through an online directory and, by serendipity, landed on Mommycast. The VC liked what she heard. So did Adam Curry. Mommycast was exactly the kind of show his fledgling PodShow Network was looking for: warm, endearing and very real. In June, Gretchen and Paige signed with PodShow Network.

That was pretty big, but the biggest break was yet to come. At the same time, Apple Computer was working on a new version of its iTunes software jukebox. The big new feature of iTunes 4.9 was that it supported podcasts. Apple was looking for podcasts to feature with the program's July launch. Apple contacted PodShow, which didn't hesitate to recommend Mommycast. iTunes spotlighted Mommycast for a week. Listenership went through the roof.

Heninger and Vogelzang haven't looked back since then. They haven't had time. Their show has become a global phenomenon, a poster child of the disruptive potential of podcasting, and the two hosts have been too busy attending to their families and sudden fame to think much about what it all means.

The two women couldn't be more different. Gretchen has the disciplined, methodical demeanor you might expect from a former ballet company director. Paige makes things up as she goes along. She admits to not having held a job more than four years. "I have ADHD," she laughs. Paige is goofy, irreverent and impulsive. Gretchen is reasoned and serious. They're perfect together.

And Mommycast has led a charmed existence. The show's format is free-ranging and informal. "We pull in some Podsafe music[1] and just talk about our lives," says Heninger. "There's no formula. I think that's one thing people like about the show; it's like listening in on a conversation." By early 2006, an estimated 300,000 people per week were listening in.

That conversation has resonated with mothers around the world and it's beginning to move markets. Last fall, the Mommycasters devoted a portion of one program to a French documentary film called *March of the Penguins*. They thought it was a great educational experience, and the kind of movie the whole family could enjoy. Ticket sales to *March* took off after the podcast was released. Warner Independent Pictures ultimately attributed a quarter of the movie's $100,000,000 gross to the Mommycast promotion.

The pair have been profiled on CBS, NBC, BBC, and in an assortment of major newspapers. They have entertained offers to take the show to terrestrial radio, but have resisted because of the fear of losing control. Perhaps they don't need to go mainstream. In late 2005, paper cup maker Dixie signed a sponsorship contract worth more than $100,000. Other sponsors followed. "We are trying to speak to the same moms and reach them in the same way 'Mommycast' does," Dixie senior brand manager Erik Sjogren told *Brandweek* magazine. In fall 2006, Dixie featured the cohosts on a printed back-to-school promotion.

All of this has been a bit overwhelming to Heninger and Vogelzang. "We're still making peanut butter and jelly sandwiches for the kids and

1. Podsafe music is provided by musicians, usually amateurs, at no charge to podcasters in exchange for promotion. Many podcasters see it as a duty to promote Podsafe in order to advance the cause of small artists, with whom they empathize.

worrying about what to make for dinner tonight," says Heninger. "We originally thought we might do maybe five shows." Mommycast posted its 100th program in June 2006.

Can we talk?

Podcasting is a craze. All but unheard of in early 2004, podcast fever gripped the Internet-using public's imagination like few tech-driven trends before it. In early 2004, there were fewer than 100 podcasts available. That number swelled to more than 80,000 by mid-2006, according to some estimates. By early 2007, estimates were unavailable. There were too many podcasts to count. The *New Oxford American Dictionary* named "podcast" its word of the year for 2005. Some top podcasts like the Ricky Gervais Show, Curry's Daily Source Code and the Onion Daily Podcast have hundreds of thousands of subscribers. Nielsen Analytics estimated in mid-2006 that the most successful podcasts were getting as many as two million downloads a month and that big companies like Sony Pictures, Shell Oil, Warner Brothers and HBO were beginning to advertise there.

But even that estimate undershoots the popularity of the medium. Many podcasts are never registered with the major directory services like Podcast Alley, Podcast Directory, iTunes and others. Some podcasts run for just a few programs and then disappear. Others

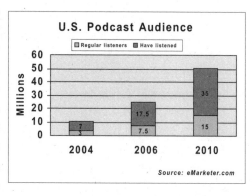

are used for internal corporate applications and aren't seen by the public. Increasingly, podcasting has become synonymous with any spoken audio program that's distributed by Internet for consumption at the user's convenience, whether on a computer or portable media player. Podcasts are already a mainstream tool for some kinds of business communication.

Podcasting is quickly developing into a powerful channel of influence and an important opportunity for marketers. The New Influencers of podcasting are people with expertise or opinions to share. Most never

The End of Radio?

Podcasting is part of the broader trend toward time-shifted media, in which programs are downloaded to a disk and played back later. The most popular manifestation of this is the digital video recorder (DVR). Wildly popular products like TiVo enable viewers to store TV programs and play them back later. Consumers like the convenience of DVRs and the capability to skip over commercials and other unwanted programming. They also like having the ability to self-edit their programs. Needless to say, this feature has given advertisers fits.

Podcasting makes time-shifted media portable. People listen to podcasts while commuting, running errands and exercising. To today's information-hungry consumer, podcasts are a way to fill the nooks and crannies of their day with more information. So far, most podcasts are audio-only, but video podcasting is growing quickly and a new generation of devices will soon make TiVo portable. Podcasts are usually syndicated via RSS.[2] Listeners sign up for a subscription and then have the shows automatically downloaded to their computers or media players.

Some people believe podcasting will quickly upend terrestrial radio. Demographic trends support that conclusion. People spend 14 percent less time listening to radio in an average day than they did a decade ago, according to Arbitron. Radio skeptics say this is due to industry consolidation, leading to safe, standardized formats and programmatic monotony.

It's a trend that podcast enthusiasts believe will lead to a boom in their medium. Ron Bloom, CEO of PodShow Network, calls it the "5/50" phenomenon: within five years, he believes, 50 percent of the content that people listen to will be generated by other consumers. In an age of information overload, "people are looking for filters to get to the highest quality of content they can," he says. Podcasting will be an essential tool for businesses making the transition to being content providers.

PodShow has set out to build a media empire around consumer-generated media. It contracts with individual podcasters to give them professional promotion and advertising sales in exchange for a cut of the business. The company has been criticized for being too heavy-handed in the way it writes contracts, but it nevertheless succeeded in signing up more than 100 podcasters in its first two years of operation.

Tuning Out

Change in time spent listening to radio spring 199 to spring 2006

	AGE
−15.0%	12-17
−15.3	18-24
−13.2	25-34
−7.9	35-44
−5.7	45-49
−3.4	50-54
−6.8	55-64
−8.1	65+

While all age groups are listening to the radio less, 12-to-34-year olds have tuned out the most. On average, they listen 17 hours a week, down 3 hours from 1999

Source: Arbitron

2. See Chapter 9 for a more detailed description of this important technology.

PodShow's Podsafe Music Network is an association of musicians who make their work available for free to podcasters who agree to credit the musicians in exchange for using their work. Podsafe music cuts out the middlemen in the recording industry and enables artists who might otherwise never have found an audience to gain exposure. Many podcasters enthusiastically endorse Podsafe artists as part of their programs.

Bloom's partner in PodShow Network is Adam Curry, the former MTV veejay who is probably podcasting's most famous proponent. Curry praises the freedom that podcasting gives content creators.

"When you're in a 'professional' broadcast environment you're always thinking about rules such as the language you can use and what the corporation wants," he says, "With podcasts, you are the corporation and your filters are all self-imposed. People can listen when they want. You're not bound by time or frequency. There can be as many shows as you want and they can be any length."

Curry thinks podcasting will redefine the economics that have homogenized broadcasting into a small number of proven formats—like talk radio or Top 40—that attract listeners. "If I have a show and ten people listen to it, that's valid," he says. "You don't have to have a certain number of listeners to stay on the air as you have to do with TV or radio. I don't think we'll have a Howard Stern of podcasting, we'll have 1,000 Howard Sterns, each with 10,000 listeners."

Curry's podcast, the Daily Source Code, exemplifies this philosophy. Between listener commentary, program requests and listener-generated comment, about half of the programming is generated by the audience. In early 2006, Curry broke new ground by inviting listeners to create audio ads for Hasbro's iDog interactive toy. Thousands of people responded with self-produced ads. Curry sees the lines between independent content and advertising blurring, with podcasters increasingly incorporating product placements into their programming. They'll do so if listeners want it. "My audience likes advertising and they want to help create it," he says.

find an audience of more than a few listeners, but some are developing passionate and responsive audiences, the type of enthusiasts that make marketers salivate.

They're people like Andrew Sims, a high school senior in Medford, Pennsylvania, who created Mugglecast, a weekly roundup of news, analysis and commentary for Harry Potter fans. A year into the program, the show had 45,000 subscribers.

Sims and six cohosts arranged from England to Kansas record a new program each Friday using Skype, a free service that makes phone calls over the Internet. Skype is an important background player in the podcasting movement. It permits people from around the globe to make high-quality calls that can be recorded with inexpensive software. Skype has dramatically lowered the cost of producing podcasts with virtual cohosts and guests. What used to require thousands of dollars' worth of professional recording equipment can now be done with an Internet connection and a fifty-dollar headset.

The Mugglecasters earn $750 a month in sponsorships and another $800 for maintaining the website, according to an August 2006 profile in the *Philadelphia Inquirer.*

It's small change to grown-ups, but a nice income for high school students who never have to leave their bedrooms.

Ordinary people like the Mugglecasters are using podcasting to reach audiences of enthusiasts around the globe with highly targeted programming. Often, their expertise is in areas that are too specific or small to support even a cable TV program. Or they've never had the chance to be "discovered" by a mainstream media outlet. But that doesn't matter. In podcasting, the listeners discover their favorite programs without the intercession of a professional programmer. And some podcasters are beginning to affect markets in noticeable ways—people like Ara Derderian and Braden Russell.

The HT Guys

The world of high-tech audio/video equipment today could confound someone with a Ph.D. in physics. There are so many choices, standards, options, cables and channels that the average consumer can't keep up with it all. Increasingly, they just hand the job over to professionals.

Ara Derderian and Braden Russell are a lifeline. They are, by their own admission, serious home entertainment geeks. For a while, they worked together at Sony Pictures, building equipment for professional moviemakers. On the side, they started a small business advising people on how to install home theatres.

It was Derderian who first heard about podcasting. It sounded like a great idea. "We wanted to spec out a system for the customer, tell them what they needed to buy and how to optimize the room. But installing it was such a headache," he remembers.

The two enthusiasts frequently talked on the phone about the latest gadgets and gear. A podcast would be like putting a microphone in the middle, and maybe a few people would actually tune in to listen. "We thought if we got two hundred listeners we'd be happy," Russell says.

The pair launched their first HDTV podcast featuring the HT Guys (HT stands for "home theatre") in March 2005. They used a modest recording setup: two good-quality microphones and an Apple Powerbook. Their goal was to demystify home entertainment, cutting through technical jargon in terms that an ordinary consumer can understand.

The pair have a great natural chemistry and voluminous knowledge. They knew a thing or two about scripting and pacing from their years in the entertainment industry. They break each show into segments to keep things moving. Derderian's the schedule freak. They check in each weekend to talk about ideas for the next episode. By Sunday afternoon, they have an outline in place. Monday and Tuesday are spent researching topics. They record on Wednesday and launch a new show every Friday. They've kept this disciplined schedule since inception. Derderian insists on it.

It wasn't long before listenership was in the thousands and e-mail was streaming in from around the globe. One listener wrote to thank them for telling him how to buy a ten-dollar cable instead of a hundred-dollar one. Another listener wrote to invite them to his house for the premier of the season finale of the TV series 24. A listener from Cedar Rapids heard Derderian mention he was coming to town and invited him to dinner. People feel like they know these guys.

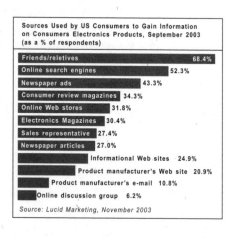

Sources Used by US Consumers to Gain Information on Consumers Electronics Products, September 2003 (as a % of respondents)

Source	%
Friends/reletives	68.4%
Online search engines	52.3%
Newspaper ads	43.3%
Consumer review magazines	34.3%
Online Web stores	31.8%
Electronics Magazines	30.4%
Sales representative	27.4%
Newspaper articles	27.0%
Informational Web sites	24.9%
Product manufacturer's Web site	20.9%
Product manufacturer's e-mail	10.8%
Online discussion group	6.2%

Source: Lucid Marketing, November 2003

"It still blows our mind that here we are a couple of guys in Orange County, California, who no one had ever heard of before and we're getting e-mails from India asking for advice," Russell says. About twenty-five e-mails arrive every day, more on Fridays, when a new show comes out.

Derderian and Russell devote about ten hours each week to the podcast, a commitment that's grown as the HDTV podcast expanded to 35,000 listeners per month over eighteen months. They dream of bigger things. Ad revenue has brought them to nearly break even but in late 2006, they were preparing to go twice-weekly. They know that their audience is a group equipment-makers want: people who are buying and installing high-end home entertainment. And they trust other users. A 2003 survey by Lucid Marketing found that 68 percent of consumer electronics buyers seek advice from friends and relatives prior to making a decision. The HT Guys are like the expert next door. "On our podcast, there is no noise; it's all signal," says Derderian, using an analogy an audio engineer would love.

But even if the big-time eludes the HT Guys, they'll probably keep plugging away. When they go to consumer electronics conferences, people recognize them. Equipment samples that they used to have to beg from manufacturers now show up at their front door. One podcast on the Blueray DVD standard got more than 25,000 downloads. For a gadget freak, it's heaven. "We get to play with cool products before anyone sees them, Russell says. "And Ara's a good friend."

The wine lovers

Joe Carpenter became a podcaster through an unconventional route. As a corporate business analyst working for a global company, his job was to investigate new technologies to deliver information. He thought podcasting was a pretty cool way to do that.

But how to learn about the medium? "The best way to drive is to get behind the wheel," says Carpenter. He wanted to podcast, but didn't have a topic in mind. He was a motorcycle racing enthusiast and he had a young daughter. He also lived in California's San Francisco Bay Area, the heart of the U.S. wine-making industry. He didn't know a lot about wine, but he reasoned that there were a lot of other people out there in the same situation. Maybe a podcast about wine for amateur wine lovers was the ticket.

On July 1, 2005, Joe Carpenter and a friend, Lori Leahy, launched A Guy, a Girl, and a Bottle (GNGNB). Billed as a review of wineries and wines "from an amateur's perspective," the weekly program had Joe and Lori visiting small wineries to sample their products, comment on the taste and go behind the scenes to learn how wine was made.

They weren't alone in the market. In southern California, a group of hard-core wine enthusiasts had launched the Grape Radio podcast six months

Nuts and Bolts of Podcasting

Podcasting took off because of a rare perfect storm of changes in technology and markets that occurred in the first half of this decade:

- Rapid declines in data storage costs made it practical for ordinary computer users to create large audio files and carry their music collections with them on portable devices.
- Low-cost or free Internet services emerged to store and distribute audio content.
- The MP3 digital audio format provided a recording standard that is universally supported by device makers.
- Really Simple Syndication (RSS) technology created a standard way for people to subscribe to podcasts and have them automatically delivered to their computers.
- Apple's iPod music player became a cultural phenomenon, selling more than 25 million units in 2005 alone.
- Free software became available to allow people to easily create, distribute and listen to podcasts.
- Major media outlets jumped on the trend early, led by National Public Radio, which now distributes hundreds of programs as podcasts.
- The listening public became disenfranchised with the increasingly formulaic format of commercial radio, making people receptive to new and experimental programming.

Audio programs have been broadcast or "streamed" over the Internet for a decade but podcasts are a major evolution in technology and convenience. Podcasts are made to be listened to offline, at the listener's convenience. People also subscribe to podcasts via RSS, insuring that the latest program is always available.

That last part is important to podcasting purists. They insist that a program isn't a podcast unless people can subscribe to it. People debate this issue, but the distinction has at least psychological importance. A subscription service invites regular updates and builds a measurable audience over time, providing an indication of listener affinity. "I'm not as interested in the 3,000 people who listen to a program as much as the 1,000 who subscribe," said Paul Colligan, author of the *Business Podcasting Bible*, in an interview on Gigavox Network.

In its simplest form, a podcast can be recorded directly into a computer using an inexpensive microphone and standard sound hardware. The sound files can be mixed and edited using a wide variety of free and commercial software programs. The files are then saved in the MP3 format and uploaded to a server for distribution using RSS. A listener who subscribes to a podcast can elect to have that program downloaded automatically to a computer or even directly to a portable media player.

Many podcasters enhance the quality and variety of their programs by adding multiple voices, whether in-studio or over the phone. Many also go on the road with portable digital recorders and then mix that content into a program. Inexpensive mixing hardware is available for less than one hundred dollars and reasonably good microphones can be had for half that price. All in all, you can launch a good-quality podcast for about two hundred dollars in equipment.

And new technology may accelerate that growth. The knock on podcasting has been that there was no way to reliably estimate audience size or characteristics. This is because podcasts are typically delivered via RSS feed, which allows listeners to remain anonymous and makes counting them very difficult. But some clever technology companies are figuring out ways to get around these limitations. Potentially, they could allow marketers to target very fine segments of listeners with targeted ads.

Both Kiptronic and PodShow have a service that inserts a short message at the beginning and end of a podcast as the program is being downloaded. It does this without the active involvement of the producer, which means that ads could be flexibly changed to complement the topic.

Another idea comes from Podbridge, which claims to have technology that can tell who has actually listened to a podcast, not just who downloaded it. Users provide demographic information when they first sign up for the service and then the Podbridge software tracks which podcasts they listen to and shoots that information back to the advertisers.

Podcast Ready gives users simple tools for subscribing to and managing their podcast subscriptions. In exchange, users provide information about the podcasts they listen to, giving advertisers valuable insight into which programs are working.

As technology problems are overcome, podcasting could become a mainstream advertising medium very quickly. The incentives are certainly there for enterprising firms to start talking.

---

earlier and was building a reputation as a kingmaker in the market of wine enthusiasts. Wine blogs were already proliferating on the Internet. But GNGNB had a special sauce: the cordial approachability of its hosts.

Armed with a portable audio recorder and microphone, Joe and Lori ventured out each week to explore the undiscovered treasures of Napa and lesser known but equally exciting wine regions. And listeners came. "At first it was about learning the in's and out's of podcasting and having fun," Carpenter says. "But as things developed, it's become more successful than I ever expected."

PodShow Network took notice of GNGNB and thought Carpenter and Leahy epitomized the grass-roots influencers the company sought to promote. The two signed with PodShow in January 2006. Today, GNGNB's audience numbers are in the tens of thousands of wine enthusiasts for each episode. Leahy left the program in early 2006 to go back to work and was replaced by Joe's wife, Pam. Despite the commitments of raising a young daughter and working two jobs, the couple still make regular forays into the California vineyards. They've ditched the weekly frequency; the schedule was just too hectic. But they've expanded the show's scope to include luscious delicacies like chocolate and fine spirits. And they're having a ball.

"If we had zero listeners, we'd still do it because it's fun," says Pam Carpenter. "We're meeting a lot of people and learning a lot of things and that, in itself, is worth it."

For Joe Carpenter, GNGNB has been a new career. He's since joined PodShow as director of podcaster relations, helping to draw more citizen journalists into the fold. The hosts get a regular stream of e-mails from listeners and vineyards, some of whom thank them for sending customers to their small businesses. "I didn't set out to become famous. I figured I'd do it for a little while and the move on," says Joe. "And now I think that as long as it's fun and engaging, I'll keep doing it."

By the people

Podcasting has captured the imagination of programmers and marketers, in large part because its roots in commercial radio are so well understood. Media and marketers took an immediate shine to podcasts. EMarketer, an online research firm, has estimated that podcasting was an $80 million advertising market in 2006 and will generate $300 million in ad revenue by 2010. That's a drop in the bucket compared to the $26 billion spent in online advertising in 2006, but notable performance for a medium that didn't even exist two years earlier.

Podcasting is perhaps the purest form of consumer-generated media. It's real people talking about stuff that excites them. People podcast for the same reason that they blog: It's a cheap, flexible form of self-expression, a way to share one's thoughts and opinions with a like-minded audience.

Because podcasts are easy to produce, quality varies widely. At the high end are the slick productions put on by major media companies, who see podcasting as a way to extend the life of their existing programs. National Public Radio, which distributes more than three hundred podcasts, has created a new business model for the medium. It aggregates productions from its member stations and then sells underwriter sponsorships against those programs. Many of the new programs are organized topically, piecing together content from multiple sources around a single theme.

At the other extreme are the thousands of programs produced by individuals on topics ranging from dieting to religion to one woman who records dogs barking. Some of these programs are terrible, but many have a gritty authenticity that's distinctive and appealing. In fact, amateur Podcasters value the rough-edged quality of independent productions, believing that it makes them more human.

"What listeners tell us is that mainstream programming converted to MP3 files and redistributed and called a podcast is interesting to a point, but it's not what they are really compelled by," Kris Jacob, a vice president of business development at PodShow, told *Online Journalism Review* in late 2005. "What they are compelled by is unique, independent niche programming that appeals to them and allows them to develop a relationship that they can't forge with mainstream programming."

Thousands of podcasters are like Dana McCurley, a technology editor in Framingham, Massachusetts, who has a passion for bunnies. She adopted her first rabbit when she was still in college. She now has four of the long-eared pets, whom she nurtures as if they were her children. She started her BunnyBlab blog in 2005 and launched a podcast series by the same name in 2006.

Each twenty-minute episode is devoted to some aspect of bunny care: choosing a pet, bringing it home, acclimating it to new surroundings, nutrition, avoiding domestic hazards and the like. BunnyBlab has only about forty listeners, but the archival value is well worth the effort, McCurley says. "People buy baby bunnies because they're so cute and then find out months late that they really require special care and attention. They end up giving them to shelters or releasing them in the back yard," she says. "A year from now, someone could be looking for help on what to do about their bunny. If my podcasts can help them prepare them for the realities of having a bunny, it's worth it."

The New Influencers of podcasting present intriguing possibilities for marketers to reach highly targeted audiences. Like bloggers, they're passionate about their audiences but not constrained by the conventions of mainstream radio. They love getting feedback from listeners and look for new ways to involve their audience more closely in their programs. Few are motivated by commercial interests.

But podcasts differ from blogs in some important ways. For one thing, they're less interactive. The back-and-forth of blog conversations are simply impossible to duplicate in a one-way audio medium. Podcasters have come up with some clever workarounds for this limitation. Most programs have associated blogs called "show notes" that outline and elaborate upon the audio content and invite commentary. Many Podcasters also set up telephone answering machines to take listeners' comments, which they play back on subsequent shows. This feedback mechanism is increasingly popular, replicating to some degree the talk radio format that's so popular in terrestrial radio. Podcasts are also more likely to be topical than blogs.

Podcasts are designed to be listened to from beginning to end. Most popular podcasts have a theme, an introduction and a consistent format. Often they include contests, listener-response segments, moderator rants and other regular features. This is an opportunity for marketers to sponsor or participate in segments that interest them. Many cash-poor podcasters are more than happy to accept giveaways or content that they believe will interest their listeners. Savvy marketers are already working with podcasters to get access to their engaged audiences, often by doing little more than donating product samples.

Podcasting certainly does have its personalities. Hundreds of thousand of listeners regularly listen in to hear what's on the minds of Adam Curry, Ricky Gervais and the Mugglecasters. But most podcasters are enthusiasts with a passion and expertise about gardening, nutrition, automotive repair or some other profession or pastime. Their audiences are small but highly engaged and enthusiastic. It is probably the most focused listener group a marketer can hope to reach.

Many podcasters don't have the standard media biases against integrating advertising with editorial content and so are willing to be creative in working their sponsors into the conversations. Popular techniques are to invite listeners to participate in creating promotions for sponsors or to work sponsor-subsidized promotions like giveaways into the programming. Podcasters are always looking for ways to build audience and keep listeners coming back, which makes them open to cooperating with sponsors on contests and promotions. This is a great opportunity to tune in to your customers' opinions about you and your product. You may also get some decent marketing material from the exercise.

Marketers need to pay attention to the audiences these people are building. While they may be small, they're focused and influential. They subscribe to podcasts because they actively want to listen. Many also have a lot of money to spend. If you're in the home entertainment business and you don't see the value of the 30,000 subscribers to HDTV podcast, you're not yet tuned in to the value of small markets.

But you need to place your bets carefully because podcasts are more combustible than mainstream radio. Most podcasters have day jobs and can't be counted on to post a new program on a set schedule. Few programmers have the week-in/week-out consistency of the HT Guys or Mommycast.

Podcasts can also be pretty uninhibited. The medium isn't regulated by any government agency, so there are no restrictions of subject matter or language. Podcasters love this freedom, of course, but it can be a little frightening to marketers seeking to align their brand with a show. Some of the most popular programs, like the Keith and the Girl podcast and the Dawn and Drew Show can be downright foulmouthed. Apple's iTunes music distribution service makes an effort to identify adult-themed podcasts, but it's not infallible. It's a good idea to get to know a podcaster before becoming involved in his or her program.

Just jump in

What may be an even more appealing opportunity for marketers is to join the party and use the medium to advance their own messages. And why not? Podcasting is cheap and fast. An interview with your lead engineer or the VP of marketing can be posted to the world in a few hours. You can also use a podcast series to grab hold of a topic that you want to "own."

Whirlpool USA did that. In mid-2005, the appliance maker launched a podcast series called Whirlpool American Family. New programs are posted about once a week.

There's nothing about home appliances in these programs. The programs are about child-rearing, schooling, health, work/family issues, nutrition and a host of other family concerns. They're the brainchild of

Audrey Reed-Granger, a Whirlpool publicist who admits that she didn't even know what a podcast was until a few weeks before she suggested the idea to Whirlpool management.

"I listened to a few podcasts and it struck me that this was the reason I got into journalism," says Reed-Granger, a former television producer. "It was very earnest, just average people reporting on things that go on in normal life. I wanted to capture that."

Her bosses liked the idea and the nominal cost. The first podcast launched in late July 2005. By September, the online buzz became apparent.

"There was a lot of blogosphere chatter about Whirlpool," Reed-Granger says. "We figured out that it was about American Family. People were endorsing the podcasts in their blogs and other bloggers were tuning in. I started getting e-mail from people suggesting speakers."

What started as interviews with friends and contacts has become an institution. Book publishers and PR agencies pitch their clients as guests on American Family podcasts. About a year into the program, Whirlpool American Family had more than 70,000 monthly downloads and was also carried on more than a dozen independent podcast sites. By mass-media audience standards, the numbers were minuscule. But the audience was highly engaged and the blog buzz was uniformly positive. "It's less about the brand than the essence of the people that market the products," Reed-Granger says. "It's made us more likeable."

Whirlpool isn't alone. General Motors complements its Fastlane blog with occasional podcasts. A spokesman told the *Wall Street Journal* that the monthly listenership has ranged from 39,000 to 87,000 people. An interview with a lead designer of the Chevrolet Corvette has logged more than 100,000 downloads. This is an example of using podcasting to reach enthusiasts. GM knows that Corvette owners are passionate about their vehicle, and a podcast is a cheap way to tap into that enthusiasm.

IBM's investor relations group ran a series of twelve podcasts that looked into the future of institutions like the home, banking, sports and even crime. The intention was to position IBM as a forward-looking company. IBM called the podcasts a success, scoring more than 50,000 downloads in the first three months. "We show that we're passionate and approachable and just excited about what we do," George Faulkner of IBM's communications group told the *Journal News*, a Hudson Valley, New York, newspaper. Emboldened, IBM launched another podcast series in mid-2006 called Shortcuts. It offered tips on how to use personal technology.

Purina launched a podcast series in 2005 and has expanded it to seven regularly updated programs, including a videocast. The company uses online media aggressively in its promotions, maintaining fifteen websites and extensive libraries of tips on pet care. It complements the podcasts with a photo-sharing site and downloadable ring tones.

One of the more interesting experiments has been by Johnson & Johnson Vision Care, Inc. In late 2005, the company launched a podcast developed by its Acuvue contact lens division and featuring two Long Island high school girls named Heather and Jonelle. Each program features the pair talking about teenage life: school, family, friends and particularly boys. Listening to it is like eavesdropping on a gabfest at the mall.

While the link between contact lenses and high school chatter may not be evident, Acuvue said the program addresses its need to find younger customers. Download with Heather and Jonelle is hardly promotional: outside of one acknowledgment of Acuvue's sponsorship, there is no discussion of contact lenses or vision care at all. But the podcast taps into a listenership that marketers want to reach. For the price of hiring a couple of average teenagers and some Internet hosting costs, Acuvue is talking to a desirable market.

Educate the consumer

This is an important point. In the best practice of social media, podcasts should be educational and actionable, but never overtly promotional. Successful corporate podcasters whom I interviewed all stressed this point. My own experience reinforces it.

In 2006, my media consulting business came to encompass a great many custom podcasts for companies in the information technology field. I worked extensively with marketers on these programs and found that their approaches varied widely. The savviest marketers saw the podcasts as an opportunity to educate customers about a problem the customers didn't know they had or didn't know how to solve. The podcasts would help them to understand the problem and indirectly suggest a solution. These marketers would take pains to suggest speakers who had a high a level of credibility with the technical audience. They included engineers, developers and product managers. In some cases, they also included customers.

One company that made anti-spyware tools offered its chief technology officer to talk about a new category of threat. The man had a doctorate in computer science and more than twenty years' experience in the field. Listening to his voluminous knowledge of the topic, you couldn't help but be impressed by the intellectual resources this company was bringing to solving this problem.

Another company, also in the computer security realm, tapped a corporate director who had previously been an information security czar in the Clinton administration. In a fascinating twenty-minute interview, he talked about the vulnerability of the nation's computers to terrorists and professional criminals. It was a little scary, but it reinforced the fact that the company had impressive expertise at its disposal.

In contrast, other vendors put forth marketing executives who relentlessly repeated the company's message. These interviews were boring, useless and even offensively self-promotional. It's one thing to hear such messaging in an ad, but what technology professional is going to voluntarily choose to listen to a marketing pitch?

For corporate marketers, podcasting is low-hanging fruit. Podcasts are cheap and easy to produce, which means you can experiment and have fun without worrying about looking bad on national television. A good start is simply to put a microphone in front of the lead engineer on the coolest product your company makes. If your customers are enthusiasts about your products, all the better. You can use podcasting to take them inside your company and show them how those products come to be.

Or you can own a topic. If you make bicycles, launch a monthly podcast on America's greatest bike routes. If you make nails, talk about home improvement. If your business is adult education, give studying tips or interview authorities in your fields of concentration. The vast majority of podcasts are just ordinary people talking about things that interest them. Nothing says your company can't be one of them.

The Sound Man

In 2003, Doug Kaye told his wife he would never start another company. Now, thanks to podcasting, he's involved in the most important startup of his life.

Kaye didn't need to prove anything at the time. He was 54. He had made enough from Rational Data Systems, which he started in 1978 and sold eighteen years later, and some dot-com IPOs to ensure a comfortable living. Since 1995, he had dabbled in a variety of Internet startups, including a dating service and one that sold art online. Only one survived to go public, but that didn't really matter. Doug Kaye was content to write books, consult and enjoy the spectacular view from the deck of his home nestled in the hills of Marin County, just north of San Francisco.

One of those book projects would eventually become *Loosely Coupled: The Missing Pieces of Web Services*. Published in 2003, it was a sort of seminal tutorial volume for managers eyeing the burgeoning field of software integration. Kaye knew next to nothing about Web services when he set out to write *Loosely Coupled*, so he networked his way through to the people who did. Through interviews with about forty very smart people, he learned the ropes. He also learned "that these people knew more about the subject than I'd ever know," he says. "I was getting in the way."

Kaye knew a lot about building websites from his days in the tech industry. He also knew a lot about sound. At one point, in fact, sound had been his career. As a kid, he had worked summers at a San Francisco company that built public address systems. After graduating from the University of California at Berkeley with a theatre degree, he had made a good living for several years engineering sound for movie crews that came through the Bay Area. At night, he ran the sound board at some prestigious local theatres.

He had pursued a graduate school program in TV and film at NYU but quit after a year because his work experience had vaulted him too far ahead of the rest of the class. ("After two weeks, they offered me a job teaching," he says.) But he remained in New York for a decade after that, working as a sound engineer, dubbing foreign language films and producing a couple of independent documentaries. When his employer decided to computerize some of its work, Kaye offered to get involved. He took his first and only programming course and wrote software for automating color correction on movie film. It involved writing an operating system, program language compiler and computer language, but that seemed natural. "No one ever told me you can't write a compiler," he says.

The road forks

Doug Kaye's life forked at that point. For the next twenty-five years, he pursued his passion for programming, built a business and made his fortune. But his passion for sound was never far away. And when it was time to write *Loosely Coupled*, it was suddenly useful again.

He started calling up the people he had interviewed earlier for the book and asked if he could come back and interview them again. Only this time there'd be quality sound equipment and scripted questions and the result would be a professional-sounding Q&A interview. Kaye rerecorded interviews with a handful of speakers (one of them Phil Windley, then CIO of the State of Utah, would later join Kaye in his new venture), and posted them on his new Blogarithms blog.

Timing counts for a lot, and Doug Kaye's timing was perfect. Web services was hot in 2003 and as news of the interviews spread through the blogosphere, people came and listened. Some wrote Kaye e-mails complimenting him for helping them shortcut the learning curve. At the same time, Apple's new iPod music player was gaining momentum and a few intrepid souls had written software that let people download what amounted to talk radio programs by subscription. The medium had even acquired a cute name: "podcasting."

For Doug Kaye, podcasting was planetary alignment. It combined his passion for sound with his love of technology. Kaye was a lifelong conference-goer and he had always rued the fact that he couldn't get to as many events as he wanted. Maybe he could find a way to record those speeches and make them available for others to listen to whenever they wanted. In June of 2003, Kaye launched a website for his burgeoning collection of podcasts. He called it IT Conversations (ITC), a riff on the "markets are conversations" theme of *Cluetrain Manifesto*, the document that many people believe kicked off the Web 2.0 phenomenon.[1]

Turn of events

ITC was a cool idea but Kaye's vision of it as a home for great thoughts from great thinkers wouldn't take shape until early 2004. O'Reilly Media's Emerging Technology Conference was building a reputation as a forum for forward-looking speakers. Kaye approached the organizers and proposed that he record the proceedings for ITC. O'Reilly hedged at first. Events organizers spend a lot of money courting attendees. It's a competitive, price-sensitive market and success hinges on attracting the right people. Even for paid events, no-show rates can approach 50 percent and one bad conference can kill a business. O'Reilly didn't want to risk the chance that people would download the content for free instead of paying to register. Kaye could record, they said, but he had to sit in the back of the room. What's more, he couldn't tell anyone in advance what he was doing.

Doug Kaye sat in the back of the room. And got lucky again. Joe Trippi, fresh from his tour as manager of the hip and digital Howard Dean campaign, gave his first detailed public account of the digital strategies that vaulted Dean to prominence. Doug Kaye was the only person in the room who recorded it. Suddenly, ITC was a newsmaker.

The O'Reilly experiment was a huge success. Conference organizers were thrilled. ITC was on the map and other event organizers began ringing Doug Kaye's number.

O'Reilly's initial fears that podcasting would cannibalize attendance were misplaced. The opposite is actually true. There's documented evidence that one hundred times as many people listen to a conference podcast as attend a conference. When deployed intelligently, recorded presentations can juice marketing from year to year. In other words, proceedings from last year's conference can raise anticipation about this year's conference. "Everybody freaks out up front," Kaye says of organizers' typical reactions to the podcasting idea, "And everybody has renewed."

O'Reilly gambled with ITC and won. They were hooked and ITC has podcast nearly every O'Reilly conference for the last three years.

1. See Appendix B.

Economics are one thing that are making podcasting so disruptive. Doug Kaye's studio is half of a converted guest bedroom in his Kentfield home. For the first three years of its existence, ITC had no offices, no overhead and no staff. Whatever revenue came from a tip jar was distributed to the volunteers. ITC's original content management system is hand-written by Doug Kaye and, until mid-2005, he screened almost all the content himself.

Economics like that create a quandary for conference organizers. "The cost of distributing a podcast is about 1 percent of the cost of putting on a conference," Kaye says. Organizers are in the difficult position of having to embrace a technology that increasingly challenges the informational value of their events. IT Conversations is demonstrating that the two businesses can be symbiotic.

Over its first three years, ITC assembled a library of more than twelve hundred recorded speeches and interviews from events and syndicated programs. A team of volunteers that grew to number more than fifty, worked for beer money and the chance to share in Kaye's vision of recording every public event in the world for education and posterity. Its most popular programs—Kaye's interview with Apple cofounder Steve Wozniak and Malcolm Gladwell's presentation to the Pop!Tech conference in 2004 top the list—have each logged north of 150,000 downloads. But the real action is in the long tail. Nearly every program in the library gets at least a few downloads each month.

The next level

In 2006, the road forked again, stoked by Kaye's entrepreneurial instincts and the chance to make ITC a very big influencer indeed. Early that year, Kaye launched the Conversations Network, a portfolio of ITC-like portals that is doing for different verticals what ITC did for technology. The first channel to launch—Social Innovation Conversations—featured content from Stanford University and was funded by grants. Kaye sees the network eventually encompassing as many as forty channels.

In July, Kaye and podcasting pioneer Michael Geoghegan teamed to launch GigaVox, Inc., a for-profit network that will have the advantage of corporate funding, venture capital and other resources to take podcasting to the mainstream. The Conversations Network remains the nonprofit arm of the enterprise, funded by grants and paid memberships.

The team of former volunteers will work for both enterprises, but now they'll have offices and equipment. GigaVox will court corporate sponsorships and venture capitalists. Benefits of the for-profit company's investments in technology and learning will percolate down to the non-profit Conversations Network.

One of GigaVox's most promising new ventures is Podcast Academy, a traveling crash course in how to create and promote podcasts. Conceived as a training vehicle for prospective volunteers, the academy has sold out in multiple cities. It could become the education arm of the GigaVox network.

Once again, time could be on Doug Kaye's side. ITC has a unique and established franchise in podspace. It's untangled a lot of the problems of creating a successful network of contributors. It's got the pole position in the race to create a new model of virtual events.

And it's got Doug Kaye, a guy who's just having an unbelievable amount of fun. "This is the most important thing I've ever done," he says. "But if I'm not working on the most important thing, I'm not happy."

CHAPTER 9
Tools of The Trade

If you've read this far, you're probably intrigued by the opportunity of joining the conversation, terrified by its unpredictability, or more likely a little of both. As a business marketer, you don't necessarily need to be a player in social media, but you should be aware of what's being said about you.

There are several high-end products and services that monitor online chatter and give subscribers reports of varying levels of sophistication. Among the providers are Nielsen BuzzMetrics with BrandPulse, Cymfony with Orchestra, Nstein with Ntelligent Enterprise Search and Factiva with a suite of tracking products. Services can run from a few hundred to several thousand dollars per month. They're mainly used by professional marketing firms and large corporations.

Fortunately, you don't have to spend a lot of money—or *any* money, in fact—to listen to the conversation. There are many free services that alert you when something is going on in the blogosphere that you need to know about.

Google Alerts are a powerful way to monitor what the media is saying about any topic. The free service essentially performs regular searches on topics that you specify and sends you an e-mail when new results pop up. The news alert feature is particularly useful. Type in your company name, product name, your name or anything else and you will be automatically notified when that term appears in a new article in

Google News's directory of more than 4,500 news sources. This service is a huge time-saver. You should have alerts set up for all the companies and brands that are important to you.

It's also worth spending fifteen minutes to familiarize yourself with the advanced search features of the engine of your choice. Most people aren't even aware of them, but they can save you hours of time over the course of a year. For example, putting quotation marks around a query will deliver a more targeted result. A search for Bill Gates will turn up every record in Google's database that includes the word "bill" or "gates." If you search for "Bill Gates," however, you'll only get results that relate to Microsoft's founder.

The "linkdomain:" command in Yahoo!'s search engine will give you a list of all links to any page or domain that you specify. You can also choose to search only on a specific website by specifying "site:" in the query. For example, if you want to know if Steve Rubel has ever mentioned your company on his Micro Persuasion blog, you'd enter your firm's name followed by "site:micropersuasion.com." This little trick will save you from scrolling through screens of irrelevant search results.

And Google and Yahoo! aren't the only games in town. Ask.com's search engine has improved greatly since its acquisition by the Barry Diller's IAC/Interactive Corp. Its search engine is not only fast, but includes a useful sidebar of related search results, extensive reference information and a built-in viewer that lets you preview a site without leaving the search results page. Amazon.com's A9 search engine lets you customize your results page to include all kinds of categories, such as blogs, news, government documents and about three hundred other sources. In the course of spending countless hours online researching this book, I found myself using Ask and Amazon search engines more and more while reducing my time with Google.

Searching blogs

Searching blogs is a little trickier. Because blogs are updated so frequently, new entries may not make it into the major search engines for days. As we've seen, a couple of days is all it takes for a blog swarm to form. Blog-specific search engines work by monitoring syndication streams called RSS feeds (more on RSS below) that most bloggers use to tell the world when their site has been updated. These search engines can grab new content less than an hour after it has been published, making them the best way to keep tabs on the blogosphere. The downside is that they are less effective at filtering results than a specialized search engine like Google or Ask. That means that you have to do more work on the back end.

Popular RSS-based search engines include Technorati, IceRocket, Feedster, and BlogPulse. There are hundreds of other blog directories and search engines, however,[1] each with a different twist. Opinmind.com, for example, classifies search results by bias. It analyzes the tone of various blog posts and displays a meter showing whether opinion is running in favor of or against the topic being searched. TalkDigger combines the results of multiple blog search engines and ranks the results by link popularity. BlogBlusiness.com is a directory of blogs about different business-related topics, organized by category.

Many blog search engines—including Technorati, Blogpulse and IceRocket—provide experimental tools to help you track conversations. Technorati has watchlists, which are the equivalent of Google Alerts for blogs. As a registered user, you can specify search terms and then tell the service to monitor blog activity for those terms. Whenever there's a hit, Technorati will notify you via an RSS message. With watchlists, there is really no excuse for being late to a conversation.

Technorati's Top 100 Blogs list is also a pretty good roundup of the most influential bloggers according to how many links they have from other bloggers. However, you can search for any blog at Technorati and find out where it ranks in the two million or so blogs that the service includes in its rankings. People debate the validity of the Technorati list but the fact is that it is currently the gold standard for tracking influence in the blogosphere. If you're trying to sort through a long list of posts about your company, searching Technorati for a blog's ranking can help you separate the wheat from the chaff. Technorati also lets you narrow your search results by the authority of the blogger. Authority is determined by a proprietary formula that factors in inbound links and the activity level of the blog. This enormously useful feature can save you a lot of time. Another search engine, Sphere.com, also returns results based on a proprietary algorithm that determines the influence of the author.

1. New media consultant and author Robin Good maintains a fantastic list of blog search engines at masternewmedia.org/rss/top55/.

IceRocket and Blogpulse have some interesting and helpful twists on the search theme. Both can track conversations over time and display the trend in graphical format, showing how many people were talking about the topic on any given day. This is useful for monitoring buzz, particularly when you're caught up in a blog swarm or active conversation. It's also an important early indicator of whether a topic is gathering steam. You should check in regularly on your company and product names. Blogpulse profiles top bloggers with information about who they are and what they write about. The service is rudimentary but promising. IceRocket indexes MySpace posts and images.

Podcasts are a different world. Searching them is difficult because the content is so hard to index. However, two remarkable search engines—Podscope.com and Podzinger.com—do a pretty fine job. Enter a search term and you're taken to a list of podcasts that mention that term. What's more, you can click on a control button and listen to the exact segment in the program where the searched-for term is spoken. The principal shortcoming of these search engines is that they don't cover every podcast out there, but the technology is uncannily good.

There are many directories of podcasts. Among the best are Podcast Alley (owned by PodShow Network), Podcasting News, Podcast.net and iPodder.org.[2]

Comments and Trackbacks—As noted in Chapter 4, comments are an important indicator of a blog's popularity. Popular bloggers tend to log a lot of comments, both because they're well-read and because commenters seek to drive traffic back to their own sites. The volume of comments can also give you an idea of how popular a topic is as well as who's talking about it.

A trackback, as defined by Wikipedia.org is "a mechanism for communication between blogs: if a blogger writes a new entry commenting on, or referring to, an entry found at another blog, and both blogging tools support the TrackBack protocol, then the commenting blogger can notify the other blog with a "TrackBack ping"; the receiving blog will typically display summaries of, and links to, all the commenting entries

2. Robin Good also maintains a comprehensive list of podcast directories at masternewmedia.org/news/2005/05/20/where_to_submit_your_podcasts.htm.

below the original entry. This allows for conversations spanning several blogs that readers can easily follow. A list of trackbacks gives you a quick look at who's discussing a topic. Be aware that not all services support them, Google's Blogger being the most notable one. But trackbacks are another way to quickly assess popularity.

What's all this about RSS?

RSS is the best technology you're probably not using. Don't feel ashamed: fewer than 30 percent of Internet denizens use RSS. It's an extremely powerful but somewhat clumsy technology that is central to the blogging movement.

RSS is a basically a personal news wire service. People who create content can use RSS to automatically notify the world when they have added information to their blog or website. Every blog or podcast service supports RSS. RSS is critical to blogging because it's timely. If you publish something to a standard website, you may have to wait days or even weeks for a search engine to come by and index it. RSS basically goes out and tells the search engines, "Hey, there's something new here. Come look right now."

You subscribe to RSS feeds by plugging the feed URL into a specialized Web service or software program. The subscription process has historically been somewhat convoluted, but new services like Bloglines and the Google toolbar are much easier to use. If a site has been recently updated, the RSS reader grabs the latest content and delivers it back to the subscriber. That information can be displayed in an e-mail message, a Web page, a specialized reader or any one of a number of other formats. RSS feeds can even be delivered via messages to a cell phone. People choose to subscribe to an RSS feed, which means they can also choose to unsubscribe whenever they want. As a result, RSS feeds cut through the piles of spam and junk mail that clutter most in-boxes.

But that's not all that RSS delivers. Content providers can also customize the RSS feeds they provide. For example, I could choose to offer a feed that includes everything I post on my blog about small business. A subscriber to that feed would then receive only my thoughts on that topic but nothing else. He or she wouldn't even have to go to my website; most bloggers deliver the full text of their entries in their feeds.

RSS has gotten a bad rap because early versions were fairly difficult to use. They tended to deliver a page full of program code, which was enough to send the average PC user running for the exits. However, RSS has gotten considerably cleaner and more transparent as new services have sprung up. New operating systems from Microsoft and Apple also integrate RSS much more tightly than they did before.

There are drawbacks to RSS, the biggest one being that actual readership can be difficult to track. RSS can tell you how many people are subscribing to your content, but there's no way to tell—other than click-throughs to your site—whether subscribers are actually paying attention. Some commercial services, including EvolvePoint's Feedback and SyndicateIQ, provide enhanced reporting and analysis that can give you insight into who's reading you.

Why should you care? Some visionaries believe that RSS will all but replace e-mail and become an intrinsic part of the way people send and receive information. Leading bloggers like Steve Rubel and Dan Gillmor have publicly said that they won't read press releases any more unless they're delivered in RSS format. While their positions may be a little extreme, the message is that marketers need to get on board with this technology.

There's actually no good reason not to enable your corporate website with RSS right now. Why hope that customers and influencers will come find you when you have something new to announce? With RSS, you can turn them into subscribers who actively choose to receive new information from you. RSS delivery should be an option on all corporate press releases.

You should be familiar with RSS as a reader, too. We've seen that the number of New Influencers in your market may run into the hundreds. There is simply no way to keep tabs on that many websites. With RSS subscriptions, you can have notifications of new postings sent directly to you and you can preview what writers are saying without visiting a website. The time savings are substantial.

Most blog search services also let you save your search terms as RSS feeds. This is the equivalent of having a standing search in place. Any time a new blog entry or podcast is posted with those keywords, you're automatically notified. That way you never have to miss out on a conversation.

And what the heck is tagging?

Tags are newer and even less understood that RSS, but they are just as powerful. Tagging is a free-form way to classify information, a form of information that techies call metadata. People attach tags to information they've found on the Web as a way of organizing and finding it later. Tags are most often applied to frequently changing information, which makes them ideally suited for social media.

Lots of bloggers and Web publishers use tags today as a way to self-classify their information. If I write an article on Volvos, for example, I might tag it "Volvo, car, sedan, European, 4WD, snow, safety, vehicle, upscale" and any other words that might remind me of Volvos. Those tags are then stored in a database—it can be mine or someone else's—and linked to the source. I can then find that information again by searching on one or more of those keywords, or someone else can do the same.

Think of tags as the Dewey Decimal System for the Internet. Only the Dewey system was limited by the fact that a book could only be in one place at one time. Tags, in contrast, can be used to "shelve" something in a lot of different places at once. So a travelogue about Italy, for example, can be found by searching on Rome, Fiat, Chianti, pasta or villas.

Many bloggers publish their tag lists on their site or on community bookmark sites like del.icio.us. You can look at a blogger's tag list to get an idea of how much he or she writes about a particular topic. Sometimes the list is just a lot of words with numbers next to them, signifying how many articles correspond to that tag. Sometimes the list is presented as a "tag cloud," where more frequently mentioned tags are in larger type than less frequent tags.

There is no standardized list of tags and any user can tag any content item any way he or she wants, even misspelling words in the process. As a result, it's possible to miss important information in a tag search if the author or referral link uses tags other than the ones you're searching for. If this sounds messy, it is. This anarchy is very Web 2.0. But it is also powerful in its elegant simplicity.

Once you understand tags, you will love them. They give insight into the unique language that individuals use to describe the topics that motivate them. More important, when shared, they can reveal trends that even the people who create content didn't see. The content creator attaches tags describing an article or blog post, but the community of readers may attach a whole different set of tags. In effect, the community decides what content is all about, even if it isn't what the creator intended.

Many Web search engines and directories support tags, but del.icio.us is the best known. It is a Spartan, text-only site where users can easily bookmark and tag items they find on the Web. They can share those tags selectively with other users or allow anyone to see them. Visitors may research original web-based items and look at the tags that have been affixed to them.

Cluetrain Manifesto coauthor David Weinberger, who is writing a book on tags, says this can be of great use to marketers. For example, if you type "McDonald's" into the del.icio.us search engine, you'll find that the most-tagged McDonald's-related Web page is an excerpt from *Fast Food Nation*, a 2001 book that was highly critical of the restaurateur. More than two hundred fifty del.icio.us members have tagged that article. A couple of pegs down the list is the Freaky Universe of McDonald's Commercials, a sarcastic send-up of the restaurant company's ads, which 119 people have tagged.

Clearly, McDonald's spoofs are popular. Type "McDonald's humor" into the del.icio.us search engine and get a list of other satiric sites. If you click on the list of who's tagged any article, you can read their comments and also what other tags they used to describe the content. You can also click into any individual user's list of tags to see what other articles they're tagging. This gives you insight into the personalities and preferences of individual influencers.

On Technorati, bloggers and their tags are tied together in a single profile. So if you want to learn more about any particular blogger, you can look at all of the posts he or she has tagged with a particular keyword as well as tags contributed by other bloggers. This begins to give you a clearer picture of who's influencing whom and whether an individual has a bias for or against your company.

Tags can also give you valuable insight into your own product and company because they're a small window on how others see you. They can help you spot opportunity. For example, if you're marketing a fruit juice for its taste but a lot of people are tagging it with health or nutrition descriptions, that's a positioning opportunity. Tags can also give early warning of a problem. If people are tagging your home page with terms like "polluter" or "sexist," then you've got issues.

They can also be used to assess the popularity of an article or blog post. Search for the article name in del.icio.us, save it and then look at how many other people have saved it. You can click down into that list and find out what comments people are making.

Tags are also a good way to find images, podcasts, video and other hard-to-search-for items on the Web. Many people who produce multimedia content attach bundles of tags to make it easy to find. Something that doesn't show up in a conventional search engine may show up in Flickr (a photo-sharing site), TagWorld or del.icio.us because of its tags.

Aggregation engines

This catchall category covers link blogs, topical blogs, and community news sites. These are sites whose basic purpose is to drive viewers elsewhere. This may sound prosaic, but these sites are probably the most important arbiters of influence in social media. BoingBoing.net, Metafilter, Waxy.org, ScienceBlogs and Fark.com are all forms of link blogs. Some may publish only a single sentence with a link to something else while others may go into detail. All this is essentially to offer a handpicked guide to what the authors of the link blog think is best, most important or most interesting in the blogosphere.

As discussed in Chapter 1, link blogs can have tremendous influence. A single mention on BoingBoing may give a story prominence that links from a hundred minor bloggers couldn't. All of these sites have a personality—BoingBoing tends toward the intellectual while Fark specializes in the bizarre—and many have preferences for certain types of stories. It's a good idea to subscribe to their RSS feeds.

A final note on influencers to watch. The blogosphere is a constantly changing ecosystem and leaders come and go. Prominent bloggers like Stowe Boyd and Robert Scoble have told me that they could fall from the top rankings in a few weeks if they failed to tend to their readers. To a large extent, this is true. For example, TechCrunch, a leading Silicon Valley blog, went from startup to one of the ten most popular blogs on the Internet in barely a year. A lot of that had to do with the notoriety of the author, Michael Arrington, a successful lawyer, but it also shows that even in a very crowded field, there's room for new entrants. While you should have your own roster of A-list bloggers, it's worth checking back from time to time to be sure a new voice hasn't entered the conversation unexpectedly.

The Toolmaker

Dan Bricklin secured his place in computer history early in life. In 1979, when he was just 28, he and Robert Frankston wrote VisiCalc, the first personal computer spreadsheet. VisiCalc was an immediate success. It gave business people a compelling reason to use a PC and was a major factor in the IBM PC's success. By a twist of fate, Bricklin and Frankston never made much money on VisiCalc, which was soon surpassed by Lotus's 1-2-3, but Bricklin has gone on to a notable career as a software developer and visionary.

A later invention, Dan Bricklin's Demo, is still legendary in the software industry for its usefulness as a design tool. Bricklin also cofounded Slate, a handwriting-recognition software company, and Trellix, which made an easy-to-use Web design authoring system. Today he runs Software Garden, a tiny developer that enables him "to do whatever I feel like," he chuckles. Right now, that's developing a spreadsheet using the shared-editing tool called a wiki. He's also an inveterate blogger and podcaster who's as likely to be seen at a conference interviewing a speaker for a podcast as talking from the stage.

Some people think Dan Bricklin is a great programmer and he certainly is that. But during an interview at his Boston-area home, it struck me that Bricklin is first and foremost a designer. His passion for information presentation is the thread that runs throughout his work. It had never occurred to me before that the spreadsheet is, first and foremost, an information design tool. Not until Bricklin mentioned it.

His insights into social media are so penetrating that I decided to discard the profile format I use elsewhere in this book to quote Bricklin directly. Here is an edited transcript of my interview with Bricklin with additional material from his presentation to Podcast Academy at Boston University in the spring of 2006.

In Bricklin's words:

I'm the son of a printer and the grandson of a printer.

I've been blogging for a long time. I was also early into video and podcasting. I like to get my hands dirty with the technology and I like to keep up to date. A lot of what makes me different from many other people is that I try to practice what I talk about and write about.

I maintain several blogs. There's my personal blog at bricklin.com/log. I share a blog with Dave Reed and Bob Frankston at SATN.org website. I use that for more policy type of stuff. Then I have a couple of little blogs associated with products and some others with groups I work with. I also have blogs and podcasts for Software Garden and other things I'm interested in.

Publicity value

I've found in business that my background is a help to publicity. So it helps to keep a public persona and to keep fresh. To do that, I have to be active, to network, and to keep visible. The original purpose of my website was as background material for press, for historical background. It's been very effective in that respect. The media now know what I'm up to and they're much more prepared when they talk to me. I have more assurance that coverage will be based on fact because of things that I've written. If there's news that I care about, I always try to have a statement on my blog.

Blogging has been phenomenal. It's let me express myself and keep up a public dialog with people in the industry. The feedback you get is phenomenal in terms of being part of a worldwide conversation.

New/old journalism

My neighbor, Chris Daly, is a journalism professor at Boston University. A lot of what I've learned about writing for the Web I learned from him. Chris was asked to write something for a newspaper on blogging versus journalism. It was called "Are Bloggers Journalists? Let's Ask Thomas Jefferson." The newspaper ended up deciding they didn't want it, so I offered to format it in HTML and upload it to his website and I would link to it.

Well, Chris heard from more people as a result of that blog entry than he ever would have heard in the newspaper. He got calls and e-mails from top people in the journalism business. Part of the article ended up in a museum exhibit about the free press and he was even quoted by name in the Congressional Record. That's incredible response from one posting pointed to by a blogger.

Chris said that journalism in Jefferson's day was very similar to what we call blogging today. They called it pamphleteering. The big media we know of today are foreign to what the founding fathers thought about. In those days, people were writing stuff and reading it and commenting on it. Journalism as it's taught in schools today is a flavor of communication, some of which is based on technology and business structures that we no longer have to follow.

Through my own blog I get e-mails from people I'd never have known about. I've met some people who were interested in accidents: things that don't work the way they're expected to work. That ended up in my essay "Software That Lasts 200 Years," which says that we need to start thinking about software more like how we think about building bridges, dams, and sewers. What we build must last for generations. This requires new thinking and new ways of organizing development.

Sometimes when I'm the only witness to something, I'll document it through the blog or podcast. I podcast a meeting with Eric Kriss from the State of Massachusetts and people from Microsoft and Adobe. It was extremely important in a discussion about open standards. [Massachusetts was notable at the time for having declared it wouldn't use Microsoft Office until it was compatible with open document standards.] It would have been a shame to have a meeting like that happen and not be able to share it with others. That podcast has been downloaded thousands of times.

Some blogging will be subsumed by other means. A blog is based on continually adding to something. The unit is a post and the page is not as important as the post. The importance of a permalink is that it permanently links to a post and has a time associated with it.

The right tool for the job

Social media has different forms and each one is useful for different things. A website is relatively stable. It has an organizational base but not a chronological base. Wikis are something else. On a wiki, the page and the links are a structure that changes over time and the unit is the page. However, a wiki keeps track of modifications by individuals. It's an entity that changes over time. The important thing is that it has a current state, which is totally different from a blog. You need blogs and wikis at different times, like you need a phone at a different time than you need a memo. We learn to use the right tool at the right time.

As blogging tools get easier to use, they'll get subsumed into other things. The idea of having a flow of chronological posts is what's important. And the formats will merge. For example, changes to a wiki can be a blog and can be presented through RSS. I see blogging as becoming more and more embedded.

People have been thinking about these things for a long time. If you look at how religious texts were done hundreds of years ago, it's amazing what they did to organize information. The Talmud deals with the kinds of issues we're discussing in how to present information in the blogosphere. There were sacred texts and commentary was included by other people. In 1554 they were using a form of hyperlinks in text, only they were referring to other books.

The Talmud was actually assembled by a particular rabbi who assembled what everyone had been discussing for generations before him. Then the students put their discussions in the next section. It was like a big wiki. They were inventing all this because before that they only had scrolls. They had to create a whole new set of rules when they went from scrolls to books.

If you look at the spreadsheet analogy, people use spreadsheets to organize data for themselves. A lot of people say they're using a spreadsheet but what they're really using is a table manager. When I was creating VisiCalc, I wanted to create a magic blackboard where things didn't have to be in a particular place. Dan Bricklin's Demo program was similar. It helped people figure out how they wanted to see things on a screen.

Podcasts and a shrinking world

I'd been involved with sound for a long time. Podcasting is another form of information presentation. How's a podcast different from radio? In a podcast, almost everybody listens right from the start. You don't have to keep repeating what you're talking about. That's a big change.

Last September, the Massachusetts Technology Leadership Council asked me to be on an open source interest group. I got the idea of podcasting the meetings. Almost immediately, more people were listening to the podcast than attending the meetings. Thousands of people downloaded a two-hour recording and it helped make decisions about a major topic.

It's amazing how fast radio is going to podcasts. It was about a year from the first NPR podcast to practically every NPR program being available as a podcast. My friend Bob Frankston says that demand creates supply. Almost everything we write now is on the Internet. Digital photography has taken over for most conventional photography. Audio players are pervasive now. For all the effort that goes into producing content, it's a shame to have it just disappear. Every public meeting should be recorded so all the people who weren't able to be there can listen to what happened.

Distance is becoming less of a barrier to sharing information and staying in touch. It's much more likely today that you can get the right information to the right person. That's making us much more efficient. Look at how the cell phone has been picked up all over the world. The ability to communicate with someone without having to make appointments and be in a particular location has liberated people in so many ways. Kids who leave high school today don't have to lose track of people. They're as up to date with their lives as if their friends were in the town next door.

CHAPTER 10

Going Viral

If you go to EthicsCrisis.com, you can read some pretty eye-popping stuff.

> "I'm going after my boss's clients," says one contributor. "I never signed a non-compete agreement that went beyond termination of my employment, so all her clients are fair game. And I know I'll do a lot better than she did."
>
> "A vendor vying for a big contract from my company sent me on vacation. But I gave the contract to someone else," reads another confession.

Is this site a tribute to pop psychology? A virtual confession booth? Actually, it's run by SRF Global Translations, a company that markets language translation services. EthicsCrisis.com is a variation on the popular PostSecret[1] blog, which has visitors admitting to their deepest, darkest secrets on elaborately designed postcards. Only EthicsCrisis allows other visitors to rate the confessions people have posted for acceptability. Some admissions have logged more than 2,000 votes.

SRF didn't even have a website until April 2006. But since Ethics Crisis launched, the blog has been visited by tens of thousands of people who are willing to share their deepest ethical secrets for the sole purpose

---

1. postsecret.blogspot.com

of getting them off their chest. There's also a lot of information about corporate ethics in general, as SRF tries to stake out this topic as a specialty. The result: Within six weeks of the launch, SRF Global had achieved top ten search engine placement for "multilanguage translations" on Google. More important, within two weeks, SRF was already getting inquiries and paid transactions via the blog. "Not bad for a $300 software license and a few thousand dollars worth of programming and design," says B. L. Ochman, who created EthicsCrisis for SRF.

Ochman is a specialist in the burgeoning field of viral marketing.[2] This specialized brand of promotion, also called "word of mouth" or "guerilla" marketing, is nothing new. Each person tells several friends and word spreads on a geometric scale. It is perhaps the oldest form of marketing, but the Internet has given it new power. If each person tells five friends and those friends, in turn, tell five more friends, more than one million people will have heard the news after only twelve tellings. Plant the right seed and watch a cornfield sprout. But you must have the right message and you must understand the medium.

Social media has completely changed the dynamics of viral marketing. What once required a phone call or a letter can now be duplicated on a large scale using e-mail. And blogs magnify the effects by orders of magnitude. Get mentioned on the right blog, and the five friends becomes five thousand. It's no wonder that specialized viral marketing firms are sprouting up all over the country.

Viral marketing is one way in which the new breed of marketers is learning to leverage the power of social media. It is an inherently risky strategy. A viable message that doesn't catch on is a waste. But the cost of viral marketing is so low—in my interviews, marketers frequently cited costs less than a thirty-second television commercial—that it's cheap to try.

Viral marketing taps an existing vein of Web users and relies on them to spread the word about a site, contest or video by e-mail and blog. The campaigns usually rely on humor, mystery or competition to motivate people to participate. Marketers are intrigued. *BusinessWeek* estimated that viral marketing was a $100 million to $150 million industry in mid-2006. There's even an industry group: the Word of Mouth Marketing Association was formed in 2004 to promote best practices through publications and events.

---

2. Her blog at whatsnextblog.com is a gold mine of good ideas.

Viral hits

B. L. Ochman's best-known viral campaign was for Budget Rent-A-Car. Called "Up Your Budget," the promotion hid $10,000 in each of sixteen cities around the US. Clues to the location of each cache were distributed by Internet video and people raced to be first to find the treasure. The whole contest was managed via a blog.

"For my life, I have no idea how people found these things," laughs Ochman. "They flew and took buses to other cites and created websites where they blogged about what the clues meant. It took on a life of its own."

The campaign, which cost less than a half million dollars to produce, drew one million unique visitors and 10 million page views to the blog in four weeks in late 2005, with traffic peaking at 20,000 unique visitors per hour. Promotion consisted of blog ads and well-placed mentions on the Adrants and MarketingVox blogs.

"To be asked to sit back and just let the viral do its job was a complete leap of faith for us," says Budget executive marketing VP Scott Deaver. "But we're very happy with the way it worked out."

When it works, viral marketing can have awesome power. In the book *Naked Conversations*, Robert Scoble and Shel Israel cite the example of ICQ, an Internet chat program developed by four young Israeli students. The group originally told forty friends about their invention and within two months 65,000 people had downloaded the software. By the end of 1998, just two years after the viral chain began, the service had been downloaded 25 million times and AOL had purchased the developers' company for $287 million.

Skype, the wildly popular Internet phone service, recorded 25 million downloads just nineteen months after startup, the authors relate. It sold to eBay in October 2005 for $2.6 billion.

In both cases, the marketing campaigns were almost entirely viral and cost next to nothing. The developers used a number of innovative marketing tactics to seed the audience. For example, each new release of ICQ was revealed to 1,000 randomly selected users, who were given the same "secret password." Creating the sense of insider awareness built excitement.

But even Skype's remarkable record was eclipsed by Firefox, an open-source software alternative to Microsoft Internet Explorer. It recorded more than 50 million downloads in the first six months, with no money spent on marketing. In fact, Firefox users were so rabid that they took up a collection to buy a newspaper ad, Scoble and Israel relate. This result would probably have been impossible to obtain using conventional marketing. The cost simply would have been too high.

These three examples aren't typical, of course. In all cases, the products were free. The revenue model was built on advertising or there was no revenue model at all. ICQ and Skype appealed to a base of cost-sensitive, mainly younger customers, which is a demographic most marketers shun. Firefox tapped a well of anti-Microsoft sentiment to stoke the feeding frenzy. These cases are unusual but they do show the potentially awesome power of viral marketing.

The first viral epidemic to hit the Internet is generally acknowledged to be "I Kiss You," a plain-looking website created by Mahir, a Turkish everyman. Its broken English, dorky photos and innocent come-ons for women to come stay with him in Ankara became a global joke in 1999. Internet eTour.com brought Mahir to the U.S. for a two-week tour and he was profiled in newspapers around the globe.[3]

Many people remember an epidemic that helped kick off the viral video craze. In the fall of 2005, 19-year-old Gary Brolsman recorded a grainy video of himself dancing to an obscure song by a Romanian rock group named O-Zone. The short video that came to be known as "Numa Numa" showed Brolsma gyrating and gesticulating from his chair in campy rapture to the music. It was hysterical. People attached it to e-mail messages, websites copied it and, as each recipient forwarded the clip to a dozen friends, Gary Brolsman's dance quickly spread across the globe. Within a few days, millions of people had downloaded and shared the video with friends. Brolsma was featured on *Good Morning America*, the *Tonight Show* and VH1's *Best Week Ever*. And within a few months, O-Zone, which was almost unknown in the U.S. prior to the Brolsma video, was on the top ten charts.

The growth of video sites such as YouTube and Revver has further built momentum behind viral marketing. It seems that everyone wants to be Gary Brolsma. Smart ad agencies no longer create commercials just for television; ad campaigns can live on the Web for months, even years. Anheuser-Busch promoted online versions of its TV commercials the week

---

3. The original site, which is at istanbul.tc/mahir/mahir/, has logged millions of visits.

before the 2006 Super Bowl and got more than 22 million visits to its website, according to the *New York Times*. More than eight hundred other websites also copied and posted the ads.

"Volkswagen, known for its distinctive advertising, keeps more than twenty commercials under the 'VW Life' section of its website," the *Times* noted. Delivery service DHL "has an extensive archive that contains ads from two years and four campaigns ago. Bud Light now allows visitors to e-mail its ads or download them onto iPods." In fact, the 2006 Super Bowl was the first in which a majority of the television ads sent viewers to an online destination.

Driving forces

Marketers' interest in viral marketing is being driven by several developments:

Declining response rates—Click-throughs to conventional banner and e-mail advertising have been declining for some time, a function of list exhaustion, customer disinterest, and spam.

Technology developments—Web 2.0 tools, falling hardware and bandwidth costs and a growing online population are making interactive media more attractive. Multimedia content like video and audio files can now be delivered quickly for a fraction of the cost of a few years ago.

Demographic shifts—It's a fact that younger consumers are consuming more information online and less through traditional media channels. An Online Publishers Association study in early 2006 found that one in four Internet users watches video at least weekly and that they are likely to be young, male and affluent. Pew Research reported that 57 percent of teenagers created and published media in 2005. Viral campaigns increasingly encourage this user-generated content.

Customer preference—It's also a fact that people trust their peers more than marketers. Research by Keller Fay Group found that 76 percent of consumers don't believe companies tell the truth in advertising. The percentage who say they trust other people "like themselves" has grown from 22 percent in 2003 to 68 percent in 2006. *MediaPost* reported that 67 percent of people polled in a 1977 research study said they were moved to take some sort of action by word-of-mouth influence. In 2003, that number had risen to 92 percent.

Low cost—Done right, a viral campaign can deliver a larger number of engaged customers than one on television and at a fraction of the cost.

With all these factors in play, it's not surprising that marketers are experimenting with viral media. A Jupiter Research study in late 2006 found that nearly one in five advertisers planned to use viral campaigns in the next year, half of them for the first time.

Viral isn't for everyone, and there are a lot of risks. The more campaigns that are launched, the more crowded the space becomes. A lot of good ideas have already been tried. Viral marketing agencies, which are usually small and specialized, are beginning to cash in on the craze. Fees of a half million dollars are no longer unusual, and that's without a performance guarantee.

For many products, viral campaigns won't work at all. A two-year study of more than 15 million recommendations by almost 4 million users of a recommendation engine (a recommendation engine gathers opinions about a product or service and boils them down to a rating, often on a five-point scale) on a retail website found that viral messaging was largely ineffective in promoting purchases. The study's authors concluded: "We find that most recommendation chains do not grow very large, often terminating with the initial purchase of a product."[4]

What's more, campaigns that are overly aggressive or provide too many incentives for viral promotion can actually backfire. "Recommendations start to lose effect after more than two or three are passed between two people," the researchers wrote. "The result has important implications for viral marketing because providing too much incentive for people to recommend to one another can weaken the very social network links that the marketer is intending to exploit." In other words, viral promotion must be grass-roots and genuine. A marketer who tries too hard to stimulate a viral campaign may only end up looking foolish and driving customers away.

4. J. Leskovec, L. Adamic and B. Huberman. The Dynamics of Viral Marketing. ACM Conference on Electronic Commerce (EC 2006), Ann Arbor, MI, 2006.

Researchers also found that viral marketing works better for some products than for others. Books, for example, were less likely to be bought as the result of a viral recommendation, while DVDs did quite well. A lot of research is still being done in this area, but reliable conclusions are few.

Early successes

Early experience from the field points to encouraging, although decidedly mixed results.

One of the best-known viral campaigns was the Subservient Chicken, a Burger King effort to promote its new line of chicken sandwiches. The company created a website where visitors could tell the chicken what to do, anything from dance to watch TV. The creative team filmed an actor in a chicken suit acting out about four hundred sequences and then programmed each into the website. The technology was slick and the novelty of the site appealed to bloggers, who quickly spread the word. The campaign logged 14 million unique visitors and more than 400 million page views over the course of a year, according to *AdWeek*. More important, sales of chicken sandwiches grew 9 percent a week in the month after the campaign debuted.

General Motors launched a website, chevyapprentice.com, to accompany its sponsorship of NBC's "The Apprentice." The site let visitors assemble their own TV ads for the Chevy Tahoe sport utility vehicle (SUV), with the best ones spotlighted in a contest. In one month, more than 22,000 ads were created.

The GM campaign drew a lot of heat because of the several thousand negative ads posted by SUV critics. "It will kill every plant in its path," read one ad, showing the Tahoe driving through an open field. GM didn't remove the negative ads and declared the campaign an unqualified success. "A few media pundits seem to think this social media program was a failure," wrote Ed Peper, Chevrolet general manager, on the Fastlane blog. "We, on the other hand, welcome the opportunity to clarify the facts…In our opinion, this has been one of the most creative and successful promotions we have done."

The create-your-own-ad approach is gaining in popularity, though. Universal Pictures encouraged fans of the horror movie *Slither* to create their own thirty-second ads, with the winner to run on TV. Universal put nearly 30 percent of its marketing budget for the film into online media, MediaPost reported. Converse, Inc. maintains a video site, conversegallery.com, where visitors can upload their own ads for athletic shoes.

USA Network launched showusyourcharacter.com, a website that enabled users to upload videos showcasing their hidden talents. The six-week program culminated in a tour and national on-air promotion of the most distinctive characters. Visitors could watch the submissions and easily e-mail them to friends. A total of 288 videos were uploaded and visits exceeded 450,000.

The California Milk Processor Board created CowAbduction.com, a spoof site that purportedly documents cattle kidnapping by aliens. Visitors are invited to submit evidence in the form of photos and videos documenting the problem. Bizarre? Sure, but the site has more than 13,000 references on Google.

Scion and Toyota Financial Services used Whyville.net, a popular site with 8- to 15-year old kids, to promote its low-cost cars. Users could figure out the price of their ideal car, design bumper stickers and learn how to finance their purchase. Ten days into the campaign, members had used the word "Scion" in chat sessions more than 78,000 times and the mini-site had 34,000 visits. Toyota called the campaign a success in its efforts to attract a new generation of budget-conscious car buyers.

Agency.com, an interactive marketing agency, created a swarm in the summer of 2006 with an unconventional video it posted on YouTube. The nine-minute serial dramatized the agency's efforts to win the advertising account for the Subway sandwich shop chain, showing a snippet of life inside an ad agency.

Reaction was overwhelming and largely negative, at least from other ad bloggers. The video is "filled with mindless business blather, self-important ad speak, fist bumps, fashionably untucked shirts and way too many utterances of the word 'dude.'" wrote Steve Hall on Adrants. "Attention ad agencies. Don't DON'T. DO NOT DO THIS."

But there's no doubt the video clip boosted Agency.com's image. Two weeks after the video was posted, a Google search on "agency.com subway" returned 133,000 results.

Australian brewer Fosters[5] teamed with Heavy.com to create a dating game with videos of ten "sheilas" (Australian slang for unattached women) posted on a site and users invited to vote for their favorites.

Peerflix, a service for buying and trading videos, conceived of a contest in which users took photos of celebrities behaving badly. Money was paid for the best photos, with a "hall of fame" for those with the most credits. The campaign recorded two million game plays over three months after its launch in January 2006. Promotion was solely online, mostly through blogs.

Frito-Lay featured a consumer-generated video for Doritos on the 2007 Super Bowl. It was reportedly the greatest-ever exposure for a work of that kind.

Snakes in the grass

Those are only a few of the scores of success stories that are described on the Web.[6] In some industries, viral marketing has become part of the landscape. The film industry was rocked by the success of *The Blair Witch Project*, the low-budget 1999 horror/thriller that grossed $140 million and was marketed heavily through viral promotion.[7] Studios now typically seed new film ideas with bloggers long before the movie is released. If buzz about a film already exists, the tactic can boost interest, although it is not yet a substitute for conventional advertising.

Websites for new films and television shows now routinely include games, trivia quizzes and prizes. When Discovery Network was promoting *Miami Ink*, a new show about the tattoo culture in Miami, it asked website visitors to upload photos of their favorite tattoo. Thousands of people responded, prompting the network to add a contest in which viewers vote on the best tattoos.

The producers of *Sweet Charity*, a 2005 Broadway musical, invited people to submit audition videos for a chance to get a one-night dance-on part in the program. The ten finalists marketed the contest heavily through local media, driving more than 250,000 video views in three weeks.[8]

New Line Cinema's *Snakes on a Plane*, released in August 2006, showed the limits of viral marketing. The film generated considerable buzz for its reliance on the blogosphere for promotion. Bloggers reportedly saved the film from the trash bin in the first place, vetoed plans to

---

5. Foster's clearly believes in the power of online media. In mid-2006 it announced it would halt all U.S. television advertising and put its entire budget online. Foster's spend $5 million on TV ads in 2005.
6. MarketingSherpa.com and MediaPost.com both have excellent archives of successful viral campaigns.
7. In the case of *Blair Witch*, producers planted rumors on websites and chat rooms that the film was a documentary. The mystery help grow anticipation prior to its release.

change the unconventional title and enthusiastically promoted the production through websites like SnakesOnABlog.com. Nevertheless, *Snakes* took in only a little more than $15 million in its opening weekend, a disappointing figure that was perhaps testament to the relatively small number of blogging enthusiasts.

"The Blair Witch Project campaign can't be made again," wrote Thord Henegren on the popular blog The Blog Herald. "Viral marketing… doesn't feel new anymore…It would be really hard to rally the blogosphere like that again." That may be the single biggest disincentive for marketers to use viral tactics. Viral campaigns must capture the fancy of the audience or they burn out quickly, and it's almost impossible to predict what people will respond to. There's also no reliable way to test a campaign in advance and once a viral campaign has run, it can't be run again.

Ford Motor Company's Bold Moves campaign, which was described in Chapter 5, had a viral element. Viewers were invited to visit the site regularly for updates to a video documentary about the auto maker's efforts to reinvent itself. However, early evidence was that Bold Moves was a disappointment. Ford's vehicle sales were down 10 percent in the quarter the campaign launched and Ford drew heat for an online effort that seemed contrived and manipulative. Auto marketing expert Art Spinella told *USA Today* that bold products would be a lot more important than bold advertising to rescue Ford's image.

Success factors

Experiments like *Snakes* and Bold Moves point to some essential truths about viral marketing:

The product had better be good. Bloggers told me this repeatedly. No amount of marketing can make a bad product sell well. Marketers must have confidence that customers will be genuinely excited about the product or the viral campaign will fall flat. In fact, most products would probably not do well if marketed virally.

The campaign must be innovative, intriguing and fun. Humor, contests and treasure hunts seem to do well in viral campaigns. Some advertisers have also experimented with serial dramas or mysteries us-

8. The viral campaign may have been more successful than the show, which closed after a few months.

ing online video. The goal is to engage the user and give her an experience she'll want to share with others. For this, you'll need insight into what motivates the people you're trying to reach (monitoring blogs is a good way to do this). The more narrowly you can define your target market and understand the needs of the people in it, the better chance you have to influence them.

Don't push it. You want a viral campaign to look genuine. Pairing it with aggressive e-mail promotion or display advertising is risky because it can make you look disingenuous. If people believe you're trying to manipulate them, they will hammer you in the blogosphere. You'll know pretty quickly if the campaign is working. If it isn't, write it off.

Reward people for coming. A funny video clip can be a reward in itself, but games, contests and make-your-own experiences need to be satisfying. Post the results of the users' interaction on a leader board, enter them in a drawing or offer points for repeated visits. GM's ChevyApprentice campaign is a good example: users could build their own ad and then save it and play it back for their friends.

Let go. Once you launch a viral campaign, it's pretty much out of your control. You're relying on people you don't know and don't manage to spread the word. This is scary, particularly to marketers who are accustomed to managing their media campaigns down to the individual insertion order. "I think you could creatively come up with a campaign for just about anything if your mind is open," says B. L. Ochman. "The problem is when the client wants things to be about total control. That just isn't realistic."

Use the medium. Use viral means to promote viral campaigns. Contact influential bloggers and give them an early heads-up about your idea. Post teasers on relevant blogs ("relevant" is important; comment spam is a bad idea), put a link on your corporate site. You're asking people to interact with you online so you need to show respect for the medium.

There's no doubt that viral marketing is on the upswing, and the costs are low enough that it's probably worth a marketer's consideration. But be forewarned: a good viral campaign requires expertise that few marketers possess, and success will become more elusive as campaigns proliferate. As Sergeant Phil Esterhaus cautioned the police squad on *Hill Street Blues* at the start of each episode, "Let's be careful out there."

The Guerilla

Outside a converted warehouse at 307 Canal Street in Greenwich Village, a low-tech circus of street vendors hawks everything from cheap umbrellas to Indian art. It doesn't look like a setting for online innovation, but in a spacious loft at the top of a long flight of stairs, a group of about thirty mostly young people is quietly challenging conventional marketing wisdom.

NightAgency does guerilla marketing. In just three years, it has assembled an impressive roster of brand-name clients, including MTV, Microsoft, Rockport Company, Heineken, Yahoo! and many more. NightAgency doesn't do any conventional advertising. Its medium is people and its tool, increasingly, is the Internet.

Guerilla marketing is a relatively new discipline but its tactics are anything but high-tech. Sometimes called word-of-mouth or viral marketing, guerilla tactics generate chatter by inserting brands and concepts into people's day-to-day lives.

For example, NightAgency promoted the opening of a new San Francisco store by beauty goods maker Sephora by slapping the company's brand on traffic barriers and cones around town. It called them "barricads." The agency also hired young women to dress as cigarette girls and stand on street corners passing out coupons from trays bearing the Sephora logo. The campaign was quirky and memorable. And Sephora had the most successful store opening in its history.

Guerilla marketing can cost next to nothing. It's all about great ideas. NightAgency never runs the same campaign twice. Its advantage is thinking differently about marketing and staying current with the latest tools.

NightAgency is the brainchild of three Syracuse University buddies—Darren Paul, Scott Cohn and Evan Vogel. Paul and Vogel cut their teeth publishing advertising-supported tourist guides to major cities after they graduated from college. It's a market where getting noticed makes all the difference.

The pair learned that they could increase circulation by placing the tourist guides in unusual places like college fairs and flea markets. They created ad buzz by videotaping readers and showing the videos to prospective advertisers. The business grew nicely.

Paul and Vogel knew their ideas about marketing were different. And they thought that maybe the ideas themselves could be a business in an advertising market that bored them. "We were totally disenfranchised by what was out there," says Paul, a 28-year-old Miami native. "We knew the stuff we were seeing wasn't very good. Ad agencies were good at creating specs but they didn't know what the ads were trying to do."

NightAgency was founded on New Year's Day 2004. Its concepts were so original that it quickly landed test campaigns from some major advertisers who were intrigued by the compelling price/performance.

For the launch of Microsoft's Zoo Tycoon simulation game, the agency persuaded zoos in seven cities to offer free tours. But what really put NightAgency on the map was an early campaign for the New York Health & Racquet Club. Paul was puzzling over ideas for the account on a plane flight when he read an article by an airline executive extolling the importance of "putting butts in seats." Hmmm, Paul thought. Maybe that's the medium.

NightAgency bought eight pairs of underwear, silk-screened the health club logo on the seat and sent people out in the streets to "flash" passersby. People loved it. The media loved it. National newspapers and broadcast networks covered the idea that came to be called "Ass-vertising." A tongue-in-cheek website, ass-vertise.com, still gets 50,000 visitors a month. Paul estimates the $5,000 campaign generated $3 million to $5 million worth of media publicity.

As technology has improved, though, NightAgency's canvas has increasingly become the Internet. Today, its ideas usually start with websites and guerilla tactics to drive traffic to them.

For the relaunch of the MTV2 station and its new logo—a two-headed dog—NightAgency built The2HeadedDog.com. MTV supported the initiative with posters plastered with the logo and URL—nothing else—on street signs and t-shirts. They took video cameras out on the street and asked passersby to sing or rap songs with "two-headed dog" in the lyrics. Then they posted the videos on the website. They invited artists to submit concept art modeled around the two-headed logo and staged an art exhibition. They invited people to submit offbeat videos. And people did.

For Rockport Company's iTravel shoe subsidiary, NightAgency launched a travel website: j3tlag.com. Then they reached out to bloggers who were travel enthusiasts and recruited them to contribute. They added a sweepstakes and street marketing to drive traffic. Word of mouth did the rest.

More ambitious was Symantec Corporation's first consumer antivirus campaign. NightAgency built a virtual city at SafetyTown.com and created a four-part cliff-hanger video series in the mold of the TV hit *24*. The idea was to engage viewers and keep them coming back week after week until the story played itself out. The branding was soft, almost like a product placement. But user paths invariably led to an offer. SafetyTown has been a home run: more than 20 percent of visitors have requested more information. That's the key, Paul says. Get the audience to interact with the product. Whether that's a scratch-and-win game card or a download, the consumer needs to get invested.

Over the last two years, the landscape of guerilla marketing has shifted. Increasingly, NightAgency builds the website first and uses street marketing to drive traffic there. Video production that once required $40,000 worth of computing equipment can be done with Apple Macintoshes at a tenth of the price. Nowhere is that more evident than at NightAgency's loft, which is decked out with a couple of dozen high-end Macs running all manner of Adobe Flash and streaming video. Broadband is changing guerilla marketing, Paul says. You can now ask people to submit their own photos and videos. Social networks are becoming the street corners of cyberspace.

Not that NightAgency didn't see stuff like this coming. When Paul was 19, he conceived of a Web community called Socite. Members would have their own domains and build their own Web pages. Nine years later, the social media phenomenon hit it big.

CHAPTER 11
Next Steps

While I was writing the last chapter of this book, a friend asked me if he should start a blog. Tom is a talented artist, a career graphic designer who is trying to make the switch to building and selling fine handcrafted furniture. His problem is that he has to spend too much time explaining to people why $2,000 isn't too much to spend on a handcrafted end table. His sales cycle is too long.

My mind immediately jumped to the possibilities. I thought of Thomas Mahon, the Saville Row tailor who reinvented his business by using a blog to tell the world about the fine points of quality tailoring. I thought of Duane Keiser, who couldn't make any money selling his art until he started selling it on his blog, and who now paints full time.[1]

Tom is a tech-savvy guy working in a low-tech field. If he started posting photos of his projects, explained the geometry underlying the crafting of a perfectly tapered table leg and delivered it all with his characteristic good humor, I believe he would quickly develop a following, maybe an army. I don't know if Tom will follow up on the suggestions, but the avenues open to a small business owner like him simply didn't exist a few years ago.

1. Both of these innovators are profiled in Chapter 6.

Joining the conversation

Many businesses are grappling with a question of whether to join the blogosphere. It's not a simple decision. As noted in Chapter 6, the decision is reasonably straightforward for small companies. If you're passionate about your work and can communicate, then you should be using this channel. Blog about your market, your employees, your opinions, your craft, your ideas, your causes, your travels, your customers or whatever moves you. Launch a monthly podcast to help your customers or your business partners work with you better. Use it to transfer some of the years of knowledge you've accumulated to the next generation. Put a microphone in front of a customer and ask them about their work. It doesn't really matter. Just do it.

If you're a large corporation, the decision is more difficult. Your entry into the global conversation will be noticed by the media, your customers, and your competitors. Once you start, there's no going back. If you launch and then discontinue your blog, the media will wonder what's wrong at the company and your competitors will ridicule you for the indecisiveness. You must make a decision you can live with.

In *The Corporate Blogging Book* (Portfolio, 2006), Debbie Weil proposes three issues to think about before you the launch a business blog . I'm paraphrasing:

Blog or be blogged. If people are already talking about you online, you need a way to respond. Choosing to remain silent will make it look like you're stonewalling. If you don't blog, you're not even in the game.

Think of blogging as a three-legged stool. The three legs are search engines, your customers, and the media. Blogging is a low-cost way to communicate with influencers in your market. Also, their exceptional search engine performance makes them a cheap way to gain visibility in this important channel to your customers.

Blogs are part of next-generation websites. Static websites are 1990s technology. The whole online trend is toward interactivity. New generations of blog-specific search engines are emerging and search is an increasingly effective way to be found online. If you don't have a stake in the blogosphere, you will increasingly become invisible to prospective customers and influencers.

In addition to Weil's solid advice, I'd ask these questions:

Does my culture value transparency? As we have seen, choosing to blog means engaging in a very open and public conversation with all kinds of constituents. You will gain valuable insight from this discussion, but you will also take your share of criticism. If your management isn't ready to respond to the skeptics humbly and constructively, your experience will quickly turn negative. You must buy into the perspective that being honest about your faults and shortcomings will create a more trusting relationship with your market and ultimately lead to better customer relations. If you don't believe that, don't get involved.

Are we good communicators? Not everyone is. As we explained in Chapter 5, for example, CEOs are often not the best people to participate in a conversation because their hands are tied by investors, regulators, and the media. Your good communicators may be buried three or four levels down in the organization. Are you willing to give them a public soap box? Do you trust them to be positive and constructive? Are you willing to accept the possibility that their celebrity will make them a target for recruiters and your competition? Not all businesses will be willing to accept this trade-off, and those that won't should seriously question whether to enter the conversation.

Can we live with the commitment? Don't start a blog because one incident motivates you to talk. Start it because you want to create an ongoing conversation about something that is important to you. You must be willing to commit to contributing new content every few days for years down the road. Your organization needs to join you in this commitment, because others will inevitably take on responsibility for continuing the conversation. This is why choosing a voice and a topic are so important.

Podcasting is a little more forgiving. You can launch a podcast of limited duration, shut it down and archive it. However, I expect you won't want to do that. Podcasting is addictive and once you start building an audience, you won't want to stop.

Do I believe that small markets are important? Most marketers over 30 were brought up in an age in which size and scale was everything. Successful companies were big. The Super Bowl was the ultimate marketing platform. It's human nature to want to define superlatives in terms of size. Even after seven years of serving small markets, I find myself doing it all the time.

In Chapter 2, we talked about the power of small markets, with their engaged audience and focused conversations. Direct marketing to these audiences can yield response rates ten times higher than those attainable with mass-market messaging. Yet many people don't instinctively believe that these markets are worth their time. And marketing budgets, skewed as they are toward broadcast and display advertising, don't reward this fine level of engagement.

John Wanamaker famously remarked that he knew that half of his advertising budget was wasted; he just didn't know which half. The Internet makes it possible to market cost-effectively to very small groups. There's much less waste and the quality of the customer relationship is greatly improved. It's hard to imagine why businesses should ever return to a model in which they had to talk to 100 people to get three to listen.[2]

Are you ready for a wild ride? No one is editing bloggers and podcasters. There are many intelligent, reasonable voices in social media, but there are also a few wackos. Fortunately, they don't build much of an audience and their potential to disrupt conversation is low. But you will encounter them and they may be hard to ignore.

Early social networks were often undermined by disruptors, but that isn't happening in the blogosphere. As more voices have joined the conversation—scholars, business leaders, authors, journalists, inventors, engineers, politicians and others—the quality of discourse has improved. The credibility of social media will be defined by those who choose to participate in it, and there is no question that the quality of those people is on the upswing. Not long ago, it was a notable event when the mainstream media picked up on a story that originated with a blogger. Now it happens all the time. Mainstream media has become so dependent on social media, in fact, that is hard to imagine that professional news organizations would let this channel go away.

In Chapter 5, we talked about the Dell blog, which drew immediate criticism in the blogosphere for being too promotional when it launched

---

2. If you are a disciple of Seth Godin, as many marketers are, then subscribe to his blog at sethgodin.typepad.com/. His latest book, *Small Is the New Big*, could change your perspective.

in 2006. I suspect Dell wasn't ready for this firestorm, but the company responded appropriately, adjusted its attitude and kept plugging away. People will be quick to forgive you if you admit your mistakes, and the voices of reason are coming to dominate the online discussion. But it helps to have some Maalox on hand in the meantime.

A bubble?

Watching the phenomenal growth of social media venues like You-Tube and MySpace, some people have come to believe that this is a bubble economy. They will choose to wait for the inevitable shakeout before deciding whether to join the conversation. They will be waiting for a very long time.

Social media isn't a bubble any more than e-mail or instant messaging were bubbles. Bubbles need air in the form of investment capital and inflated investor expectations. There simply hasn't been much investment in this market because there isn't much money to be made. As we saw in the chapters on enthusiasts and podcasters, most social media practitioners aren't in it for the money. Rather, they seek recognition, a chance to meet others and the opportunity to influence markets.

As one speaker at the 2006 BlogHer conference put it, "I'd rather have ten readers who are really interested in what I'm saying than 100,000 who aren't." Social media is simply an electronic version of interactions that have been going on for a long time. A good analogy is the campfire, probably the oldest social venue on the planet. People like to converse one-on-one and in small groups. They learn from people they trust and they trust the people they know. The top-down style of communication that has defined mass media for 150 years is artificial, but it was the best we could do given the limitations of technology. Now technology has changed the rules, and it becomes possible to recreate the campfire in cyberspace.

It's true that the environment is still pretty chaotic and lacks the checks and balances of mature media. But those issues will be resolved over time. Harvard Business School professor Clayton Christiansen has observed that disruptive new technologies usually aren't very good at first. But they succeed because they give people the capacity to do something they couldn't have done before. Automobiles, radio, television, air travel, telephones, personal computers and the Internet were all clunky and awkward to use in their early iterations. Yet their value exceeded the inconvenience of using them. Social media is in the second inning of its game and it will become stronger and more functional as time goes on. Talk to an enthusiastic blogger and you'll hear terms like "empowerment," "expression," "community" and "conversation." You will have to pry blogging tools out of their cold, dead hands.

Predictions

In talking to scores of bloggers, podcasters and the people who watch them, I've arrived at a set of conclusions about changing influence patterns in social media that I feel pretty confident about.

This trend is unstoppable. All the demographics are lined up to support that assumption. Study after study has demonstrated that people born after 1980 read fewer newspapers and magazines, watch less scheduled television and spend more time online than people born before them. My teenage kids don't know what a jump page, section front or pull-quote is. They barely even know how to read a newspaper. All their news comes to them online and on-demand. So it is for all their friends as well.

What they do well is maintain a half dozen simultaneous instant messaging sessions, navigate through their friends' pages on MySpace and find video on YouTube. They use "Google" as a verb. They expect all the information they want to be right there when they need it.

Technologies that enable people to communicate more freely and flexibly inevitably succeed. In the process, they reshape institutions in fundamental and unforeseeable ways. Experience has also shown that technologies that empower people to do things themselves, rather than rely on institutions to act for them, almost always succeed.

MIT professor Thomas Malone has pointed out that more than 150,000 people make their living doing business on eBay. "If those people were employees of eBay, it'd be one of the largest employers and retailers in the world," he told the 2004 Supernova conference. "But they're not employees. They're independent store owners, and they have all the freedom independent store owners have." This business model couldn't have existed without personal publishing and the Internet. Will the eBay model spread to other businesses and markets? It's likely.

Media institutions will matter less and less. Beginning about 150 years ago, influence began to become concentrated in the hands of fewer and fewer entities, mainly media companies. There were sound economic reasons for this. Publishing and broadcasting were expensive and few people could afford the cost of producing, distributing and supporting a viable media product. This meant that the true influencers—the people who shaped opinions—were beholden to their corporate parents, who often had an interest in marginalizing their identities in order to make them replaceable. What was important was the publication, not the writer or broadcaster.

Unfortunately, this created conflicts and inefficiencies. Even those influencers who enjoyed strong name recognition were aware that their soapbox was owned by someone else, someone who could silence them if they went astray. Many media outlets subjected their reporters to restrictive political or commercial agendas. And the unassailable dominance that big media enjoyed ultimately led to laziness and scandals such as the *New York Times'* Jayson Blair incident.

The economics of the New Influencers turns the mainstream media model on its head. With the cost of entry so low, the need for institutions has diminished. That means the New Influencers don't need corporate parents and corporate pressure. A few entrepreneurs have created social media conglomerates—Weblogs, Inc. and Gawker Media are two notable successes—but there hasn't been a gold rush to this business. Maybe someone will figure it out, but the business model isn't self-evident.

There are big implications for marketers in this evolution. The centers of influence in most markets are shifting from organizations to individuals. It will be much harder in the future to identify who the real influencers are because they aren't aligned with branded institutions. On the other hand, the traditional media gatekeepers, with their predefined biases and agendas, are fading away. There's a chance to start over and build centers of influence based upon the quality of what people say rather than who they work for.

Mainstream media will be around for a long time. It will change and adapt to a new world. But it will become less and less relevant to markets.

Very few traditional media will make the shift. Mainstream print and broadcast companies are caught in the headlights of an oncoming train and they don't know what to do about it. Most are placing their bets on social media, adding bloggers to their home pages and tacking on discussion forums. But they have an inherent disadvantage that will doom most of them: they are addicted to a business model that is increasingly irrelevant and they don't have time or investor latitude to make the shift.

In that model, sky-high ad rates finance large and expensive production and distribution networks to deliver a message. Until recently, that infrastructure was needed because the cost of disseminating information was so high. But that just isn't true any more. Low-cost Internet publishing, combined with sophisticated search technology and community rating engines means that the costs of producing and distributing content in the future will be orders of magnitude less than it is today. It will be cheaper for advertisers to find customers online than through broadcast or print outlets.

This is happening today. The TechCrunch blog is arguably more influential in Silicon Valley business than the *San Jose Mercury News*, yet it has a total staff of six. Social media services are disintermediating an expensive delivery layer by concentrating around online channels. Content publishers no longer need a big organization to publish. They can do it all themselves.

An early 2006 report from Blackfriars Communications forecast a huge drop in business spending on traditional media. Companies allocated about 31 percent of their marketing spending to traditional advertising in 2005, but expected that number to fall to 22 percent in 2006, the report said.

The Project for Excellence in Journalism documented the declines in a 2006 report called *The State of the News Media*:

> There are roughly half as many reporters covering metropolitan Philadelphia, for instance, as in 1980. The number of newspaper reporters there has fallen from 500 to 220…The local TV stations, with the exception of Fox, have cut back on traditional news coverage. The five AM radio stations that used to cover news have been reduced to two.
>
> As recently as 1990, the Philadelphia Inquirer had 46 reporters covering the city. Today it has 24…The former dean at the Columbia University Graduate School of Journalism, Tom Goldstein would conclude, "Unless they urgently respond to the changing environment, newspapers risk early extinction."

Major media companies are trying to make the shift. One heartening trend has been robust growth in their online revenues. Newspapers' online ad revenue grew 35 percent to $613 million in the first quarter of 2006, according to a report by the Newspaper Association of America.

However, these numbers are still a drop in the bucket compared to the huge—and still hugely profitable—revenues that newspapers generate from print advertising. In order to adjust to an online-driven model, these institutions will they need to jettison vast numbers of sales, editorial, production and marketing staff and fundamentally remake their businesses. I think a lot of media executives understand this, but they're powerless to do anything about it. Their investors don't have the patience to endure the short-term losses they'll have to take to make the transition. So they'll milk profits out of declining markets rather than position themselves for growth in new ones, which is a sure formula for failure.

This is an alarming trend. As we've seen, mainstream media has a vital role to play in disseminating information. They are the fact-checkers and the validators. They apply professional standards that don't exist in the blogosphere. But their cost structures are increasingly a liability. Let's hope they can make the transition because without a vibrant mainstream media, we are all worse off.

Everyone will need to work really hard for a while

We're in the teeth of a seismic shift, and that will be very stressful to everyone for a while. Content creators can't be nearly as comfortable as they were in the past. The leading voices in the blogosphere are mostly individuals or small groups. As a rule, they have little or no administrative, marketing, sales or circulation support. Their source of influence is links and comments and if they can't keep up the engine that constantly generates new links, they will die. Prominent blogger Stowe Boyd told me that if he takes just a week off from blogging, his Technorati ranking drops from 2,100 to 2,300. Take off a month and you're in trouble; six months and you're invisible and starting from scratch again. Many A-list bloggers I talked to for this book said they haven't taken a real vacation in years because they're concerned about their popularity ranking.

In short, the days when Johnny Carson or Dan Rather could disappear on vacation for a couple of months and count on the network to cover for them are gone. When there's no network, there's no safety net. Influencers will increasingly be solely responsible for keeping their names before their constituents and ensuring their relevance to the conversation. Perhaps, in time, new brands will emerge that have the staying power of the old networks, but it's going to take a while to get there.

For marketers, the task of finding the New Influencers is going to be difficult. As we explored in Chapter 4, the metrics for assessing influence in social media are imperfect and still evolving. And the proper metrics for the long tail may never evolve. In other words, if your company makes industrial welding equipment, you may never find a search engine that really tells you what you need to know about the influencers in your business. The discipline of finding those people may be manual for a long time to come.

But maybe that's not so bad. Marketing, after all, is the art of establishing relationships with customers. Because of business pressures, it has evolved into the science of managing lists and measuring response. But does that mean it can't return to its (more interesting) roots? The metric-driven culture of direct marketing has come to dominate the marketing field. Maybe it's time to relegate that overly simplistic discipline to the trash bin, where it belongs.

Reinventing marketing

In my twenty-four years in publishing, I've had the chance to meet several thousand sales and marketing people. I've observed that the relationship between these two groups is often pretty badly broken. Marketing supports sales. Its job is to deliver a message, which many marketers still interpret as meaning they should blanket the largest possible universe in hopes that 2 or 3 percent of the recipients will respond. These leads get thrown over the wall to a largely disinterested sales force, which doesn't trust marketing very much, anyway. Often the leads are never even followed up. And a big reason, of course, is that the leads aren't very interested; they're responding to a message, not engaging in a conversation. Salespeople spend a lot of time chasing dead leads until they conclude that the leads aren't even worth chasing any more.

In my years as a journalist, I was often amazed at how little knowledge marketers had of their products and their customers. What they knew was gleaned from sales reports and the little bit of information that product developers shared with them. It seemed that many saw their job as stuffing as many buzzwords as possible into a few message points and then urging their executives to recite those messages as often as possible.

Why would anyone be satisfied with a role like that? In my view, marketers are ideally positioned to be the chief liaison between customer and company. They should be charged with understanding what customers need and translating that into product requirements. Sales is too focused on tactics to play this role. Marketers are in a position to nurture the conversation that leads to sales. Social media offers them an unprecedented opportunity to do that.

A lot of marketers, maybe a majority, won't be able to make this transition. Stowe Boyd tells of how he participated in an American Marketing Association press tour to explain social media but dropped out early after it became clear his audience wasn't interested. "They were basically interested in doing as little as possible to prepare for it," he says. The inertia of the marketing profession toward online channels is also evident in the continuing low profile of search engine optimization (SEO) in their priorities. It's hard to imagine why direct, outbound marketing still gets so much attention when SEO techniques are far more effective at reaching customers at the exact moment they're actively asking for information about a product.

A CMO (Chief Marketing Officer) Council survey of 550 marketing professionals released in April 2006 found that nearly three-quarters didn't utilize a customer advisory board or a formal online community of customers. Only 6 percent of those who did said it was critical to their work. Nearly 30 percent said someone else in the company determines customer segmentation and targeting and that most customer interactions are driven by the sales organization.

I don't believe these shortcomings are due to laziness but rather to resource constraints and micromanaging by CEOs and other executives. Even if they wanted to change their tactics, most marketers can't get out from under the constant demand for leads called for by their internal constituents. They're fighting with one hand tied behind their backs.

The global conversation is a chance for marketing to break out of this stalemate and regain control over customer conversations. My personal experience has been that marketers do understand the changes that are going on around them and want to adapt. They want to find and talk to the New Influencers. They are overwhelmed by the enormity of this task and confused about where to begin. That may make them look disinterested, but I believe most are still just struggling to understand these shifts. In the next couple of years, they will start to change their way of doing business and I suspect that innovations will emerge from that. We're just in a difficult transition period right now.

Traditional marketing and traditional media will always have a role to play in commerce. They will morph and adapt to changing demographic trends. But it is clear that growth will be centered around conversation-based tactics. The next generation of customers will want to interact with businesses in very different ways. The New Influencers are here to stay. Your challenge, and your opportunity is in learning how to influence them and becoming an influencer yourself.

APPENDIX A
The Numbers

Who, exactly, are the people using social media? MySpace demonstrates that a lot of them are teenagers, but for the purposes of this book, we've focused on the business influencers.

There have been several attempts to define the demographics of the blogosphere and get at the motivations of the people who are active there. Edelman's 2005 blogger survey[1] recorded 821 responses to a series of questions about blogging and business. BlogAds.com got a massive 38,000 responses to a survey of people who read political blogs;[2] however, more than four in five of those respondents weren't bloggers. I also conducted a much smaller (163 responses) survey of bloggers, focusing on their motivations and influences. In addition, Technorati publishes a regular State of the Blogosphere report that often has interesting statistics about the blogosphere's overall health.

Here are some generalizations based on the published research about bloggers.

They're aware. Respondents to my survey said they were most likely to post when a personal experience or observation moved them (79 percent). They also write when they see something on another blog (70 percent) or in mainstream media (57 percent). Press releases regularly prompt only 18 percent of the bloggers to post entries. If you needed any more evidence that blogging is social, you need only look at response to the question: "Have you ever met with or telephoned someone you met through blogging?" More than 60 percent said they had.

Edelman inquired about trust, and there the bloggers affirmed the importance of their peers. Asked, "When looking for product information, which do you trust most?" almost 63 percent cited "other bloggers" while only 31 percent noted company websites or press releases. The results confirm the assumption that bloggers are a community bound together by trust. This affinity creates an environment in which one blogger is able to influence many others, leading to vigorous discussion and the occasional swarm. More than half the respondents to the BlogAds research said they spent more than ten hours each week reading blogs, although the finding that 14 percent spend 19 or more hours each week in that pursuit strains credulity. The blog network also influences purchase decisions. A 2006 survey by KnowledgeStorm and ad agency Universal McCann found that 69 percent of people who read blogs daily said their purchase behavior was affected by bloggers.

They're well off. Bloggers skew toward the high end economically, with 26 percent of the people who responded to my survey earning more than $100,000 annually and 42 percent making $70,000 or more. More than two-thirds of the BlogAds respondents listed family income of more than $60,000. With numbers like that, it's easy to see why bloggers have captured the attention of marketers.

They're skeptical of marketing. Edelman's research focused on how bloggers interact with business and the story isn't good for marketers. Asked to rate the trustworthiness of a message from a PR firm on a 1-to-10 scale, respondents assigned an average value of 4.6. Messages that come directly from a company fared somewhat better at 5.5. But part of this skepticism could be caused by the gulf that exists between marketers and bloggers. More than 79 percent of the Edelman respondents said they're contacted by companies less than once a week, with more than 48 percent saying they've never been contacted. Yet 47 percent of the respondents also said they write about companies and products at least once a week.

The good news there, I suppose, is that there's nowhere to go but up.

APPENDIX B
Leveraging Technology

Small changes in underlying IT have the ability to create huge disruptions in our work and personal lives years after they happen. And these changes may seem so insignificant at the time that we don't even notice them. Their consequences are rarely predictable and often evident only in hindsight. This cycle plays out again and again in ways that fundamentally alter our lives. It is one of the most exciting dynamics of IT.

You've probably heard of Moore's Law, the principle defined in 1964 by Intel cofounder Gordon Moore. He predicted that computer processing power would double every eighteen months. And so it has, for more than forty years. Exponential growth is very powerful. A unit of computing that cost one million dollars when Moore made his prediction costs less than a penny today. And eighteen months from now, the industry will have again doubled all the progress of the last forty-three years.

The improvements aren't confined to just processors. Memory and storage costs have also declined at similarly prodigious rates. In 2003, IBM estimated that the amount of disk storage contained in a standard PC hard drive would have required more than a square mile of power-hungry storage in 1957, when disk storage was invented. And the price of that technology has declined more than 90 percent since the IBM estimate. Off-the-shelf PCs today come with more than 1,500 times as much memory as PCs of twenty years ago and cost only a third as much. The decline in the cost of computer power is the most dramatic deflation the world has ever seen. And it shows no signs of abating.

These factors combine to make it possible for new computer applications to emerge with breathtaking speed. Products and services that were economically impractical just a few years earlier can suddenly become viable, triggering a wave of new activity and competition. I would argue that social media was in the right place at the right time, but that the seeds that allowed it to prosper in the first decade of the twenty-first century were planted by rapid advances in technology.

Examples of technology leverage

Let's look at a few examples of the power of technology leverage to understand why this occurred.

The IBM personal computer was barely noticed when it was announced in August 1981, meriting only a short, inside story in the *Wall Street Journal*. It was considered so unremarkable, in fact, that internal IBM projections held that the PC would sell no more than 50,000 units.

But the sequence of changes initiated by the PC ultimately transformed the corporation and the home, reordered the power structure of the computer industry (which led to the ascendance of Microsoft and Google) and ultimately introduced the Internet and social media. The IBM PC wasn't the first or the best product of its kind. In fact, desktop computers had existed in one form or another for over a decade. The PC was successful—and ultimately transformative—for a variety of reasons that had nothing to do with the product. It came from a company with a good reputation, was priced right and quickly developed a following among software developers. It was in the right place at the right time.

Another example of technology's magnification power is the Transmission Control Protocol/Internet Protocol (TCP/IP) standard. Prior to the early 1990s, the high-tech industry engaged in protracted battles over proprietary standards from Novell, IBM, Digital Equipment Corporation and others. When a few big players finally threw in the towel and cast their lot with the TCP/IP standard, the Internet was effectively born as a business and consumer medium. The digital lifestyle we enjoy today would never have happened without that agreement.

The value of standards

Important technology changes aren't confined to the technology itself. Legislation and standards can have an even more powerful long-term effect. For example, the U.S. Federal Communications Commission's ruling in the 1980s that local phone calls should be exempt from access charges made it possible for Internet service providers to spring up offering cheap network access. The explosion of Internet use in the mid 1990s vaulted the U.S. to leadership in Internet innovation, a position it still holds. Had local phone calls not been free in the U.S., the Internet might have caught on much more slowly.

Another example is fax machines. They had existed in one form or another since the nineteenth century. But until the mid-1980s they were expensive and slow and, in most cases, could only communicate with other faxes from the same manufacturer. In 1983, the Group 3 fax standard was ratified, providing a means for all fax machines to communicate quickly. Within two years, the fax went from expensive luxury to office necessity. That, in turn, sparked huge changes in document-intensive industries such as financial services and shipping, which found they could speed up their processes and gain a market edge by deploying this technology more effectively than their competitors did.

But legislation works both ways. The Digital Millennium Copyright Act, passed in 1999, significantly strengthened copyright protection for intellectual property. Countries like Canada, which have looser copyright restrictions, or China, which effectively has none, may be able to leverage their less restrictive laws to build more robust information-based industries.

Technology adoption can also be influenced by geographic factors. Korea has the highest penetration of broadband Internet usage in the world, a leadership position that is greatly influenced by the fact that more than three-quarters of the population lives in high-rise apartment buildings. Whether it can exploit that fact to create a competitive advantage is still an open question. The point is that serendipity and timing usually have at least as much to do with technology adoption as the technology itself. And when the right technology arrives at the right time, the long-term impact can be enormous.

Social media's time arrives

People are natural born publishers. Children bind their schoolwork and crayon drawings into makeshift books. We slip family newsletters into our holiday greeting cards. When we have good news to report, we send it out to an e-mail list. As a teenager in the pre-PC era, I stole time on my employer's mimeograph machine to publish songs and short stories to distribute at school.

Until a decade ago, the technology of publishing had advanced little since Benjamin Franklin's day. Ink was still the dominant means of expressing written information and the airwaves were open mainly to those wealthy enough to afford a broadcast license. Even if you did have a press or a ham radio, the number of people you could reach with that medium was limited. Even if you could publish printed information economically, distribution was limited by the cost and speed of the mail system.

In the 1970s, a shift toward low-cost electronic media began with two consumer media innovations. The VCR introduced the concept of time-shifting and individual choice in media consumption. Then, in the late seventies, the recording industry began the move from vinyl LPs to compact discs. As with most disruptive technologies, few people realized at the time how momentous these two developments would become.

Music was the first medium to make the jump from analog to digital format. The record companies liked the fact that the disks were cheaper to produce and distribute and that customers would actually pay more for them. What they didn't foresee was that digital music could also be copied, edited and shared quickly and cheaply. In pioneering the shift from analog to digital media, the record companies inadvertently sowed the seeds of future financial despair. But they also planted the seeds of a revolution.

The shift toward digitization spread into other areas. Beginning in the early 1980s, people began to shift to creating new information digitally—on computers—instead of on typewriters and notepads. Once text was digital, it could be easily copied and edited and shared and, yes, searched. Laser printers and desktop publishing software gave ordinary people the power to produce professional-looking newsletters. VCRs and affordable video cameras put video production in the hands of amateurs.

In the mid-eighties, the first standardized, consumer-priced modems hit the market. Text-based online services like Compuserve and

The Source made it possible for people to publish electronically, albeit it to limited audiences. Online services like MCI Mail introduced the idea of e-mail, if only between subscribers of the same e-mail service. Now-ubiquitous fax machines made people realize that documents could be converted to digits and reprinted somewhere else in just a few minutes. Slowly, the concept of online publishing was being born.

The trends that would eventually give birth to personal publishing accelerated in the 1990s. Digital cameras hit retail stores and consumers discarded film en masse. In Switzerland, a scientist named Tim Berners-Lee combined the well-established concept of hypertext with the growing usage of the Internet and created the Worldwide Web. The innovation enabled the Internet to move out of the rarified academic atmosphere and into the mainstream. Internet service providers popped up everywhere, offering dial-up connections for less than twenty dollars a month. People got their first glimpse of the Web. E-mail addresses became standard business card fare and "www" began turning up on billboards and delivery trucks.

The bubble grows

The Internet bubble was inflating. In 1996, Nicholas Negroponte of the MIT Media Lab predicted that there would be a billion people online by 2000 (that milestone was reached, but not until 2005, according to the *Computer Industry Almanac*). In 1996, Microsoft built a free Web browser into Windows. Services like Angelfire, Tripod and Geocities made it possible for ordinary people to build their own websites for free. Most of them looked awful. They were cumbersome to build and difficult to maintain and those early services ultimately flamed out. But they made an important contribution by giving ordinary people their first taste of online publishing.

The early Web certainly had an interactive component. Public discussion boards called Usenet newsgroups had been part of the Internet since 1980. Proprietary services like Compuserve, Prodigy, and America Online also emerged during the eighties and nineties, each with its own interactive components. The early days of the consumer Internet, in fact, became the golden age of electronic discussion. Web portals like Yahoo!, Excite, and Lycos built their own forums and a host of niche services added discussion in focused domains.

Discussion was and continues to be an important part of the Internet experience, but the limitations of the discussion format and structure left open an opportunity for social media to fill. For one thing, discussion groups and forums were relatively impersonal. While frequent visitors could create a kind of online persona, frequent contributors had little or no personal identity. Whatever voice they had was secondary to the topic of the forums in which they participated. Oversight of the services was also confined to those who owned them. Get out of line and you'd get kicked out. People could speak, just not very freely.

Another creeping problem was vandalism. As Usenet's visibility grew, so did postings by spammers. Usenet spam became such a problem that by the early 2000s, many consumer Usenet services became almost unusable. The junk content overwhelmed legitimate discussion. Because the barrier to membership was low or nonexistent, vandals crept in and began to disrupt or derail discussions. Some important forums, like those devoted to stock trading, were overrun by people trying to plant rumors, flame legitimate commentators, or just shout obscenities. Good information was out there, but it was increasingly hard to find. Because there was no central directory of private and semipublic services, users had to troll search engines and directories to find the information they wanted. Early search engines were rudimentary and subject to manipulation by spammers.

Three critical innovations

The term "weblog" was coined on December 17, 1997, when programmer and philosopher Jorn Barger started a website called Robot Wisdom, consisting of short entries and links to interrelated sections. In May 1999, website developer Peter Merholz noted on his weblog, "I've decided to pronounce the word 'weblog' as 'wee'-blog[sic]. Or 'blog' for short." The blogging phenomenon had begun.

Blogs didn't solve the problems of discussion groups, but they did fulfill a critical need. First, they gave online discussion a face. For the first time, people could gather together their thoughts and observations and photos and easily put them on a website that was all theirs. Discussion boards were topical but blogging was personal. Blogs were also much more flexible than discussion groups. You could post about whatever you wanted when you wanted. You didn't have to answer a question or launch a thread or even expect a response from anyone. You just talked because you wanted to talk. Compared to the hierarchy of structured discussion groups, it was incredibly liberating. Third, new technologies let readers subscribe to blogs, meaning they could choose to receive new entries without having to go look for them. Controlled, personal and easily distributed, blogs were the essence of publishing.

Three innovations came together to give birth to personal Web publishing. The first was the relentless march of price/performance improvements in data storage. As noted earlier, the decline in storage costs in the last twenty years has been astonishing. A megabyte of consumer disk storage that cost $10 in 1985 cost only $2.50 in 1995. A decade later, it cost one-twentieth of a penny. That's a 20,000-fold improvement in just twenty years. And as storage has become effectively free, new businesses have sprouted to take advantage of it.

The second was open-source software. Open source introduced the idea of community software development to the world. There was nothing new about computer users being able to see and change the software that ran on their computers—IBM had published the instructions to its mainframe programs in the early 1980s—but the Internet made it possible for improvements to be quickly disseminated around the globe, spawning another round of revisions.

Open-source software made it possible for entrepreneurs to quickly and cheaply develop and release new software products into the market. Software increasingly would be constructed from building blocks of robust open-source components with a little fairy dust to differentiate one from the other. And the concept of releasing incomplete or "beta" software on the Internet—a practice popularized by Google—meant that users began to become comfortable working with software that wasn't fully ready. It may not have been perfect, but it was good enough.

Open-source software has led to an explosion of innovative and cheap web-based services. Today, for example, there are more than fifty websites you can use to build online surveys. More than thirty services will do your accounting for you via a website. And there are scores of small companies that will conduct your e-mail campaigns. Almost any business application you can imagine, in fact, is available as a Web service, most priced for just a few dollars a month.

Or free. And that's the third big innovation. In March 2003, Google rolled out AdSense, a feature that allowed publishers to earn money by displaying ads from Google's advertising network on their sites. In *The Search*, an unofficial history of Google, John Battelle writes:

> *AdSense allowed third-party publishers large and small to access Google's massive network of advertisers on a self-serve basis—in minutes, publishers could sign up for AdSense, and AdSense would then scan the publishers' Web sites and place contextually relevant ads next to the content…There was a significant difference to AdSense—it was driven not by the intent-based queries of consumers, as search is, but rather by the content of a site. The presumption was that if a reader was visiting a site written about, say, flowers, advertisements about flowers from Google's networks would be a good fit.*
>
> *By nearly any measure AdSense was a hit—thousands of publishers signed up for the services, most of them tiny sites that previously had no way to monetize the small amount of traffic they had garnered. This was particularly true for blogs…For many, AdSense was the equivalent of magic—they added a few lines of code to their sites, and in a month or so checks from Google started showing up in the mail.[2]*

AdSense, affiliate marketing and other innovations gave small site operators an incentive to publish. Their cost of sales was effectively zero and the upside was substantial. Some people began to make money blogging; a very few made good money. Perhaps more important, Google's innovations solidified in many advertisers' minds the value of small markets. Instead of blasting out hundreds of thousands of messages to a largely disinterested audience, they could target a focused group of prospects at a lower cost and get the same or better results. At the same time that AdSense began to revolutionize the economics of marketing to small markets, blogs made it possible for new influencers to emerge in those markets. AdSense alone was expected to generate $4 billion in sales in 2006, according to *Business 2.0* magazine.

The Web regroups

This convergence of factors made it much cheaper to launch and maintain a website—and to make money from it—as the Internet regrouped following the market crash of 2001.

2. *The Search: How Google and its Rivals Rewrote the Rules of Business and Transformed our Culture*, by John Battelle [Portfolio, 2005], p. 152.

Two early applications of social media brought all these forces together. One was photo-sharing. As digital cameras went mainstream, consumers looked for cheap and simple ways to show their snapshots to friends and family without having to e-mail the bulky files as attachments. Photo-sharing sites offered disk storage for a nominal cost or even free. And as people began to upload their photos to Flickr, Picasa and the many other sites that sprang up, they noticed that not just family and friends were looking at them. Photos could be organized and combined with personal commentary to create ad hoc websites that told stories: my vacation, my kid's graduation, dad's retirement party. They could be grouped together with other people's photos through the growing practice of "tagging." If your photo essay was interesting enough, people would send around links by e-mail and you could get a great deal of traffic in a short time.

The other was audio. The explosive popularity of Apple's iPod portable music player—which reached its peak at the holidays of 2005, when Apple sold 14 million of the devices in a single quarter—kicked off a whole new trend in offline audio. People had had the ability to produce audio programs and distribute them via Internet for years; webcasts were already a mainstream advertising vehicle and streaming audio had been part of the Internet landscape since the early days. But the iPod added a new dimension. People could now download good-quality audio and play it back on their personal devices whenever they wanted. In fact, a new technology called Really Simple Syndication (RSS) made this process transparent. You simply subscribed to the program, band or channel that interested you and new content was loaded into your audio player automatically. It was like getting a customized radio program. And people loved it.

The iPod is a classic example of technology leverage. There was no breakthrough technology in it. MP3 players had been around for almost ten years and other companies were selling hard disk-based music players before Apple did. The iPod's stunning success was due to its stylish design, aggressive price, smart marketing and companion iTunes software. There was also a hard-core base of Apple fans who promoted the product for free. But basically, Apple was in the right place at the right time.

The leverage effects of the iPod's success will be felt for years. It was a milestone in consumers' adoption of time-shifted media, the concept that was pioneered with the VCR and advanced by digital video recorders like TiVo. The idea that people can download media and consume it whenever and wherever they want is incredibly disruptive to mainstream media organizations and a huge opportunity for people and organizations to reshape the way they share information. It will shake some industries to the core and it will drive the next revolution of social media. Whether or not the iPod ultimately emerges as the king of digital media players, its contribution to the evolution of social media can't be underestimated. On the flip side, the role of MP3 players in the profusion of media piracy and intellectual property violation is something the media and entertainment industries will struggle with for many years.[3]

3. The topic of intellectual property theft is outside the realm of this book but is a critical one to the future of media. It's mentioned here in passing only to illustrate the fact that disruptive inventions like the iPod and the MP3 protocol can just as easily foment chaos as bring about progress.

Glossary

Prepared by the editors of whatis.com,
an online encyclopedia of technology terms

AdSense—Google's online advertising program that delivers contextually relevant advertising on websites and pays on a per-click or per-impression basis. Many bloggers use AdSense to generate revenue from their blogs.

advocacy blog—A blog with a mission. The author's purpose is to advance a particular point of view and influence public opinion. Advocacy blogs are often used to raise money for a cause, either through partnership programs, contextual advertising, sponsorships or direct donations.

Alexa.com—A website popularity engine owned by Amazon.com. Alexa is best known for allowing a user to view a site's traffic patterns, inbound links and competitors.

A-list—Jargon for an influential blogger, generally used as an adjective: "A-list blogger."

bandwidth—A term for data transfer rate (DTR), the amount of data that can be carried from one point to another in a given time period (usually a second).

banner ad—A graphic image advertisement used on Web pages. When a visitor views the ad on the page, it's called an *impression*. If the visitor clicks on the banner and is sent to the sponsor's website, the event is known as a *click through*.

blog—Short for *Web log*. An online journal that is frequently updated and intended for general public consumption. Blogs are defined by their format: a series of entries posted to a single website page in reverse-chronological order.

blogswarm— An event in which thousands of bloggers comment on the same story or news event, usually with strong opinions. A blogswarm can become the "hot topic" of the day in both the blogosphere and mainstream media.

blogger—(1) Someone who writes for or maintains a blog. (2) A free blog hosting service owned by Google.

blogosphere—The online community of bloggers and the content they publish.

BlogPulse—Blog search engine operated by Nielsen BuzzMetrics. BlogPulse is best known for its trend analysis and data mining tools.

category—In blogging software, a feature that allows a blogger to group posts together by topic. Categories can be labeled by short descriptions called *tags* or *elements*.

citizen journalist—An amateur journalist who usually publishes online by using a blog or community website.

click—The action of clicking on a banner or text advertisement. A click triggers an event, such as starting a video or sending the visitor to the sponsor's website.

comment—In blogging, a software feature that allows the reader to publicly respond to a blogger's post. Comments may be published automatically or moderated (filtered) by a human being or computer program.

comment spam—Messages and links posted in blog comment fields by robot programs ("bots"} to promote products or to improve the spammer's website search engine rankings.

company blog—A type of blog maintained by an organization to publish news and opinion about itself or an issue. Company blogs frequently have multiple authors, most of them employees.

consumer-generated media—Also called user-generated media. A broad term referring to content posted on blogs, message boards, discussion boards and review sites. The term includes articles, photographs, audio recordings and video.

conversation—(1) In a social media context, refers to two-way communication facilitated by blogs and other personal publishing tools. (2) In marketing, the evolution of a message or sales pitch into a discussion with customers.

Creative Commons—A nonprofit organization devoted to promoting an alternative copyright framework. Based on a similar public license for software, Creative Commons seeks to expand the range of creative work available for others to legally build upon and share, as long as the reuse is not for commercial purposes.

Del.icio.us—A social bookmarking website that allows members to store, categorize, annotate and share favorite Web pages.

Digg.com—A self-described "social news site" in which users submit and vote on online content. The more popular the Web page, the more prominent its position on the site.

eBook—Short for *electronic book*. An eBook can be downloaded and read on an electronic device such as a desktop computer, pocket PC, eBook reader, Internet-capable cell phone, PDA or notebook computer.

executive blog—A blog written by a high-ranking official in a business or organization.

feed—Push technology used to syndicate Web content. Users subscribe to feeds through an aggregation program, which periodically polls all the servers in the user's feed list and downloads new content.

group blog—A blog with more than one regular contributor.

hosting site—A website that houses, serves and maintains files for other websites. Blogger and WordPress are two popular blog hosting sites.

hyperlink—An icon, image or text link that, when clicked upon, brings the reader to a different part of the page, or to an entirely new Web page. Most hyperlinks appear as underlined and/or colored text on a Web page.

iPod—A popular portable digital media player and data storage device from Apple Computer.

link blog—A blog that primarily contains links to other websites. Some of the most popular blogs on the Internet are link blogs. However, this format can also be used by spammers to generate traffic to advertising sites.

long tail—A frequency distribution pattern in which most occurrences cluster near the Y-axis and a long distribution curve tapers along the X-axis. The term was first used by *Wired* magazine to describe the business models of online retailers, many of whom derive a large percentage of their income from sales of low-volume products.

mainstream media—Broad term used to describe major print and broadcast outlets.

moblog—A blog that is maintained by using a mobile device such as a PDA (personal digital assistant) or cell phone. In theory, any blog can be a moblog.

Moveable Type—Business blogging software developed by Six Apart, Ltd. Best known for the *trackback* feature, which enables bloggers to know when other bloggers have linked to their posts.

MP3 player—A portable digital audio device that stores, organizes and plays digital audio files.

MySpace—A popular social networking website where members occupy individual "spaces" and selectively share information with friends. Originally founded as a venue for aspiring musicians and bands to share music and concert dates, MySpace is now the most popular community site on the Internet. Acquired by News Corp. in 2005.

page view—A request to load a single HTML page. website traffic expressed in terms of page views is a widely accepted indicator of online popularity.

PageRank—A Web page's prominence in Google search results determined by Google's proprietary algorithm. The formula is a secret, but is known to include factors like page title, keywords and the number and prominence of other sites that link to a page.

permalink—Short for *permanent link*. A unique URL assigned to an individual blog post.

podcast—Digital audio or video programming that can be streamed over the Internet or downloaded to a portable device. Podcasts differ from streaming audio or video in that podcasts use a subscription mechanism—RSS—to deliver content to subscribers.

podosphere—The community of people who create and use podcasts.

PodSafe—A trademarked term referring to licensed content that may be legally used in a podcast, usually without a fee.

post—When used as a verb, the act of publishing online content. When used as a noun, a single online content item.

RSS—Abbreviation for Rich Site Summary or Really Simple Syndication. RSS is a publish-and-subscribe mechanism that delivers information automatically to a subscriber.

server—A program that awaits and fulfills requests from client programs. A Web browser is simply a client that requests HTML files from Web servers.

show notes—Online text summaries of podcast or videocast episodes that document or provide additional information about the recorded information. Show notes often include time stamps to allow users to fast-forward to specific parts of the show.

snarky—Early twentieth century British slang for "to nag" or "to find fault with." In the blogosphere, it is frequently used as an adjective for cynical or sarcastic.

tag—A keyword label that a user can assign to online content. Tags can be used to categorize, sort and search information and can also be shared to help others find related content.

tag cloud—A visual representation of a website's or blog's content as determined by the number of tags assigned to that content. Frequently used tags appear larger than other tags, making it easy for a visitor to determine what topics the author covers.

Technorati.com—A popular search engine for blogs.

time-shifted media—Audio or video content that is downloaded and stored locally for playback at the user's convenience.

topical blog—A highly focused blog whose contributors limit their posts to a narrow range of topics.

trackback—A protocol for an Internet program that lets a blogger know when another blogger has linked to his or her posts. Software that supports the protocol will display a TrackBack URL at the end of each post.

transparency— In blogosphere jargon, an honest and forthright attitude about one's beliefs, motivations and practices.

Usenet—Abbreviation for *user network,* or a collection of electronic bulletin boards. Messages on this distributed discussion network are organized hierarchically by subject. Each topic is known as a newsgroup. Messages posted to a newsgroup are usually distributed to other members in the group by e-mail.

viral marketing—Any marketing technique that encourages the spread of information by word of mouth. Also called *buzz* or *guerilla* marketing.

visitor—A person or robot program that comes to a site. A *unique visitor* is one who visits a site at least once in a specified time period (usually 24 hours).

vlog—Short for *video blog;* a blog that is composed of video content or has video as well as text posts.

Web 2.0—A popular term for Internet technology and applications where users are actively engaged in creating and distributing Web content. Includes blogs, wikis, podcasts, videocasts, RSS and social bookmarking.

wiki—A server program that allows users to collaborate in forming the content of a website. With a wiki, any authorized user can edit the site content, including other users' contributions, by using a regular Web browser.

Wikipedia—A free, open content online encyclopedia created through the collaborative effort of a community of users.

Wordpress—An open source blog publishing and hosting site distributed under the GNU General Public License.

XML—Abbreviation for *Extensible Markup Language*. XML is a flexible way to create common information formats and share both the format and the data on the World Wide Web, intranets and elsewhere.

YouTube—A video sharing site. YouTube is often held up as an example of a success story for user-generated content. It was acquired by Google in October 2006.

Index

24 146, 193
43 Folders 12
43folders.com 120
60 Minutes 12

A
A-list 1, 2, 17, 21, 22, 23, 26, 27, 42, 54, 58, 69, 71, 75, 129, 171, 203
A9 search engine 164
ABC 31, 86
ABlogAboutBlogging.com 39
Abramson, Andy 50, 129, 130
ACM Conference on Electronic Commerce 184
Acocella, Bart 26
Acuvue 101, 155
AdAge Digital 138
Adamic, Lada 68, 184
Adams-Wade, Norma 48
Adar, Eytan 68
Adobe 175
Adobe Flash 193
AdRants 17, 42, 55, 181, 186
AdSense 215
advertisers 20, 43, 49, 65, 66
advertising 66, 149, 182, 187, 191, 202, 203
AdvertisingAge 43
AdWeek 185
Agency.com 186
Air Conditioning Contractors of America 84, 93
Akre, Brian 80
Alexa 72
Alexa.com 19, 29, 66
Altria 53
Amazon.com 164

America Online 1-3, 44, 61, 72, 74, 126, 181, 213
American Family (Whirlpool) 101, 154
American Marketing Association 205
Anaheim, California 44
Anderson, Chris 4
andyabramson.blogs.com/voipwatch 129
Angelfire 32, 213
Annheuser-Busch 182
Apple 8, 84, 107, 140, 148, 153, 158, 160, 168, 217
Apple Macintosh 34, 193
Apple Powerbook 146
Arbitron 143
Arc-Zone 91
"Are Bloggers Journalists? Let's Ask Thomas Jefferson 175
Arrington, Michael 75, 171
Ask 165
Ask Dave Taylor 27
Ask.com 164
AskPatty.com 119
ass-vertise.com 192
"ass-vertising" 192
Associated Press 124
AT&T 104
"Attack of the Blogs" 22, 58, 75
Audacity 121
Autoblog 10, 11, 12

B
backfence.com 18
Baker, Stephen 80
Ballmer, Steve 111
Barger, Jorn 214
Baron, Andrew 66

"barricads" 191
baseball 34
Basturea, Constantin 125
Battelle, John 41, 115, 216
Bay Area 58, 157
BBC 13, 141
Bellevue, Washington 117
Benetton 82, 87, 88, 90
Benetton Talk 90
Berners-Lee, Tim 126, 213
Berry, Jon 35
Best Week Ever 182
Beta login 52
Blackfriars Communications 202
Blackshaw, Peter 22, 86
Blair, Jayson 75, 201
Blair Witch Project campaign 188
Blair Witch Project, The 187
Blendtec 31
Blockbuster, Inc. 39
Blodgett, Renee 130, 131
blog 1, 6, 8, 23, 33, 38, 40, 43, 46, 47, 59,
     64, 68, 79, 80, 86, 88, 89, 91, 92, 94,
     95, 96, 97, 98, 100, 105, 108, 110, 111,
     116, 119, 120, 123, 127, 129, 135, 150,
     158, 164, 167, 176, 181, 195, 197, 202,
     214
blog, company 99
Blog Herald, The 188
blog platform, company-wide 100
blog, skunkworks 92
blog swarm 3, 73, 74, 75, 76, 85, 164,
     166
BlogAds 208
BlogAds.com 207
Blogarithms 158
BlogBlusiness.com 165
BloggerBusiness.com 38
bloggers 1, 5, 7, 8, 9, 11, 12, 13, 15, 17,
     18m 19, 22, 23, 25, 26, 27, 34, 39, 42,
     47, 50, 51, 52, 66, 67, 68, 69, 70, 72,
     73, 75, 77, 83, 85, 89, 99, 107, 108,
     117, 124, 125, 128, 129, 130, 136, 151,
     154, 164, 165, 166, 169, 173, 185, 186,
     187, 189, 198, 200, 202
blogging 5, 23, 34, 35, 37, 40, 45, 50, 54,
     57, 67, 75, 81, 83, 90, 95, 97, 98, 100,
     111, 129, 135, 137, 203, 207, 208, 214
blogging movement 167
BlogHer conference 199
Bloglines 51, 167
blogosphere 3, 4, 9, 10, 11, 13, 15, 17,

18, 20, 22, 23, 26, 27, 37, 39, 42, 43,
     50, 51, 52, 53, 57, 58, 60, 67, 70, 75,
     76, 80, 82, 83, 84, 85, 90, 91, 95, 97,
     98, 100, 102, 105, 111, 115, 124, 129,
     130, 135, 136, 154, 158, 165, 171, 176,
     187, 188, 189, 196, 198, 203, 207
BlogPulse 4, 20, 34, 50, 71, 165, 166
blogroll 70
blogroll links 70
blogs 5, 7, 11, 14, 19, 24, 37, 49, 50, 53,
     71, 73, 77, 81, 82, 84, 90, 115, 125,
     135, 152, 154, 166, 174, 180, 187, 189,
     215, 216
blogs, advocacy 7, 8, 9, 12
blogs, business 6
blogs, corporate 81, 83, 84, 87, 88, 94,
     98, 109
blogs, cultural 6
blogs, employee 101
blogs, executive 99
blogs, gadget 71
blogs, gossip 6
blogs, link 6, 7, 8, 9, 33, 171
blogs, personal 121, 126
blogs, photo 6
blogs, political 6
blogs, spam 21
"Blogs to Riches," 57
blogs, topical 7, 8, 9, 10, 12, 99, 171
blogs, travel 6
blogs, video 6, 66. *See also* vlogs
blogs.technet.com 105
blogsouthwest.com 99
blogspace 84
blogvines 4
Blood, Rebecca 98
Bloom, Ron 143, 144
Blueray DVD standard 147
BobParsons.com 97
Boese, Alex 33, 34, 36
BOGU 110
BoingBoing 74
BoingBoing.net 2, 8, 66, 171
Bold Moves 89, 188
book publishers 154
BootsNAll.com 72
Borland International 100, 101, 103
Boston 42, 74, 173
Boston Globe 13
Boston University 173, 174
Boutin, Paul 59
Boyd, Stowe 203, 205

Bradbury, Nick 110
Brady, Jim 25
BrandPulse 163
Brandweek magazine 141
Bricklin, Dan 173
bricklin.com 174
"Brief [and Subjective] History of Corporate Blogging" 110
Brolsma, Gary 182
Brooklyn 60
Brooks, Vincent 74
Bud Light 183
Budget Rent-A-Car 181
Bulldog Reporter 132
BunnyBlab blog 151
Burger King 30, 185
Burlington, Vermont 117
Business 2.0 magazine 66, 216
Business Podcasting Bible 148
BusinessWeek 7, 13, 80, 137, 180
Butler Sheetmetal 118
buzzmachine.com 7, 85

C
cable channels 126
Calacanis, Jason 60, 136
California Milk Processor Board 186
Canada 211
Capitol Hill 91
Carmen Electrode 91
Carpenter, Joe 147, 150
Carpenter, Pam 150
Carr, Nicholas 26
Cars.com 11
Carson, Johnny 203
CBS 12, 141
Cedar Rapids 146
CGM 55
Channel 9 89, 106
Chevrolet Camaro 84
Chevrolet Corvette 91, 154
Chevy Tahoe 185
ChevyApprentice 189
chevyapprentice.com 185
Chicago Tribune 54
China 211
Chrysler 89
Cirque du Soleil 132
Clark, David 15
Cleartype 106
Cleary, Pat 90
click-through 93, 168, 183

ClickZ Network 86
Cluetrain Manifesto 131, 158, 170
CMO (Chief Marketing Officer) Council 205
CMP 135
CNBC 2
CNet 4, 61
CNET News.com 32
Coca-Cola 31
Cohn, Scott 192
Columbia University Graduate School of Journalism 202
Comcowich, Bill 77
commenting 24-26
Commercial Alert 32
Communitree 16
Compuserve 212, 213
Computer Industry Almanac 213
Comunicano 129
Congdon, Amanda 66
Congress 90
Congressional Record 175
Consumer Electronics Show 61
consumer-generated media (CGM) 55
Consumerist 2, 36
consumerist.com 2, 36
Conversations Network 160
Converse, Inc. 186
conversegallery.com 186
CooperKatz 135
Corante 19
Corporate Blogging Book, The 88, 95, 196
CourtingDestiny 7, 36
CowAbduction.com 186
Craig, Mel 114
Creative Commons license 51
creativecommons.org 51
Crunks, the 48
Curry, Adam 21, 140, 144, 152
Curry's Daily Source Code 142
CyberAlert 77
cyberspace 77, 193, 199
Cymfony 11, 53, 82, 86, 163

D
Daily Kos 8
Daily Source Code 144
DailyComedy.com 30
Dallas Morning News 48
Daly, Chris 174, 175
Dan Bricklin's Demo 176
Danbury, Conneticut 37

data storage 148, 215
davelippman.com 36
Dawn and Drew Show 153
Dean, Howard 159
Deaver, Scott 181
Del Mar, California 129
del.icio.us 50, 169, 170, 171
Dell blog 198
Dell Computer 7, 76, 82, 84, 99, 199
Dell Hell 7, 76
Denton, Nick 59, 60
Derderian, Ara 145, 146, 147
DeVere, Jody 119, 120
DHL 183
Di Renzo, Renzo 87
Diageo North America 91
Digg 50, 74, 77
digg.com 2, 19, 77
digital cameras 35
Digital Influence 128
Digital Influence Group 71, 72, 127
Digital Millennium Copyright Act 211
Digital Research 110
digital video recorder (DVR) 143
digitization 212
direct2dell.com 99
DirectoryM 64
Discovery Network 187
Disney 44, 101
Disney Blog, The 45
Disney World 46
Disneyland 44, 45, 109
Dixie 141
Dobbs, Lou 91
DOS 110
dot-coms 60
dot-com IPOs 157
dot-com meltdown 132
Down the Avenue 130
Download with Heather and Jonelle 155
Ducati Motor Holding S.p.A. 98
DVD-by-mail 37, 38, 39
DVRs 143
Dynamics of Viral Marketing, The 184

E
e-mail thread 126
eBay 4, 64, 67, 117, 181, 200
Economist 107
Edelman 53, 95, 100, 129, 207, 208
Edelman, Richard 128, 137
Edelman Trust Barometer 98

Editor & Publisher 47
EMarketer 150
Emerging Technology Conference 159
Encyclopedia Britannica 18
Engadget 9, 12, 57, 58, 60, 61
Engadget.com 8
England 144
Engler, John 91
EnglishCut.com 116
enthusiasts 36, 37, 40, 41, 46, 49, 50, 53,
    54, 57, 58, 59, 115, 145, 156, 199
Eons.com 30
espn.com 31
Etech conference 16
EthicsCrisis 180
EthicsCrisis.com 179
EvolvePoint 168
Excite 213

F
Fabrica 87
Facebook 32
Facebook.com 30
Factiva 163
Fark.com 2, 8, 66, 77, 171
Fast Food Nation 170
FastCompany 43
Fastlane 79, 80, 84, 86, 89, 95, 101, 154,
    185
Faulkner, George 154
fax machines 211, 213
Federal Communications Commission
    31, 211
FeedDemon 110
Feedster 165
Fennessey, Pat 53
Ferrari, Vincent 1, 2, 3, 74
Financial Times 59, 130
Firefox 181
fishing 34
flame wars 23
flame-mail 20
flamers 16
Flickr 171, 217
Florida 102
Forbes 22, 27, 58, 75
Ford Motor Company 89, 188
Foremski, Tom 130
Forrester Research 102
Fortune 500 81
Fortune 30
Fosters 186

Fox 202
Fox News 47
Framingham, Massachusetts 151
Franklin, Benjamin 212
Frankston, Robert 173, 174, 177
Freaky Universe of McDonald's
    Commercials 170
Friedman, Thomas 79, 80, 90
Friendster.com 32
Frost, John 44, 46
FTC 81
FX 30

G
Gadflyer 26
GarageBand 20
Gates, Bill 26, 61, 109, 110, 111, 164
Gather 19
Gawker Media 9, 19, 60, 201
Gawker.com 8
General Motors 79, 80, 81, 84, 86, 88,
    91, 95, 101, 138, 154, 185, 189
Genzyme 127
Geocities 32, 213
Geoghegan, Michael 160
Gervais, Ricky 152
GigaVox, Inc. 160
Gigavox Network 148
Gillmor, Dan 18, 22, 168
Gizmodo 57, 59, 61
Gladwell, Malcolm 160
Glance, Natalie 24, 70, 71
Global PR Blog Week 125
GNGNB. *See* A Guy, a Girl and a Bottle
GoDaddy 26
GoDaddy.com 26, 31, 86, 97
Godin, Seth 63, 124, 198
Gomes, Lee 4
Gomes, Phil 137
Gondutra, Vic 105
Good Morning America 182
Good, Robin 165
Goodman, Sarah 37
Google 2, 7, 22, 29, 30, 38, 40, 41, 50,
    53, 67, 84, 92, 93, 97, 99, 101, 107,
    113, 115, 116, 165, 167, 180, 186, 200,
    210, 215
Google Alerts 163, 165
Google Base 41
Google Blogoscoped 40, 41, 52, 66, 74
Google News 164
Google Video 31, 121

googleblog.blogspot.com 99
Grammy Awards 132
Grand Californian hotel 45
Grantham, Christian 75
Grape Radio 147
Great Plains Software 104
Greene, Vic 44
Greenwich Village 191
Groton, Massachusetts 42
Group 3 fax standard 211
Guardian 47, 118
guerilla marketing 191, 193
guerilla tactics 192
Guinness 82
Guinness & Co. 91
Guy, a Girl, and a Bottle, A (GNGNB)
    147, 150

H
HackingNetflix 7, 25, 40
HackingNetflix.com 38, 66
Hall, Steve 17, 42, 43, 55, 186
Hamilton, Heather 107, 108
Handspring Treo 34
Harley-Davidson 8
Harris Interactive 81
Harris, Steven 79, 80
Harry Potter 144
Harvard 58
Harvard Law School 102
Hasbro's iDog 144
HBO 142
HDTV 146, 153
Heavy.com 186
Heineken 191
Henegren, Thord 188
Heninger, Paige 139, 140, 141
Herald-Tribune 102
Hewlett-Packard 68, 100, 101
HeyLetsGo.com 30
Hilf, Bill 96
Hill, Bill 106
Hill Street Blues 190
Hofstra 135
Honda 30
house painting 34
HT Guys 146, 147, 153
Huberman, B. 184
Huffington Post 8, 12
Hughes 37
Hummer SUV 34
Hyperion 4

hypertext transfer protocol 67

I
"I Kiss You" 182
"I Love Wawa" 30
IBM 100, 101, 102, 103, 104, 110, 154,
    173, 209, 210, 215
ibrattleboro.com 18
IceRocket 21, 165, 166
ICQ 182
iDog 144
Iles, J. D. 117
Imagineer 44
independent software vendors (ISVs)
    104
India 146
Influence 2.0 11
influencers 39, 64, 72, 73, 77, 83, 85, 94,
    102, 118, 125, 126, 128, 130, 133, 150,
    168, 171, 196, 201, 203, 207, 216. *See
    also* New Influencers
Influentials, The 35
information technology (IT) 64
InformationWeek 66
Infoworld 66
Inside Google 41
Insignificant Thoughts 1, 2
Instapundit 8, 9, 12, 67
Intel 209
Intelliseek 22
Internet 2, 5, 6, 8, 11, 15, 19, 20, 23, 26,
    30, 31, 32, 33, 43, 58, 59, 60, 65, 66,
    67, 74, 84, 94, 97, 103, 113, 114, 125,
    129, 132, 133, 140, 142, 145, 148, 149,
    155, 157, 169, 171, 177, 180, 182, 183,
    191, 192, 198, 199, 200, 210, 211, 213,
    214, 215, 216
Internet eTour.com 182
Internet marketing 50
Internet publishing 202
Internet video 181
Interpublic Group 126
Intuit's QuickBooks Online Edition 92
Ipex bra 37
iPod 114, 148, 158, 183, 217
iPodder.org 166
iPressroom 86, 132
Israel, Shel 98, 111, 116, 181, 182
IT 209
IT Conversations 158, 160
ITC 159, 160
iTravel 193

ITToolbox 73
iTunes 140, 142, 153, 217
iUpload 101

J
j3tlag.com 193
Jacob, Kris 151
Jarvis, Jeff 7, 54, 76
Johnson & Johnson Vision Care, Inc.
    155
Journal News 154
Jupiter 82
JupiterResearch 81, 184

K
Kalehoff, Max 54
Kaltschnee, Mike 25, 37, 38, 66
Kansas 144
Kaye, Doug 157, 158, 159, 160, 161
Keiser, Duane 117, 195
Keith and the Girl 153
Keller, Ed 35
Keller Fay Group 183
kenradio.com 129
Kentfield 160
Kerley, Christina 39, 47
Kiptronic 149
knitting 34
Korea 211
Kriss, Eric 175

L
Las Vegas 45
Lauer, Matt 2
LaughingPlace.com 45
Leahy, Lori 147, 150
Lenssen, Philipp 40, 42, 52, 74
Leskovec, J. 184
Lessig, Lawrence 5, 26
Lewis & Clark College 44
Li, Charlene 102
Lifehacker.com 8, 120
Lincoln, New Hampshire 117
link charts 22
link farms 70
linkdomain: 164
links 21, 22, 26, 51, 67, 68, 70, 85, 110,
    124, 136, 164, 171, 176, 203, 214, 217
Linux 104, 109
listservs 73
Little, Cinny 71, 72, 128
LiveJournal.com 30

logosphere 24
"lonelygirl15" incident 32
Long Island 135, 155
Long Island Press 36
long tail 4, 160, 204
Long Tail: Why the Future of Business Is Selling Less of More 4
Loosely Coupled: The Missing Pieces of Web Service 157, 158
Los Angeles 131
Los Angeles Times 17
Lotus 173
Lucid marketing 147
Lutz, Bob 84, 95
Lycos 213
Lyons, Daniel 75

M

Madison Avenue 90
magazines 11, 12, 65, 80
Mahir 182
Mahon, Thomas 116, 195
mainstream media 2, 9, 11, 13, 23, 53, 54, 70, 71, 73, 75, 76, 80, 123, 125, 127, 128, 130, 133, 198, 201, 203, 218
Make 9
Malkin, Michelle 8, 12, 74
Malone, Thomas 200
March of the Penguins 141
Marin County 157
Market Sentinel 76
marketers 6, 8, 14, 23, 26, 28, 29, 31, 32, 34, 36, 39, 41, 46, 49, 50, 51, 55, 57, 61, 64, 65, 67, 70, 73, 75, 76, 80, 92, 94, 101, 106, 107, 108, 113, 116, 124, 127, 131, 142, 150, 151, 152, 153, 155, 163, 168, 170, 180, 182, 183, 184, 188, 189, 198, 201, 204, 205, 208
Marketing Profs website 124
Marketing Shift 92
MarketingSherpa 43
MarketingSherpa.com 187
MarketingVox 181
MarketWatch 4
Marqui 4
Massachusetts 175
Massachusetts Technology Leadership Council 177
McCurley, Dana 151
McDonald's 53
MCI Mail 213
McLeod, Hugh 116, 129

me2revolution 129, 137
Medford, Pennsylvania 144
Media magazine 53
MediaPost 54, 183, 185
MediaPost.com 187
Mentos 31
Merholz, Peter 214
Merrill Lynch 64
metadata 169
Metafilter 74, 171
Metafilter.com 2, 8
Miami Ink 187
micro media 136
Micro Persuasion 23, 67, 72, 85, 135, 136, 137, 164
micro-markets 65
Microsoft 18, 84, 89, 96, 100, 101, 103, 104, 105, 106, 107, 108, 112, 136, 164, 168, 175, 182, 191, 192, 210, 213
Microsoft Internet Explorer 181
Microsoft Office 175
Microsoft Office 12 106
Microsoft's Xbox 61
Mini-Microsoft 111
Minoli, Federico 98
Mishne, Gilad 24
MIT 15, 126, 200
MIT Media Lab 213
Mommycast 140, 153
Moncrief, Neil 115
Montreal 47
Moore, Gordon 209
Moore's Law 209
Moreover 59
Mosher, Sue 109
Mossberg, Walt 13, 57
Motley Fool 4
Motorola 30
MP3 148, 151, 217, 218
MSN Virtual Earth 106
MTV 140, 144, 191
MTV2 193
Mudville Gazette 74
Mugglecast 144
Mugglecasters 145, 152
Museum of Hoaxes 34, 36
MySpace 5, 29, 30, 32, 166, 199, 200, 207

N

Nail, Jim 53

Naked Conversations 98, 111, 116, 181
Nancy Boy 117
Napa 149
Napster 20
National Association of Manufacturers (NAM) 90
National Public Radio 47, 137, 148, 151
National Public Relations Achievement Award 128
Nature 18
Navision 104
NBC 2, 141, 185
NEC 105
Negroponte, Nicholas 213
Netflix 7, 37, 38, 39
NetflixFan 25
Netscape 103
New Influencers 27, 49, 72, 115, 127, 132, 142, 151, 168, 201, 204, 205, 206. *See also* influencers
New Line Cinema 187
New Orleans 18
New Oxford American Dictionary 142
New Rules of PR, The 123
New York 59, 61, 116, 157
New York Health & Racquet Club 192
New York magazine 57, 69
New York Post 2
New York Times 2, 7, 13, 47, 53, 75, 77, 79, 80, 81, 90, 183, 201
New York Times Company. 164
NewInfluencers.com 102
News Blog 91
Newspaper Association of America 203
newspapers 11, 12, 13, 23, 46, 54, 64, 74, 76, 80
Nielsen Analytics 142
Nielsen BuzzMetrics 20, 24, 54, 67, 70, 86, 163
NightAgency 191, 193
Nightline 2
Nike 30, 84
Nokia 50, 51, 130
Novell 103
NPR 177
Nstein 163
Ntelligent Enterprise Search 163
"Numa Numa" 182
Nuts about Southwest 91, 99
NYU 157

O
O-Zone 182
Ochman, B. L. 89, 180, 181, 189
Office 103
OhMyNews 18, 75
OMMA magazine 31
On the Record…Online 133
Onalytica and Immediate Future, Ltd. 76
One2One 99
Onion Daily Podcast 142
online diaries 6, 7, 9
Online Journalism Review 151
online media 64
Online Publishers Association 183
online publishing 65, 213
online video 189
Opinmind.com 165
Orange County, California 146
Orchestra 163
O'Reilly 159
O'Reilly Media 100, 159
O'Reilly Web 2.0 conference 29
Orlando 45
Outlook 109
Owens Corning 91

P
PageRank 67
Paine, Katie 92, 93, 94
Painting a Day, A 117
pamphleteering 175
Paris 111
Parmet, David 117
Parnell, Korby 108
Parsons, Bob 26, 86, 97
Paul, Darren 192, 193
PC Magazine 61
Peerflix 186
Peper, Ed 185
Pepper, Jeremy 125
Perfetti Van Melle USA 31
permalink 7, 175
Pew Internet & American Life Project 5, 34
Pew Research 183
Philadelphia 202
Philadelphia Inquirer 145, 202
Phillip Morris 53
Picasa 217
Pink Panther mascot 91
Playboy 97

playing the trombone 34
Pluck 19
Podbridge 149
Podcast Academy 161, 173
Podcast Alley 140, 142, 166
Podcast Directory 140, 142
Podcast Ready 149
Podcast.net 166
podcasters 19, 27, 66, 86, 143, 144, 147,
    149, 151, 152, 153, 155, 173, 198, 199,
    200
podcasting 5, 81, 83, 98, 121, 129, 131,
    132, 139, 141, 142, 143, 145, 147, 154,
    156, 157, 158, 160, 174, 177
Podcasting News 166
podcasts 27, 73, 82, 89, 92, 101, 111,
    114, 115, 116, 125, 129, 133, 139, 140,
    141, 143, 145, 146, 147, 148, 149, 150,
    151, 152, 153, 154, 155, 156, 166, 168,
    171, 173, 175, 177, 196, 197
Podsafe 144
Podsafe Music Network 141, 144
Podscope.com 166
PodShow 149, 150, 151
PodShow Network 20, 140, 143, 144,
    150, 166
podspace 161
PodTech.net 111
Podzinger.com 166
Pop!Tech conference 160
Port 25 96
Porter Novelli 82, 86
Portland, Oregon 44
Post 25
PostSecret.com 179
Potter, Harry 144
"Power Laws, Weblogs, and Inequal-
    ity" 68
Powers, Stephen 113, 114, 115
Poynter Institute 137
press releases 123, 124, 128, 132, 168,
    208
Prodigy 213
Project for Excellence in Journalism
    202
public relations agencies 154
public relations 39, 42, 92, 117, 123,
    124, 125, 126, 128, 129, 130, 131, 133,
    135, 136-139
public relations professionals 122
pug dogs 34
Purina 155

R
Radiant Marketing Group 117
radio stations 11
Rather, Dan 12, 203
"Rathergate" 12
Rational Data Systems 157
recommendation engine 184
Red Herring 58
Redmond, Washington 107
Reed, Dave 174
Reed-Granger, Audrey 154
RegretTheError.com 47
Reuters 47, 123, 124
Revver.com 182
Reynolds, Glenn 9, 74
Richmond, Virginia 117
Ricky Gervais Show 142
Rightlook Radio 114
Rightlook.com, Inc. 113
RobotWisdom 33, 214
RobotWisdom.com 8
Rocketboom 66
Rockport Company 191, 193
ROI 82, 83, 92, 95
Rojas, Peter 10, 57, 58, 59, 60, 61
Roos, Eric 117
RSS 106, 109, 135, 143, 148, 149, 167,
    168, 169, 176, 217
RSS feeds 39, 136, 164, 167, 171
RSS message 165
RSS-based search engines 165
Rubel, Steve 23, 42, 68, 72, 85, 124, 129,
    135, 136, 164, 168, 171
Ruckus Network, Inc. 32
Ruskin, Gary 32
Russell, Braden 145, 146, 147
Russinovich, Mark 12

S
SafetyTown.com 193
Saint Louis 37
Salt Lake City Olympics 132
San Diego 113
San Francisco 59, 117, 157, 191
San Francisco Bay Area 147
San Francisco Chronicle 47
San Jose Mercury News 18, 202
Santa Maria, California 117
satellite radio 126
SATN.org 174
Savage, Pia 36
Saville Row 116, 195

Schwartz, Jonathan 86, 97
Schwartzman, Eric 37, 86, 131, 133
Schwartzman PR 132
ScienceBlogs 171
Scion and Toyota Financial Services 186
Scoble, Robert 18, 26, 89, 98, 105, 106, 107, 108, 109, 111, 116, 136, 171, 181, 182
Scott, David Meerman 123, 124
Scrabble 34
search engine company 128
search engine optimization (SEO) 205
Search Engine Watch 41
search engines 1, 4, 33, 40, 41, 94, 115, 118, 120, 121, 164, 165, 166, 167, 170, 171, 180, 196, 204, 214
Search, The 115, 216
Searchblog 41
Searles, Doc 37, 109
Sephora 191
sethgodin.typepad.com 198
Sharpe, Kathy 31
Sharpe Partners 31
Shaveblog.com 117
Shell Oil 142
Shirky, Clay 16, 17, 68
ShopFloor.org 90
Shortcuts 154
showusyourcharacter.com 186
SignsNeverSleep 117
Silicon Alley Reporter 60
Silicon Valley 22, 130, 171, 202
Silicon Valley Watcher 130
Silverman, Craig 47, 48
Sims, Andrew 144
Sjogren, Erik 141
skunkworks blog 92
Skype 144, 181
Slack Barshinger & Partners, Inc. 42
Slashdot 74, 109
Slashdot.org 13, 77
Slate 4, 173
Slither 185
Small Block Engine 95
Small Is the New Big 63, 198
Snakes on a Plane 187
SnakesOnABlog.com 188
soccer 34
Social Innovation Conversations 160
social media 2, 3, 5, 11, 14, 18, 20, 21, 24, 27, 29, 30, 31, 37, 44, 53, 63, 66, 67, 68, 69, 71, 77, 81, 83, 84, 88, 92, 93, 94, 95, 100, 102, 115, 117, 120, 122, 124, 125, 126, 127, 129, 131, 132, 133, 135, 136, 137, 138, 139, 155, 163, 169, 171, 176, 180, 185, 193, 198, 199, 200, 202, 204, 205, 207, 210, 214, 217
Socite 193
software 4, 6, 7, 13, 17, 35, 44, 66, 77, 96, 100, 104, 119, 121, 145, 148, 149, 157, 158, 167, 173, 175, 181, 210, 212, 215
software, "beta" 215
software developers 105
Software Garden 173, 174
software, open-source 215
"Software That Lasts 200 Years" 175
Sony 12
Sony Pictures 142, 145
Source, The 213
Southwest Airlines 82, 91
spam 20, 25, 42, 183, 189, 214
spam blogs 70
spammers 16, 21
Sphere.com 165
Spinella, Art 188
Sprawl Busters 36
sprawl-busters.com 36
SRF Global 179, 180
Stanford University 5, 160
Starbucks 30
Starz cable network 43
State of the Blogosphere 207
State of the News Media 202
Stern, Howard 144
Stone, Oliver 43
Stonyfield Farms 90
Stormhoek 116, 117, 129
Stringer, Howard 13
Su, Philip 110, 111
Subservient Chicken 185
Subway 186
Sun Microsystems 86, 97, 102
Super Bowl 31, 86, 183, 197
supernodes 68, 70
Supernova conference 98, 200
Surowiecki, James 15, 17
Sweet Charity 187
Symantec Corporation 193
SyndicateIQ 168
Syracuse University 192

T

"tag clouds" 50, 169
tag lists 169
tag search 169
tagging 169
tags 169, 170, 171
TagWorld 171
"Talk of the Nation" 137
TalkDigger 165
Talmud 176
Taylor, Dave 27
Taylor Made blog 99
taylormadeblogs.com 99
TechCrunch 9, 75, 171
TechCrunch.com 8
Technology Review magazine 127
Technorati 1, 4, 9, 10, 20, 34, 39, 43, 50, 57, 67, 71, 72, 75, 99, 129, 131, 135, 137, 165, 170, 203, 207
Technorati.com 108
TechTarget 4, 64, 65, 66
The2HeadedDog.com 193
TheDisneyBlog.com 45
TheFirehouse.biz 89
TheRegister.com 13
Thomas, David 10
Thomas Nelson Publishers 100, 101
Thompson, Clive 58
Thompson-Frenk, Mary Ann 48
"throttling" 38
Time magazine 74, 133
Times of London 118
Tinbasher 118, 120
TiVo 143, 218
Today 2
Tolomelli, Valentina 98
Tonight Show 182
Top 100 Blogs 165
Toronto Globe and Mail 124
Toyota 79, 186
TrackBack 7
trackback 122, 166, 167
"TrackBack ping" 166
TrackingTraderJoes.com 39
Trader Joe's 40
Transmission Control Protocol/ Internet Protocol 210
transparency 23, 24, 83, 90, 102, 112, 197
travel 34
Trellix 173
Treynor, Jack 16

Tripod 213
Trippi, Joe 159
Trust Barometer survey 128
Twentieth Century Fox 29
Typepad 92, 119

U

U.K. 116, 118
U.S. Army 74
U.S. copyright laws 51
U.S. Department of Justice 103
United Airlines 36
Universal McCann 208
Universal Pictures 185
University of Amsterdam 24
University of California at Berkeley 157
University of California at San Diego 33
University of Sussex 58
University of Tennessee 9
Untied 36
untied.com 36
USA Network 186
USA Today 117, 133, 188
Usenet 214
Usenet newsgroups 19, 213
Utah 158

V

VCR 212, 217
VH1 182
Victoria's Secret 37
video podcasting 143
videocast 115, 155
videocasting 5
viral campaigns 184, 188, 189
viral marketing 180, 181, 182, 183, 184, 187, 188, 189, 191
viral media 184
viral messaging 184
viral promotion 187
viral video 182
Virginia 139
Visa International 127
VisiCalc 173
vloggers 27
vlogs 6. *See also* blogs, video
Vogel, Evan 192
Vogelzang, Gretchen 139, 140, 141
Vogelzang, Paul 139, 140
voice 10, 11, 115, 197

VOIP Watch 129
Volkswagen 183
"VW Life" 183

W
W2Group, Inc. 126
W3C 109
Wal-Mart 8, 36, 53, 84
Walker, Leslie 6
Wall Street Journal 4, 13, 57, 125, 127, 133, 154, 210
Waltham, Massachusetts 71
Wanamaker, John 198
Warner Brothers 142
Warner Independent Pictures 141
Washington 75
Washington Post 5, 7, 25, 32, 91
Wawa 30
Waxy 74
Waxy.org 8, 171
Web 2.0 89, 124, 159, 169, 183
Web videos 32
web-presence 117
web-tracking metrics 93
webcasts 217
Weber Group 126
Weber, Larry 76, 126, 127, 128
Weblog Handbook, The 98
weblogs 25, 26, 27, 70, 117, 131, 214
Weblogs, Inc. 10, 19, 60, 61, 136, 201
websites 2, 5, 6, 11, 39, 44, 64, 65, 77, 80, 82, 89, 93, 101, 109, 113, 116, 118-120, 124-128, 130, 132, 140, 145, 155, 157, 158, 164, 167, 168, 174-176, 182, 183-187, 192, 196, 208, 213, 214, 216
Weil, Debbie 88, 95, 196
Weinberger, David 170
Wendy's 30
Whalen, Kevin 73
Whirlpool 101, 154
Whirlpool American Family 153, 154
Whirlpool USA 153
Why I Hate Wal-Mart 36
Whyville.net 186
wiki 17, 173, 176
Wikipedia 6, 166
Wikipedia.org 18, 77
Wil Wheaton 7
Wiley 124
Wiley, Michael 95, 101, 138
"Will it Blend?" 31
Windley, Phil 158

Windows 213
Windows platform 104
Windows Vista 110
wine 34
Winer, Dave 37
winescene.com 129
Wired 59, 133
Wisdom of Crowds, The 15, 19
Wizbang 74
Woodhouse 118
Woodhouse, Paul 118
Word of Mouth Marketing Assocation 180
WordPefect 103
World Trade Center 43
Worldwide Web 67, 126, 213
Wozniak, Steve 160

X
XMen: The Last Stand 29

Y
Yahoo! 16, 22, 43, 99, 102, 123, 164, 191, 213
Yarn Harlot 7
Yon, Michael 74
YouTube 5, 29, 30, 31, 32, 121, 186, 199, 200
YouTube.com 182

Z
Zoo Tycoon 192

About the Author

Paul Gillin has been reporting on the impacts of technology and media for 25 years. Before focusing full-time on social media, he was the founding editor-in-chief of TechTarget, one of the most successful new media entities to emerge on the Internet. Previously, he was editor-in-chief of *Computerworld*.

In 2008 Gillin's book *Secrets of Social Media Marketing*, the follow-up to *The New Influencers*, was published. He now advises marketing executives and CEOs on how to turn the new social media to their advantage.

Visit NewInfluencers.com

- Regularly updated list of articles, podcasts, and useful links about:
    - podcasting
    - blogging
    - small business blogging
    - viral marketing
- Tips and tricks for using online services to monitor online conversations
- Our favorite marketing videos
- Frequently updated list of conferences and seminars about new media
- Audio interviews with many of the people who are profiled in this book